Software Architecture Interview Questions

By

Shivprasad Koirala

Sham Sheikh

www.bpbonline.com

REPRINTED 2025

FIRST EDITION 2008

ISBN: 978-81-8333-280-4

LIMITS OF LIABILITY AND DISCLAIMER OF WARRANTY

The information contained in this book is true to correct and the best of author's and publisher's knowledge. The author has made every effort to ensure the accuracy of these publications, but publisher cannot be held responsible for any loss or damage arising from any information in this book.

All trademarks referred to in the book are acknowledged as properties of their respective owners but BPB Publications cannot guarantee the accuracy of this information.

Distributors:

BPB PUBLICATIONS
20, Ansari Road, Darya Ganj
New Delhi-110002
Ph: 23254990/23254991

DECCAN AGENCIES
4-3-329, Bank Street,
Hyderabad-500195
Ph: 24756967/24756400

MICRO MEDIA
Shop No. 5, Mahendra Chambers,
150 DN Rd. Next to Capital Cinema,
V.T. (C.S.T.) Station, MUMBAI-400 001
Ph: 22078296/22078297

Published by Manish Jain for BPB Publications, 20 Ansari Road, Darya Ganj, New Delhi-110002 and Printed by him at Repro India Ltd, Mumbai

www.bpbonline.com

Important Note

We would like to highlight a important point before you start reading this book. A normal thinking all over the industry is that architecture thinking should be independent of technology. This statement is true 80 %, but then he should know about the technology in depth to envision a proper architecture for a project. In this book we have used C# to show samples, but that should not discourage people working in JAVA and C++ to compare the same fundamentals with their respective technologies. We have tried to keep the same as generalized as possible, but it's possible that at some instance we can be tied up with a particular technology. In such instances please do try to map it logically with your technological implementation.

Team Members

It's great to see Quest pond progressing year by year. A book is not one mans job it's a team work. Below are the team members who helped us to bring this book to reality:

Published and marketed by: Mr. Manish Jain (Bpb)

Primary Author: Shivprasad Koirala

Image editor: Khadak Bist

Marketing: Raju Bist

Hindi division: Sham Sheikh

Reviewer: Raman Roy and Mr. Tanvir Singh

Spell check: Kadambari

What's in the CD

- Sample code in C# for all design patterns.
- Interview rating sheet to judge yourself. Keep practicing until you are confident.
- In the CD we have given a simple excel sheet 'SalaryCalculation.xls' which can help you extract the on-hand component from your salary slip.
- Enterprise architect tool which will help you in using UML to a great extent. We have shipped a trial version. Thanks to http://www.sparxsystems.com to give us an opportunity to give this tool for trial to our readers.
- We have shipped a free Estimation book in 'Quotation PDF CD Data' folder , this E-book will give you extra confidence while doing estimation.
- Sample resume which you can use to make your resume instantly.

Features of the Book

- If you are looking for an architecture job role then this the book. It concentrates on technical and non-technical points to be looked out when you are looking for architecture role. We are sure this will be the only friend during your success and failures while searching an architecture level job.
- Book starts with basic architecture interview questions and covers OOP, UML, Design Patterns, SOA and Estimation sections.
- Design patterns is one the most asked section when you go for an architect position. A complete chapter with 30 patterns does full justice to this section.
- Design document is one of the biggest deliverable from a technical architect. No design document is complete with out UML diagrams and no technical architect interview will be complete with out UML. A complete chapter on UML diagrams will upgrade you in few hours to face any kind of UML questions.
- SOA is one of the most popular section in every architect interview. A dedicated chapter on SOA covering ESB, WS -*, Governance etc does full justice to this section.
- A technical architect is not supposed to handle project management activities in ideal world, but he will always be a part of the estimation section of the project during project proposal. Nice and sweet chapter on estimation covering function points, use case points and COCOMO does full justice to the estimation section.
- Even though OOP are basics many architects fail to answer them. It's mandatory that a technical architect should be able to answer all OOP interview questions. We have dedicated a complete chapter for OOP which covers the most asked question in OOP.
- The best part of the book is other than technical aspect it also covers points regarding salary negotiation, salary break ups according to industry standards, resume making and salary standards for technical architects.
- Load balancing questions tests how architecture can scale his project. We have covered load balancing questions which will give extra confidence to the readers during architect interviews.
- 'Points to be remembered during Interviews' section covers golden points which a HR will ask you. This section will make you aware of non-technical questions where you can slip and get trapped.
- In the CD we have given a simple excel sheet 'SalaryCalculation.xls' which can help you extract the on-hand component from your salary slip.
- Sample C# code for all 30 design pattern is available in the CD.

- Thanks to http://www.sparxsystems.com/ to allow us to give the UML tool in the CD. It's an evaluation version, but you can still use it to gain confidence in UML using tools.
- Sample resume is shipped with the CD to give you a quick start to prepare your own resume.
- Do not miss the Interview rating sheet in the book. Keep practicing it, until you are confident.

Acknowledgments

This book is dedicated to my kids, Sanjana and Simran, whose play-time has been stolen and given to the creation of this book. I am also thankful to my wife for constantly encouraging me, and also to BPB Publication that gave a newcomer like me a platform to perform. Last, but not the least, I would like to thank my mom and dad for constantly blessing me. I am indeed lucky to have my brother, Raju, who always keeps my momentum preserved. I am also grateful to Bhavnesh Asar who initially conceptualized the idea of this series of books on interview questions. And before I forget, thanks to Shaam for all the effort he has put in. It was his tiresome three months of continuous writing that made sure that we made it in time. Tons of thanks to my reviewers whose feedbacks were an essential tool that helped improve this book.

Shivprasad Koirala

The credit of being a part of this book goes to three persons: my mom, dad, and Mr Shivprasad. I mentioned my mom and dad because of all that they did for me and the sacrifices that they made for me, and I mentioned Mr. Shivprased because it was he who taught me how to share knowledge through books. I thank him from my bottom of my heart for giving me an role to play in the creation of this book. And above all, I thank the almighty Lord sitting above all of us for showing his presence, and showering his blessings and love in the form of these three persons. In case you want to get in touch with me, mail at ahteshamax@hotmail.com.

Sham Sheikh

About the Author

Shivprasad Koirala works in a multinational company and has extensive experience in the software industry. He is presently working presently as a project lead, and has, in the past, led projects in banking, travel, and financial sectors. But all in all, he is still a developer at heart working an 8-hour job. Writing is something that he does on the side because he loves writing. The author understands that nobody is perfect. He is, therefore, open to and welcomes any and all comments and criticisms, which can be mailed to shiv_koirala@yahoo.com. The author would like to reassure his readers that all bouquets and brickbats would be received with love and shall be treated with topmost priority.

The author understands that writing an interview question book is a big responsibility. He has tried to cover the maximum number of questions for each the topic in this book. But it is pretty much impossible to cover all questions that can probably be asked. So if any reader comes across any such questions during an interview, that reader is requested to mail it to shiv_koirala@yahoo.com .Who knows, that question can probably secure someone else's job!

Questpond Institute

We are proud to announce that we have opened our own computer institute in Mumbai. We take courses for both corporate as well as freshers.Shivprasad Koirala himself conducts these courses, please mail shiv_koirala@yahoo.com for further details. You can also visit http://www.questpond.com for further details.

Organizational Hierarchy

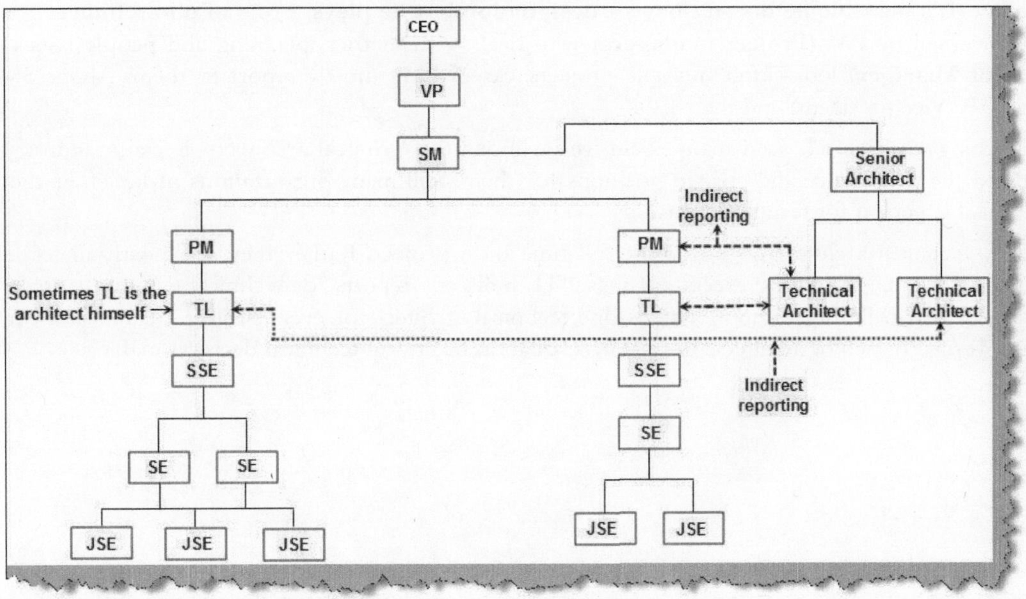

Figure: Technical architect

> **Note:** *In small-scale and mid-scale software houses, chances are that they expect a technical architecture to also do coding. But in big software houses the situation is very much different, interview are conducted according to positions applied for.... Unless the interviewer changes the rule.*

> **Note:** *There are many small and medium-sized software companies that do not follow the hierarchy ahown in the figure above, and have their own* adhoc *way of defining positions in the company.*

So why is the need of hierarchy in an interview? *"Interview is a contract between the employer and candidate to achieve specific goals."*

So, an employer is looking for a suitable candidate and a candidate is looking for a better career. Normally in interviews, the employer is very clear about what type of candidate he is looking for, but 90% of the time, the candidate is not clear about the positions he is looking for. How many times has it happened with you that you have given a whole interview and when you mention the position you are looking for... pat comes the answer, "we do not have any requirements for this position." So be clear about the position right from the start.

We have shown a general project hierarchy. Please note it can vary from organization to organization. On the ground level we have **JSE (Junior Software Engineers)** who are basically in to only execution and coding, they are normally fresher's. JSE are monitored by **SE (Software engineer)** who has around 3 to 4 years of experience. SE's are governed by **SSE's (Senior Software engineer)** who have around 5 to 7 yrs of experience. SSE's are governed by **TL (Team leads)**, they have 6 to 8 yrs of experience and are expected to be technically strong. **In many projects TL himself is the architect of the project. It's possible he doesn't have a designation but he plays a role of an architect**. Projects are governed by **PM (Project managers)** who deals with metrics, planning and people issues. **SM (Senior Manager)** looks after multiple projects. So all PM's mostly report to them. Above SM we have VP (Vice president) and the CEO.

First thing we have not seen many exclusive positions for technical architects. Recently industry has realized the importance and created positions for them. Still many organizations make TL as the sole responsible person for technical decisions.

Ideally technical architect do not work full time on a project. Rather they are mostly in to design phase or helping TL during execution phase. TL indirectly reports for technical decision to technical architect. Normally organization assigns one technical architect for every project. Technical architects are governed by senior architects in case of escalation or critical technical decision making.

Guidelines to a Good Resume

Note: *First impression the last impression.*

Note: *A sample resume is provided in the CD from project management perspective.*

Even before the interviewer meets you, he/she will first meet your resume. An interviewer looking at your resume is almost 20% of the interview happening without you knowing it. I was always bad guy at preparing resumes. Now that I am writing a series of book on interviews, I thought that I should devote a section to resumes. You can skip this part if you are confident about your resume. There is no hard and fast rule that you have to follow, but just see if the following points hold true for your resume.

- Use plain text when sending resumes through email. For instance, if you create your resume using Microsoft Word, what happens if the interviewer is using Linux? He will never be able to read your resume. And what if you create your resume in MS-Word 2000 and the interviewer has Word 97? Ouch!
- Always attach a covering letter to your application. It looks traditionally formal and is really impressive. Attach a covering letter even if you are sending your CV through email.

Given below is a check-list of what you should have in your resume:

- Start with an objective or summary, for example:
    - ❑ Working as technical architect for more than 4 years. Was a active participant in driving technical documents and code review.
    - ❑ Followed the industry's best practices, and adhered and implemented processes that enhanced the quality of technical delivery.
    - ❑ Pledge to deliver the best technical solutions to the industry.
- Specify your core strengths at the top of the resume by which the interviewer can decide whether you are eligible for the position.

For example:

- Looked after the day to day reporting of metrics from project management perspective.
- Played a major role in technical implementation and making team follow proper coding standards.
- Worked extensively with design patterns and UML.
- Well versed with architect processes like togaf.
- Looking forward to work as a Senior architecture.

This is also a good position to specify your objective or position which makes it clear to the interviewer whether he should call you for an interview. For example, if you are looking for senior positions, specify it explicitly. Any kind of certification, such as, togaf, etc, should be made visible in this section.

- Once you have briefly specified your goals and what you have done, it's time to specify what type of technical activities you have worked with. For example UML, design patterns , SOA etc.
- After that, you can run the interviewer through of your experience (what companies you have worked for, from what date to what date, etc.) This will give an overview of your experience to the interviewer. Now its time to mention all the projects you have worked on till now. This list should be in reverse chronological order, starting with your latest project.

For every project, try to put these things

- Project Name/Client name (It's sometimes unethical to mention client names; I leave it on the reader to decide.)
- Team strength for each project.
- Time taken for each project.
- Tools, language, and technology used to complete each project.
- Brief summary of the project. Senior people who have vast experience will tend to lengthen their CV by putting in summaries for all projects. Best for all is to just put in descriptions of the first three projects in reverse chronological order, and the rest can be put forth verbally during the interview. I have seen 15-page CVs, but I honestly doubt whether anyone reads them.
- Finally comes your education and personal details.
- If you are trying for onsite postings, do not forget to mention your passport number.
- There are few who try to make their CVs as long as possible. I personally think that a CV should not be more than 4 to 5 pages long.
- Do not mention your present salary in CV. You can talk about it during the HR-round of your interview.
- When you are writing summaries of projects that you have handled, make it effective by using verbs, such as, managed a team of 5 members, architected the project from start to finish, etc.
- Take 4 to 5 photocopies copies of your resume whenever you go for an interview. You may need them.
- Just in case, take at least 2 passport-size photos with you. You may need them too.
- Carry all your current office documents, especially your salary-slips and joining letter.

Salary Negotiation Skills

Ok, the long and the short of it is that we all do it for money! Not everyone maybe, but still, money matters. And salary negotiations are probably the weakest area of the IT professional. They DO NOT make good negotiators. I have seen so many who at the first instance will smile and say "Negotiable."

So, keep the following key points in mind when negotiating for money:

- Do a study of what the salary trend is. Have some kind of baseline in mind. What is the salary trend based on the number of years of experience? Discuss things with your friends beforehand.
- Do not mention your expected salary on the resume.
- Let the employer first make an offer. Try to delay the salary discussion till the very end.
- If they ask you how much you expect, come out with a figure that is a little towards the higher end and say that it is negotiable. Remember, never say negotiable on the figure that you actually want, the HR guys will always bring it down. So negotiate on what you want +a little bit extra.
- The normal trend is that they look at your current salary and add a little it so that they can pull you in. Do your homework. Say clearly that my present salary is this much and I expect this much. I will not come down below this.
- Do not talk harshly during salary negotiations.
- It's good to aim high. For instance I want a billion dollars every month, but at the same time, be realistic also.
- Some companies have those little hidden costs attached to the salary. Clarify it, rather than be surprised when you get your first pay packet.
- Many companies add extra performance compensations to your basic, which can be surprising at times. So, ask for a detail breakdown beforehand. It is best to discuss in-hand salary, rather than NET or CTC.
- Find out what the frequency of hikes and appraisals is.
- Take everything in writing, go back to your house and have a look with a cool head. Is the offer worth it? Give it a good thought.
- Do not forget that once you have job in hand, you can always go back to your current employer and negotiate.
- Remember, cribbing about the fact that your colleague is getting paid more than you is highly unprofessional. So be careful during interview, or be sportive, or be a good negotiator in the next interview.

- One very important thing is that the best negotiating ground is not the new company that you plan to join, but the old company which you are leaving. So, once you have an offer in hand, go back to your old employees, show them the offer, and only then make your next move. It is my personal experience that negotiating with an old employer is easier than with a new one. Frankly, if approached properly, rarely will anyone will say 'no,' as you have spent quiet some time with them. Just do not be aggressive or egoistic that you have an offer in hand.
- Last but not the least, sometime something's are worth more than money: **JOB SATISFACTION** being one of them. So, if the difference is money is not that much, go for job satisfaction. It is, at times, worth more than money.

The Salary Slip (CTC, Gross and Net)

Mr. Raju left his old organization where he had a package of 400000 INR and joined a new organization with a package of 600000 INR. In his old company he was getting 40000 INR on hand. At the first glance Mr. Raju felt like he has received a 50% hike. When he received the first salary in the new company he got 36000 INR on hand, SHOCKED!

We are sure many will feel cheated, but it's not the organization it's your mistake to not analyze your salary slip properly.

It's a psychology of every employee to look at what he gets on hand. First thing when you get your salary do not accept it, take it home and dissect it. Try to extract what you will get on hand rather than looking at the CTC.

> **Note:** *We have written this tutorial according to Indian corporate industry. But the basic concept will hold true even for other geographical corporates.*

We will devise a simple methodology by which we can conclude our on-hand component easily. Every salary slip has lot of components like basic, HRA, PF etc. Every salary slip component falls in to five categories as shown in figure 'Five categories'.

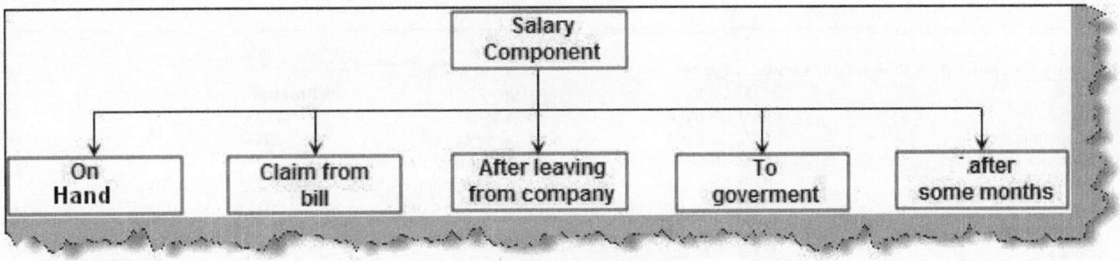

Figure: Five categories

On hand: Salary components which you get on hand needs to be pushed in to this category. Some of the examples are basic, HRA etc. This component is something which you get fixed every month and directly in to your hand.

Claim from bill: There are some salary components which we get after submitting bills. Please note this is not a monthly on-hand component, rather it's a claim which you get after submitting bills. Some of the examples of this category are LTA and phone bills.

After some months: There are salary components like bonus or some organization call them as retention bonus which is received after some months. This can be in a form of yearly or quarterly bonus. Bonuses depend on company policies and many companies add this to your CTC. Again this amount is not received in the same month itself and they do not form the monthly on-hand component.

After leaving company: There are some salary components which we get after leaving the company. For example provident fund (PF). Again this component does not add to your on-hand monthly, rather its something you will get after resignation.

To government: Some of the salary components go to the government like PT (professional tax), IT (Income tax) etc. You will never get this amount. It's something you pay to the government for the facilities they provide or you can say for running the country.

Now that we have segregated our components in to the above five categories, its time to understand three principles **CTC, Gross and Net**.

CTC is everything that company spends on us. Many professionals get carried by the CTC figure and hop the jobs. CTC is the addition of all the five components. Yes, you guessed it right it also has the salary component which you will not get on hand.

CTC = on hand + Claim from bill + after leaving company + to government + after some months.

Gross is only on hand. This is the figure on which you should negotiate. Many times company try to shuffle the salary components in the above categories to come to this figure, be careful and alert when they do so.

Gross = on hand

Net is what you get exactly on hand after Income tax deduction.

Net = Gross – Tax on gross.

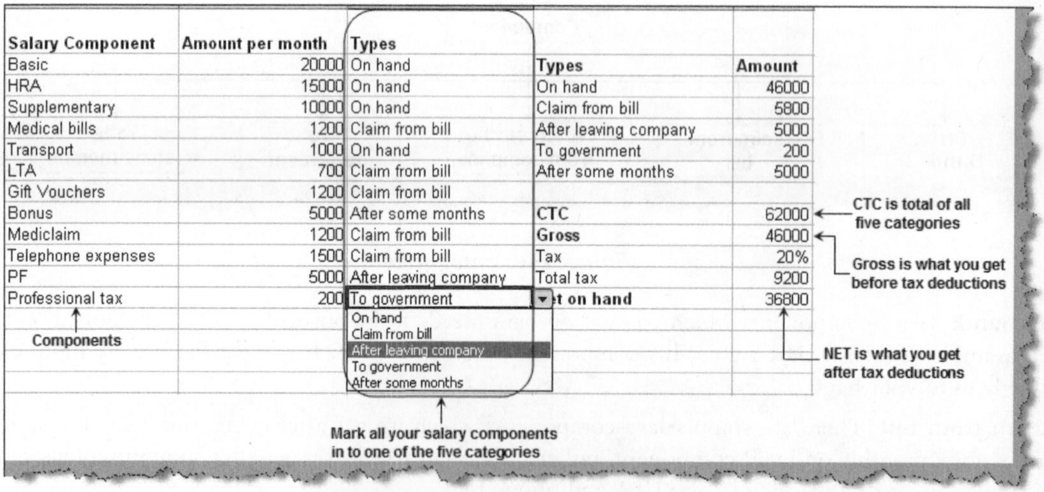

Salary Component	Amount per month	Types
Basic	20000	On hand
HRA	15000	On hand
Supplementary	10000	On hand
Medical bills	1200	Claim from bill
Transport	1000	On hand
LTA	700	Claim from bill
Gift Vouchers	1200	Claim from bill
Bonus	5000	After some months
Mediclaim	1200	Claim from bill
Telephone expenses	1500	Claim from bill
PF	5000	After leaving company
Professional tax	200	To government

Types	Amount
On hand	46000
Claim from bill	5800
After leaving company	5000
To government	200
After some months	5000
CTC	62000
Gross	46000
Tax	20%
Total tax	9200
Net on hand	36800

Figure: Salary calculator

In the CD we have given a simple excel sheet 'SalaryCalculation.xls' which can help you extract the on-hand component from your salary slip. You just need to enter all components and select from the combo box in which category the components belong. This sheet is a sample sheet, so probably you will need to add and remove some components according to your slip. Also you need to adjust the tax value according to your salary range.

Above is a snapshot of the salary calculator EXCEL sheet.

Broad Salary Structure

Given below, in a tabular form, is the salary structure for technical architects. This data is from the perspective of the Indian market. Amounts given below are annual CTCs (Cost-to-Company).

Note: *The below salary structure is not an industry standard. We have seen some architects getting mind blowing salaries even in small scale companies. The below sheet is from the authors knowledge point of view which he has gained from his friends and IT people he knows in the industry. You can take it as bench mark but not as an IT standard.*

	Mid/Small level IT Companies (CTC p.a.)	**Large Scale IT companies (CTC p.a.)**
Technical Architects	700000 - 800000 INR	800000 - 1200000 INR
Senior Technical Architects	1000000 - 1300000 INR	1200000 - 1500000 INR
Chief technical architects	We have not seen chief technical architects in mid-scale companies.	1500000 - 2000000 INR

Figure: Salary Card for Architects

Interview Rating Sheet

In the CD, we have provided an Interview Rating MS-Excel sheet. This sheet will help you in gaining an insight into how much you are ready for Software testing, JAVA, .NET , SQL Server , Networking or project management interviews. In the excel sheet, we have thirteen sections:

- Guidelines
- JAVA
- Java Results
- .NET
- .NET Results
- SQL Server
- SQL Server Results
- Software Testing
- Software Testing Results
- Networking
- Networking Results
- Project Management
- Project Management results
- **Architecture**
- **Architecture Results**

The guidelines-sheet defines the guidelines for rating. For every question asked, you can rate yourself on a scale of 1 to 5. The following guidelines are to be followed when you rate yourself:

- 0-You have no idea about the question.
- 1-You know only the definition.
- 2-You know the concept but do not have in-depth knowledge of the subject.
- 3-You know the concept and have partial knowledge of the concept.
- 4-You know the concept and have in-depth knowledge of the subject.
- 5- You are an expert and no one can touch you in this area.

The remaining 10 sections are questions and results. For example, we have the Architecture section and the Architecture results Section. The project management section will take in the rating inputs for every question, and project management result will show the output. Same holds true for .NET, JAVA, SQL Server, Software Testing and Networking.

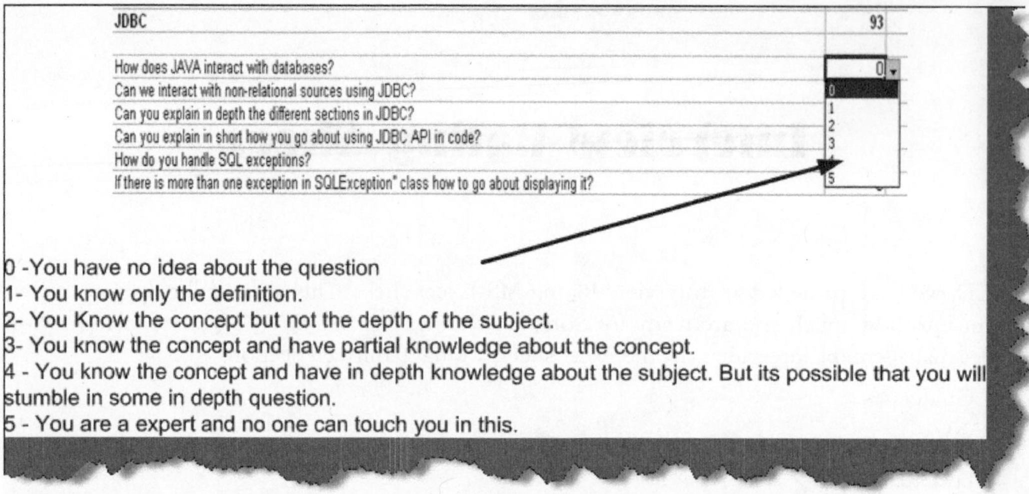

Figure: Rate Yourself

For every question asked, you need to rate yourself. So go through every question and see how good you are. You do not have anyone to supervise you, but remember that at the end of the day it is you who has to clear the interview. So be fair to yourself.

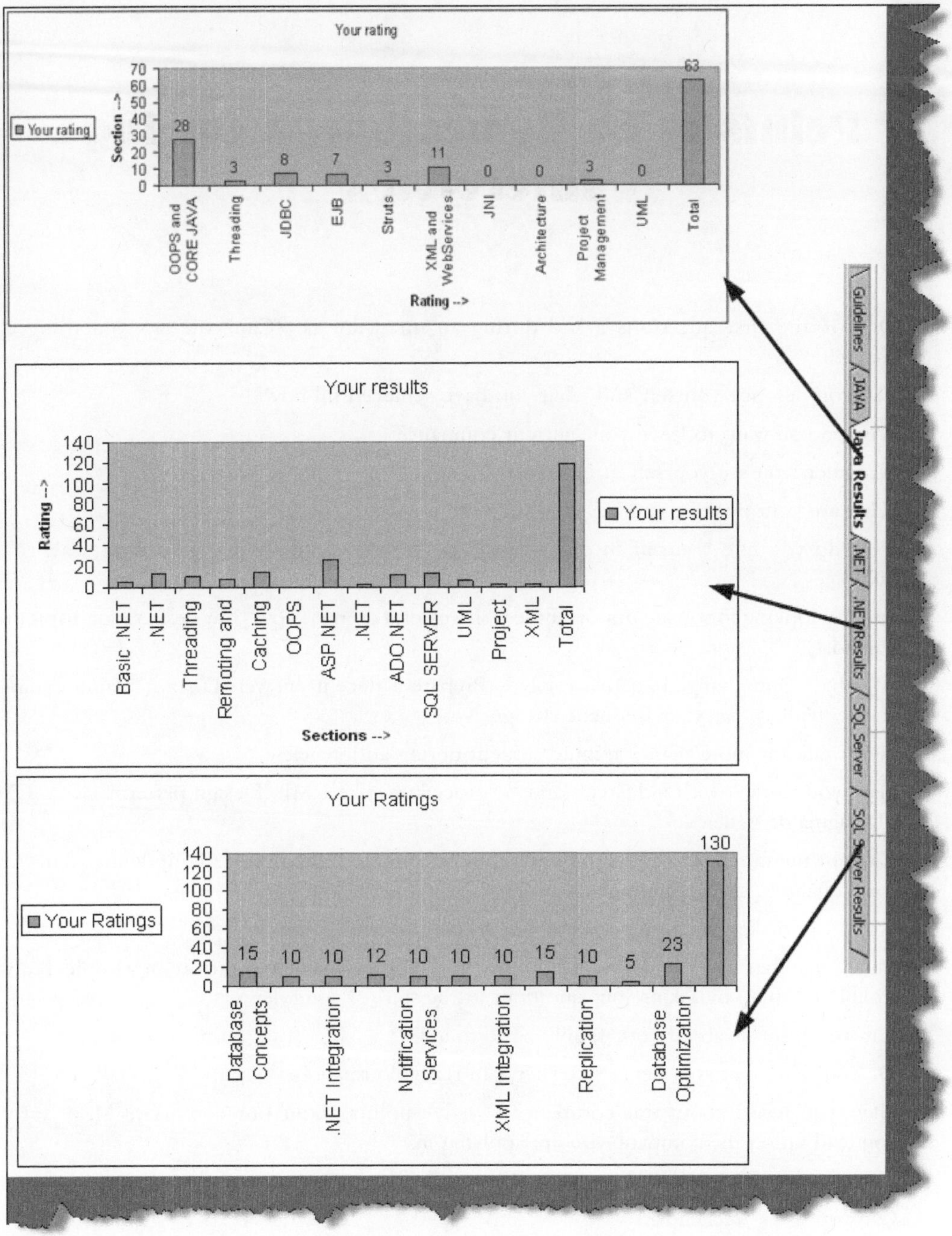

Figure: Overall Rating Values

The figure above shows how you have performed in each section, and your overall rating.

Points to be Remembered During Interviews

- One of the first questions asked during an interview is, "Can you say something about yourself?"
- Can you describe yourself and what you have achieved till now?
- Why do you want to leave your current company?
- Where do you see yourself after 3 years?
- What are your positive and negative traits?
- How do you rate yourself in organization process level implementation on a scale of 1 to 10?
- Are you looking for onsite opportunities? (Be careful do not show your desperation for journeys abroad.)
- Why have you changed so many jobs? (Prepare a decent answer. Do not blame companies and individuals for your frequent changes.)
- Never talk for more than 1 minute straight during an interview.
- Have you worked with industry standard procedures like UML, Design patterns, SOA, CMMI, SIX sigma or Agile?
- Do not mention client names in your resume. If asked, say that it's confidential. This brings forth qualities, such as, honesty.
- When you make your resume keep your recent projects at the top.
- Find out what the employer is looking for (router implementation or simple Network troubleshooting) by asking him questions at the start of interview.
- Can you brief us about your family background?
- Do you think that you, being a fresher, can really do this job?
- Have you heard about our company? Say five points about our company? Make sure that you read up on the company you are applying in.
- Can you describe your best project?
- Can you work weekends?
- What is the biggest team size you have worked with?
- Describe your current project.

- How much time will you need to join our organization? What's the notice period in your current organization?
- What certifications do you hold? MCAD,JCP certification etc,
- Do you have your passport-size photos, final-year mark sheet, and employment letters from previous companies, last month's salary-slip, passport, and other necessary documents.
- What motivates you the most?
- Why you want to leave your current organization?
- Which type of job gives you the greatest satisfaction?
- What type of environment are you looking for?
- Do you have any experience in enterprise architecture?
- Do you like to work as a team? or as an individual?
- Describe the best manager you have worked for?
- Why should I hire you?
- Have you ever been fired?
- Can you tell us about a few important points that you have learnt from your past project experiences?
- Have you gone through some unsuccessful projects,? If yes, can you tell us why they failed?
- Are you comfortable relocating? If you have personal problems, say 'no' right at the beginning, or else within two months you may have to read this book again.
- Do you work late nights? The best answer to this is that you can if there is a project deadline. Do not show that it's your culture to work nights.
- Tell us about your special achievements. Here, say something about your best project.
- Do you have any plans of opening your own software company? Beware! do not start pouring out your Bill Gates' dreams, this can create a wrong impression.

How to Read This Book

If you can read English, you can read this book! Just kidding! There are some legends that will make your reading more effective. Every question has a simple tag that rates the question.

These rating are given by the author, and can vary according to companies and individuals.

(B) **Basic Question:** 'Basic Question' means that it is a fundamental question and should be answered. For example, 'Explain SDLC cycle?' Stumbling on these questions will rarely see you pass Project Management interviews.

(I) **Intermediate Questions:** These are mid-level questions, and you are expected to answer them if you are looking for a decent position in the company.

(A) **Advanced Questions:** These are advanced level question that are expected when they are looking for specialists in the field.

> **Note:** *While reading, you will come across sections marked 'Note,' which highlight special points of that section. One advice, do not read this book from start to finish. Go through the index and see which sections you are targeting and revise those.*

Contents

1

Basic Architecture Interview Questions

(B) What is the definition of software architecture?

Software architecture means to describe overall design and structure of a computer system. To describe this system you can either use UML, free text, control flow diagram etc. For instance figure 'basic architecture' shows how we have represented a simple order and payment processing software using block diagrams.

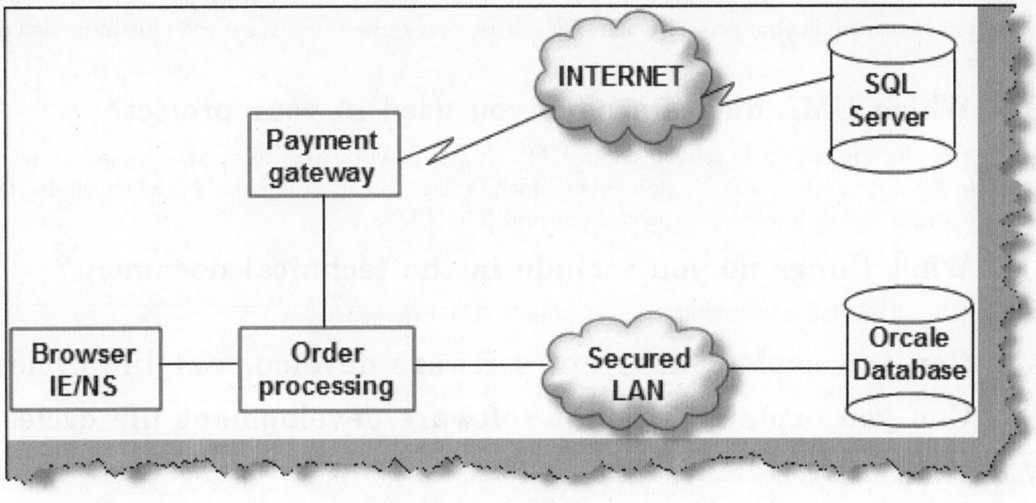

Figure: Basic architecture

(B) Can you explain your current project architecture?

This answer will depend completely on individual experiences. You can answer it in three phases. **First** describe in short (really short) your project domain. If you have already explained your domain, do not repeat it you can go for the second step. **Second** describe an overall high level view of the project technically. If possible draw a diagram. We are sure the interviewer will stop you here and go in to details in one the project sections technically. In case he does not , then move to the **third** step, start going in to low level explanation.

Below is a simple example of how an order processing system is explained.

Step 1 (Domain): It is a simple order processing system made for Koirala limited. End customer will log in to the website and order product by using local banks payment gateway.

Step 2 (High level): The whole system stood up on a basic three tier system i.e. the UI , business components and the database layer. System also had a basic rules engine which worked on reflection. Some services of the system where exposed using web services for third party organization.

Step 3 (Low level): XML was used to pass data between business components and database layer to enable loose coupling. Web services exposed to the third party followed WS-* specifications.

> **Note:** *In 90% interviews interviewer will ask question depending on your current project. So highlight those points which you are sure and strong on.* **Best is stand before a mirror and explain your project properly.**

(B) Which design pattern have you worked with?

Please do not boast that you know all design patterns. We are sure that interviewer will not like it. We have dedicated a complete chapter on design patterns. Run through it once and see which design patterns have you implemented in your project practically and say only those. This way it will look more practical and impressive.

(B) Which UML diagram have you used in your project?

Again please do not boast you have used all UML diagrams. We have dedicated a complete chapter on this. In the same chapter we have defined in which project scenarios we should used which diagram. So try to answer this with more scenario based approach.

(I) What things do you include in the technical document?

Left to the reader as this answer will depend on individual experience.

(A) Can you explain different software development life cycles?

(A) Can you explain different software development life cycles ?

> **Note:** *This questions is asked to test that as a technical architect do you have a know how of all the project life cycles. Even though not a technical topic interviewer expects you to answer.*

SDLC (System Development Life Cycle) is overall process of developing information systems through multi stage process systems from investigation of initial requirements through analysis, design, implementation, and maintenance. The days are gone when one COBOL programmer used to analyze, test, and implement software systems. Systems have become complex, huge team members are involved, architects, analyst, programmers, testers, users etc. To manage this number of SDLC models have been created.

Following are popular models, which are listed:

- Waterfall Model.
- Spiral Model.

- Build and Fix model.
- Rapid prototyping Model.
- Incremental Model.

This section we will go into depth of different SDLC models.

Water Fall Model

This is the oldest model. It has sequence of stages; output of one stage becomes input of other.

Following are stages in Waterfall model:

- System Requirement: This is initial stage of the project where end user requirements are gathered and documented.
- System Design: In this stage detail requirements, screen layout, business rules, process diagram, pseudo code, and other documentations are prepared. This is first step in technical phase.
- Implementation: Depending on the design document, actual code is written here.
- Integration and Testing: All pieces are brought together and tested. Bugs are removed in this phase.
- Acceptance, Installation and Deployment: This is final stage where software is put in production and runs actual business.
- Maintenance: This is least glamorous phase, which runs forever. Code Changes, correction, addition etc are done in this phase.

Waterfall is suited for low risk in areas of User Interface and performance requirements, but high risk in budget and schedule predictability and control. Waterfall assumes that all requirements can be specified in advance. But unfortunately, requirement grows and changes through various stages, so it needs feedback from one stage to other.

Spiral Model

Spiral Model removes the drawback of waterfall model, by providing emphasis to go back and reiterate earlier stages a number of times as project progresses. On broader level, it is a series of short waterfall cycles, each producing an early prototype representing a part of entire project. It also helps demonstrate a Proof of Concept at early software life cycle.

Build and Fix Model

This is the way free-lancers work Write some code and keep modifying it until the customer is happy. This approach can be quite dangerous and risky.

Rapid Prototyping Model

This model is also called as Rapid Application Development. The initial emphasis is on creating prototype that look and acts like the desired product. Prototype can be created by using tools, which is different from those used for final product. Once the prototype is approved, its discarded and real software development is started from scratch. The problem with this model is that sometimes the prototype moves ahead to become the final live product, which can be bad from design point of view. It is a effective model but can have higher costing than other models as you require programmers during the initial phase of the software cycle.

Incremental Model

In this model, we divide products into builds, where section of product are created and tested separately. Here errors are found in requirement phase itself, user feedback is taken for each stage and code is tested after it is written.

(I) What is a definition of enterprise architecture?

Before defining enterprise architecture lets first define what an enterprise is. It is a collection of organization which has common set of goals. Enterprise architecture defines the IT infrastructure architecture for the collection of organization with common set of goals.

(B) What is TOGAF ?

TOGAF is a framework - a detailed method and a set of supporting tools - for developing enterprise architecture.

(I) Can you explain OOA and OOD ?

OOA looks at the problem domain with the purpose of creating a model. OOA only creates a model and does not look in to the implementation details of the same.

OOD takes the model derived from OOA and get in to technical implementation details like transactions, language, platform etc.

In short OOA gives us a model while OOD defines the details technical implementation of the model.

(A) What is the concept of load balancing?

Many times your application should have the capacity to handle huge client load. This is where load balancer comes in to picture. So we deploy load balancer on the front and we have web farms of

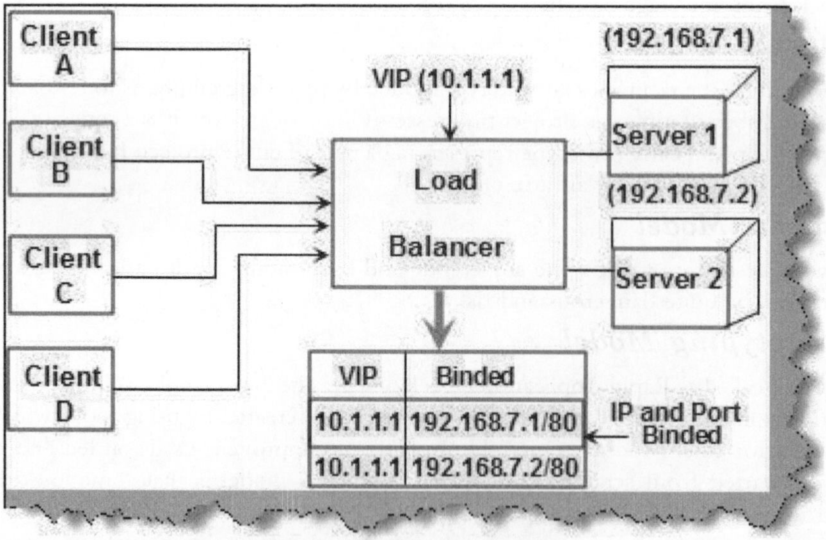

Figure: Load balancer

server at the back of the load balancer. Load balancer can be a software or a hardware , depends on what solutions you take. VIP (Virtual IP address) is assigned to the load balancer. This VIP is then binded with server and the port. For instance in the figure 'Load balancer' we have assigned VIP as '10.1.1.1'. We have two servers behind the load balancer. This VIP is binded with the two servers with IP and port. So now when the first client connects the load balancer redirects to the server 1. When the second client connects it redirects to server 2. This redirect depends on the load-distribution method used by the load balancer.

(A) Can you explain stateless load balancing?

Stateless load balancer uses the hashing algorithm. It takes packet from the client and selects fields from the packet to be hashed. For instance from each client it can take IP address and port number and hash them in to an integer between 1 to number of servers. You can see from the figure we have four servers. So the load balancer takes the IP address and port and hashes them with a number between 1 to 4. Depending on the number the client is directed to the server. For instance client A is directed to server 2, client b to server 1 and so on. Once the client is connected to a server it is always redirected to the same server.

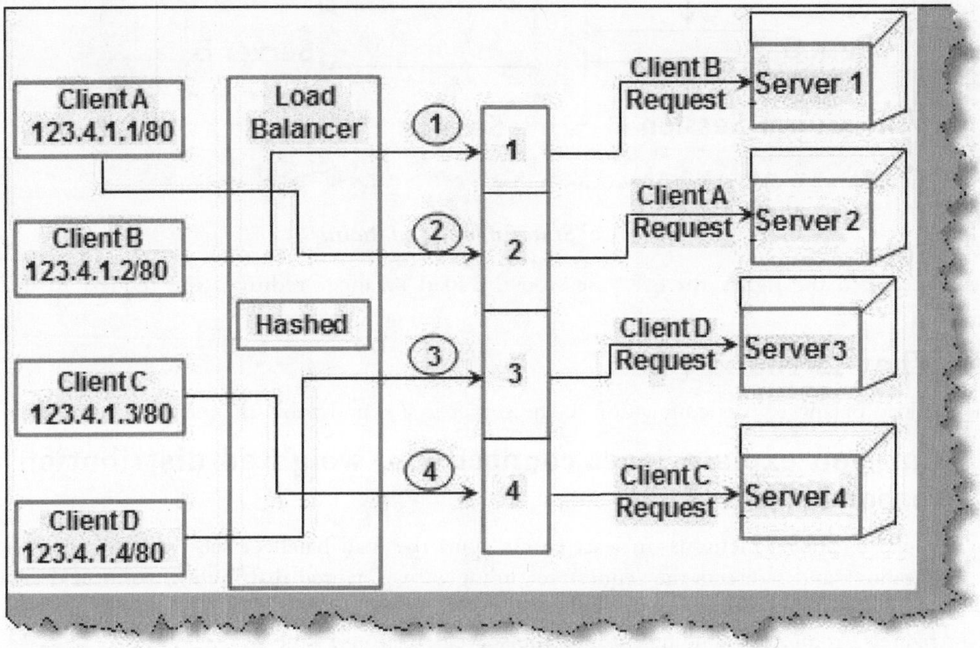

Figure: Stateless load balancing

Advantage of stateless load balancing is that it's simple. The biggest disadvantage is that it treats all clients equally and connects one client to one server always. That is if client A is connects to server 2 it will always connect to server 2. This is irrespective of how many times client A sends request. So if client A sends 100 request and client B sends 10 requests even then client A will be sent to server 2 for all the 100 request and client B to server 1 for all 10 requests.

(I) Can you explain stateful load balancing?

In stateful balancing the load balancer looks at each session and assigns it to the appropriate server based on load. In order that the load balancer can track each session it needs to know when the session starts and when it ends.

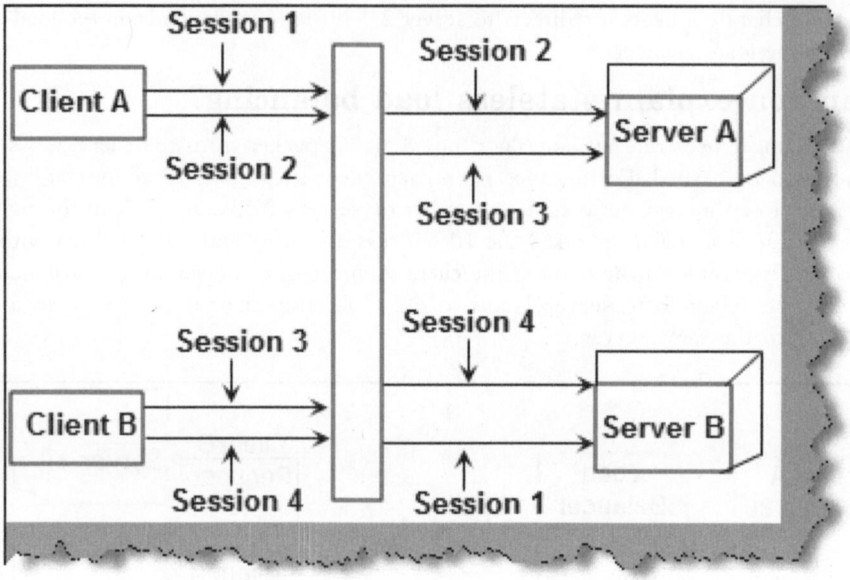

Figure: Stateful load balancing

You can see from the figure for every session the load balancer redirects the request to different servers.

(I) What is round-robin?

In this the load balancer gives connection to the server in a round-robin manner.

(A) Can you explain least connections, weighted distribution and response time ?

These are load balancing methods. In least connections the load balancer sees which server has least client connections and redirects the request accordingly. In weighted distribution you can define how much a server will be loaded depending on power and capacity of the servers. In response time load balancer redirects request depending on how the server's response time is.

> **Note:** *We have covered just the fundamentals of load balancing. There are many load balancing softwares available like Microsoft load balancer. Which ever load balancer you use the fundamentals of load balancing methods remain same. We would strongly suggest you to go through one of the load balancers to be confident during interviews. Every architect is supposed to know how to scale an application, so load balancer becomes a favorite question for every one.*

2

OOP

(B) What is OOP?

OOP is an approach towards software development. In this approach we think software as objects which interact with each other to complete a task. One of the main goals of OOP is to map software architecture with the real word. In real world we interact with objects and the object with other objects to accomplish a task. For instance currently you are currently interacting with the book object and the book is interacting with the pages object to accomplish the reading activity.

(B) What are the characteristic of OOP?

There are four main characteristics of OOP:

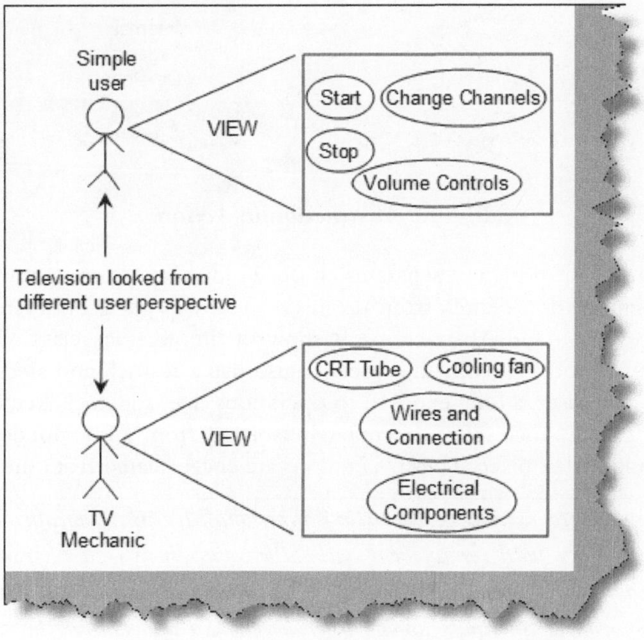

Figure: Abstraction Perspective

Abstraction: Abstraction filters un-necessary information from the user's perspective. It just gives enough information to the user rather than giving him unnecessary information by which he can get confused. Abstraction can be different from different user perspective. For instance figure 'Abstraction perspective' shows how a simple user looks at a television and how a TV mechanic looks at the television. From a simple user perspective he only needs to start,stop,change channels and control volume. But when a TV mechanic looks at the box he is concerned with details like CRT,Electrical Components,Wires,connection,cooling fan etc. So abstraction is about two things one is show only what is needed and second the need should be from end users perspective.

Ok, now how does that fit in to the software world. When we design components we should know what type of user will be using the component. Figure 'Abstraction in action' shows how the customer components has different view of abstraction for the internal and external developer.

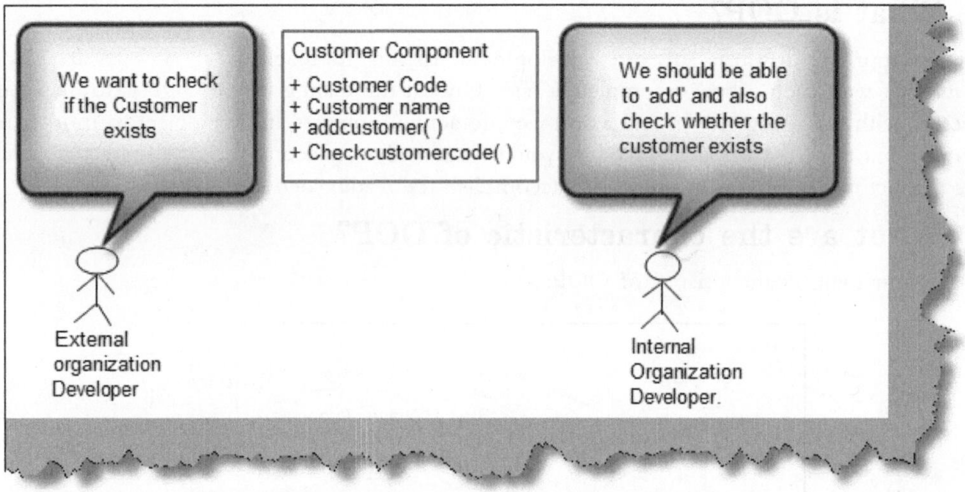

Figure: Abstraction in Action

- **Encapsulation**: Encapsulation separates an object interface from its implementation. It hides internal implementation details from the users. You can get a better feel by looking at the figure 'Encapsulation and Abstraction'. It shows a simple stock class which allows a user to add and remove products from the stock. It also has a restock and alert in case products are out of stock. End user is only exposed to operations like 'addstock','removestock' and get the current level of the stock. He is completely isolated from auto functionalities like how the restock operation takes place. These operations are encapsulated from the end user perspective.

Note: *Abstraction means to expose the necessary functionalities while encapsulation means to hide the complexity. They both complement each other, but there is a huge difference in terms of thinking approach. In interviews* **'difference between abstraction and encapsulation'** *is one of the favorites questions among interviewers. So understand the concept fundamentally as you can get in to long talks of confusion with the interviewer.*

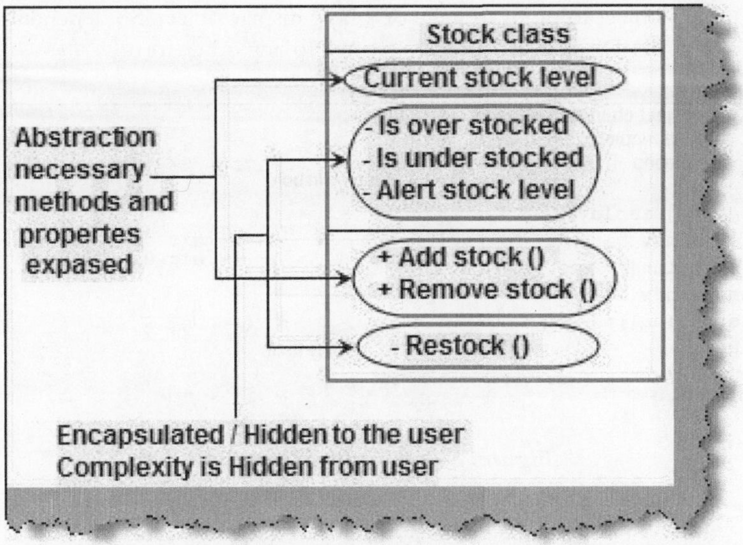

Figure: Encapsulation and Abstraction

In java or C# encapsulation is achieved by using private, public and protected access modifiers.

- **Inheritance**: OOP is all about mapping with real world. One of the relationships in real world is parent child relationship. Inheritance is a methodology by which you can form new classes using existing classes as base. For instance figure 'Inheritance in action' shows we have created a parent class called as 'ClsDisplay'. We can inherit from 'clsDisplay' and create bold and italic display classes.

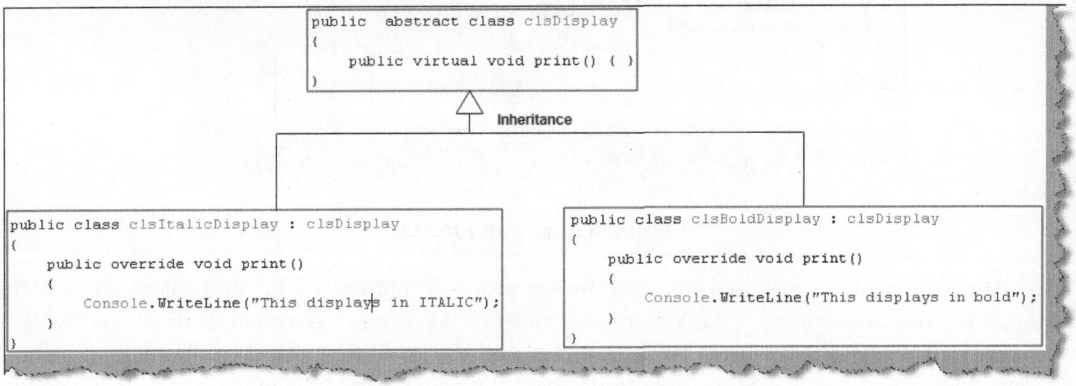

Figure: Inheritance in action

- **Polymorphism**: Polymorphism means one object can exist in different forms. It refers to ability of the object to take different forms depending on situations. For instance we can use the 'clsDisplay' object to point to italic or a bold display object. So depending on the situation the parent class 'clsDisplay' can morph/change to any other form.

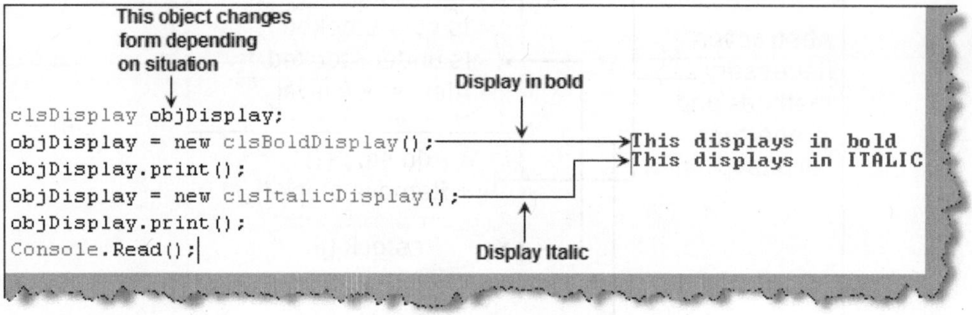

Figure: Polymorphism in action

> **Note:** *You can get source code of the same in C# in OOPs folder.*

(I) Can you explain interfaces?

In real world interface allows two disparate/ different objects to communicate with each other. For instance a human is a very different object when compared to television object. But they can still use the remote control interface to communicate with each other. Same holds true for interfaces in software, it defines a communication vocabulary between objects. Interfaces have empty methods and we can not create an object of interface.

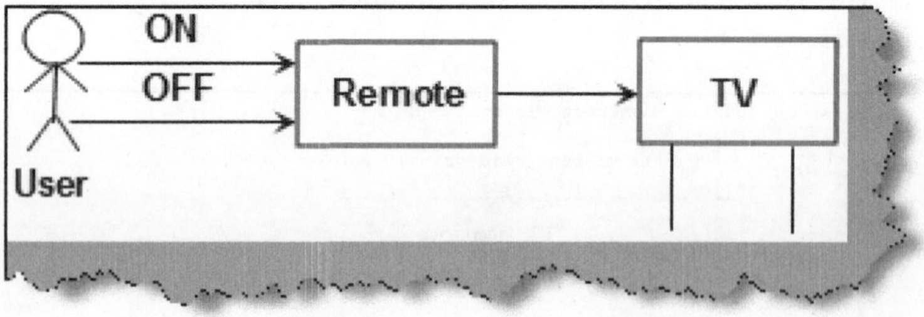

Figure: Television interface

The other important thing is that interface brings in lot of uniformity in the project. They define common way of communication. Let's consider a situation where you have multiple developers working on customer and supplier classes. You want that every developer should define the method name as 'Update' when these classes add the data to database. Developers are human's so some would name it as update and some as add. You can tackle this situation by defining an interface with a method called as update. Now all the classes inherit from the same interface thus making update method constant through out the classes. You can also see how the client code methods are looking consistent in naming convention thus enforcing consistent communication interfaces across all classes.

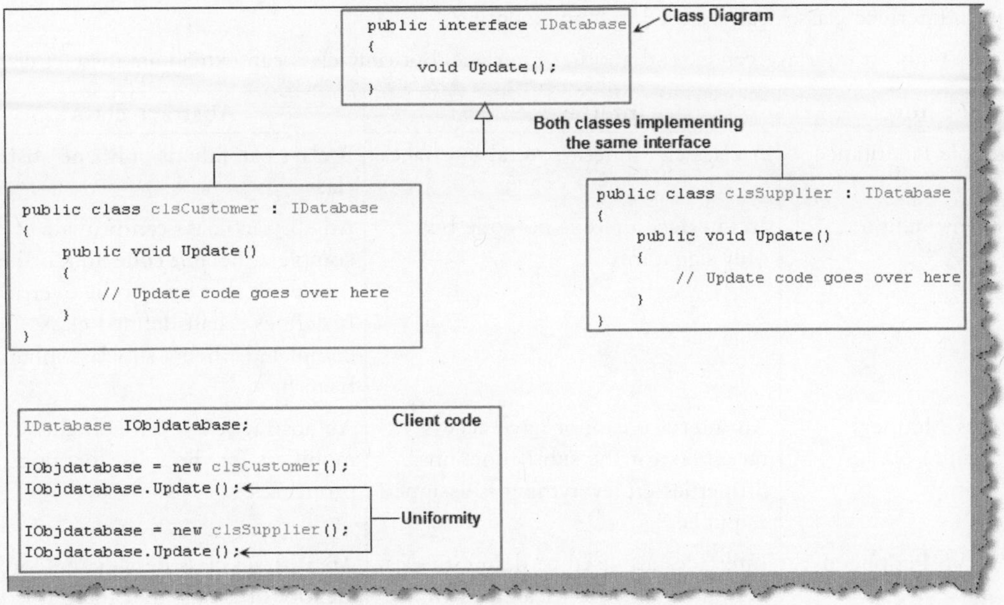

Figure: Interface fundamentals

(B) Can you explain aggregation and composition ?

This has been answered in the UML chapter.

(B) What are abstract classes?

Abstract class is designed to act as a base class (to be inherited by other classes).Abstract class is a design concept in program development and provides a base upon which other classes are built. An abstract class is a special kind of class that cannot be instantiated. So the question is why we need a class that cannot be instantiated? An abstract class can only be inherited. In other words, it only allows other classes to inherit from it but cannot be instantiated. The advantage is that it enforces certain hierarchies for all the subclasses. In simple words, it is a kind of contract that forces all the subclasses to carry on the same hierarchies or standards.

(B) What's the difference between abstract classes and interfaces?

Below are the differences between abstract classes and interfaces:

- An abstract class defines the generalization/specialization relationship. Interfaces define common interfaces by which classes can communicate in a uniform manner.
- Abstract classes can have implementations for some of its methods, but the interface class can't have implementation for any of its members.
- Abstract class defines few or none of the methods, but interface defines all the methods.
- Abstract classes are used by sub classing / inheritance.

- Interface classes can be used by implementing.
- Only an interface can extend another interface, but only class can extend an abstract class.

Feature	Interface	Abstract class
Multiple inheritance	A class can inherit several interfaces.	A class can inherit only one abstract class.
Implementation	In interface there is no code but only signatures.	An abstract class can provide complete, default code and/or just the details that have to be overridden. It defines a half defined class which completed when a subclass inherits from it.
Access Modfiers	An interface cannot have access modifiers for the subs, functions, properties etc everything is assumed as public	An abstract class can contain access modifiers for the subs, functions, properties
Core VS Peripheral	Interfaces are used to define the peripheral abilities of a class. In other words both Human and Vehicle can inherit from a IMovable interface.	An abstract class defines the core identity of a class and there it is used for objects of the same type.
Homogeneity	If various implementations only share method signatures then it is better to use Interfaces.	If various implementations are of the same kind and use common behaviour or status then abstract class is better to use.
Adding functionality (Versioning)	If we add a new method to an Interface then we have to track down all the implementations of the interface and define implementation for the new method.	If we add a new method to an abstract class then we have the option of providing default implementation and therefore all the existing code might work properly.
Fields and Constants	No fields can be defined in interfaces	An abstract class can have fields and constraints defined

(I) Can we create a object of a class whose constructor is private?

No

3

UML

(B) Define UML?

Unified Modeling Language, a standard language for designing and documenting a system in an object-oriented manner. It has nine diagrams which can be used in design document to express design of software architecture.

(I) Can you explain use case diagrams?

Use case diagram answers what system does from the user point of view. Use case answer 'What will the system do?'. Use cases are mainly used in requirement document to depict clarity regarding a system. There are three important parts in a use case scenario, actor and use case.

Scenario: A scenario is a sequence of events which happen when a user interacts with the system.

Actor: Actor is the who of the system, in other words the end user.

Use Case: Use case is task or the goal performed by the end user. Below figure 'Use Case' shows a simple scenario with 'Actor' and a 'Use Case'. Scenario represents an accountant entering accounts data in the system. As use case's represent action performed they are normally represented by strong verbs.

Actor's are represented by simple stick man and use case by oval shape as shown in figure 'Use Case' below.

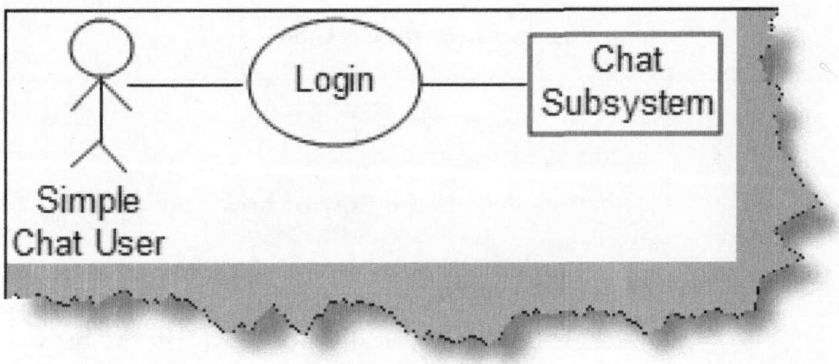

Figure: Use Case

(I) Can you explain primary and secondary actors?

Actors are further classified in to two types primary and secondary actors. Primary actors are the users who are the active participants and they initiate the user case, while secondary actors are those who only passively participate in the use case.

(I) How does a simple use case look like?

Use case's have two views of representation in any requirement document. One is the use case diagrams and the other is a detail step table about how the use case works. So it's like a pair first an over view is shown using a use case diagram and then a table explaining the same in detail. Below is a simple 'login' use case shown diagrammatically and then a detail table with steps about how the use case is executed.

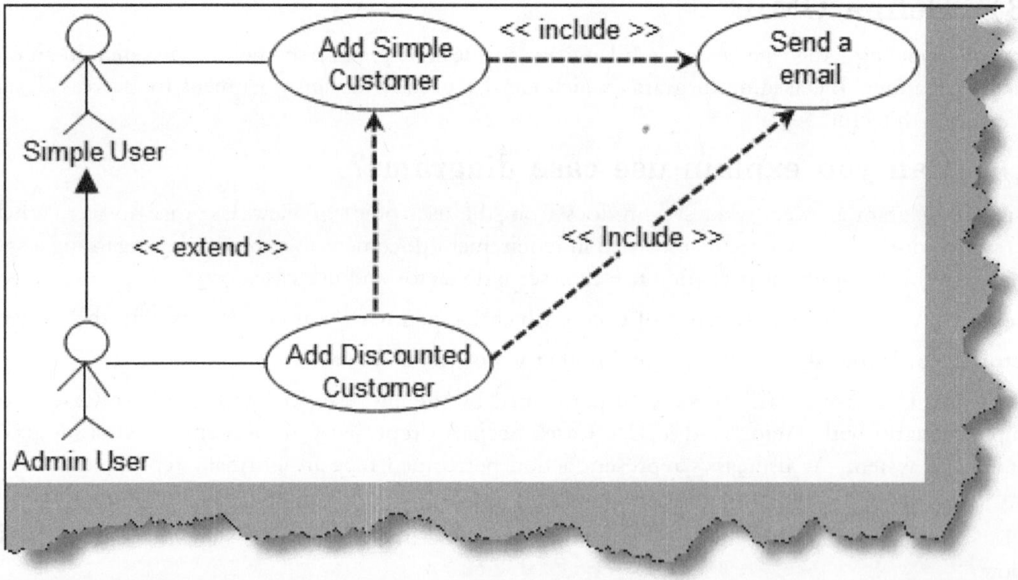

Figure: Login Use Case

Use Case	Rel001
Use Case Name	Login
Description	This uses depicts the flow of how user will log-in into the chat application.
Primary Actor	Simple chat user.
Trigger	User types chat application on URL of the browser.
Pre-condition	NA
Assumption	No password is currently present for the system Rooms will remain constant as explained in the assumption section of this document

Failed End conditions	Duplicate user name is not allowed in the chat application.
Action	User clicks on the log-in button.
Main Scenario	• User types chat application on URL of the browser which in turn opens the main page. • In the main page of application user is popped up with 'Enter user name' option and various 'rooms' option drop down menu. • User then types the name and selects one of the room from drop down menu and then clicks on the 'Log-in' button. • Application then checks whether the user name is unique in the system if not then user is popped up with error message that "user already exist". • After entering the unique name the user is finally logged in the application.
Action	NA
Alternate Scenario	NA
Success Scenarios	1. Opens page of a selected room in that other user names and their messages can be seen.
Note and Open Issues	NA

Table: Login use case table

> **Note:** *You must be wondering why we have this pair why not just a use case table only. Use case diagrams are good to show relationship between use case and they also provide high over view. The table explanation of a use case talks details about the use case. So when a developer or a user is reading a requirement document, he can get an overview by looking at the diagram if he is interested he can read the use case tables for more details.*

(I) Can you explain 'Extend' and 'Include' in use cases?

'Extend' and 'Include' define relationships between use cases. Below figure 'Extend and Include' shows how these two fundamentals are implemented in a project. The below use case represents a system which is used to maintain customer. When a customer is added successfully it should send an email to the admin saying that a new customer is added. Only admin have rights to modify the customer. First lets define extend and include and then see how the same fits in this use case scenario.

Include: Include relationship represents an invocation of one use case by the other. If you think from the coding perspective its like one function been called by the other function.

Extend: This relationship signifies that the extending use case will work exactly like the base use case only that some new steps will inserted in the extended use case.

Below figure 'Extend and Include' shows that 'add customer' is same as the 'add discounted customer'. The 'Add discounted customer' has an extra process, to define discount for the discounted customer which is not available for the simple customer. One of the requirements of the project was that when we add a customer, the system should send an email. So after the customer is added either through 'Add simple customer' use case or 'Add discounted customer' use case it should invoke 'send a email' use case. So we have defined the same with a simple dotted line with <<include>> as the relationship.

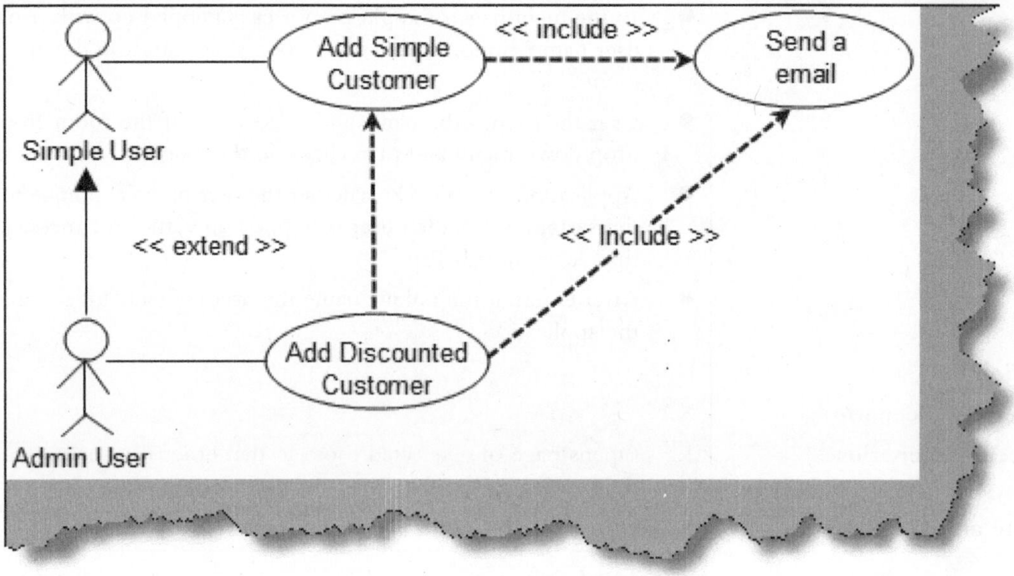

Figure: Extend and Include

> **Note:** *One of the points to be noted in the diagram 'Extend and Include' is we have defined inheritance relationship between simple and admin user. This also helps us defining a technical road map regarding relationships between simple and admin user.*

(I) Can you explain class diagrams?

Class diagram

Class is basically a prototype which helps us create objects. Class defines the static structure of the project. A class represents family of an object. By using Class we can create uniform objects.

In the below figure you can see how the class diagram looks. Basically there are three important sections which are numbered as shown in the below. Let's try to understand according to the numbering:

- Class name: This is the first section or top most section of the Class which represents the name of the Class (clsCustomer).
- Attributes: This is the second section or the middle section of the class which represents the properties of the system.
- Methods: This section carries operation or method to act on the attributes.

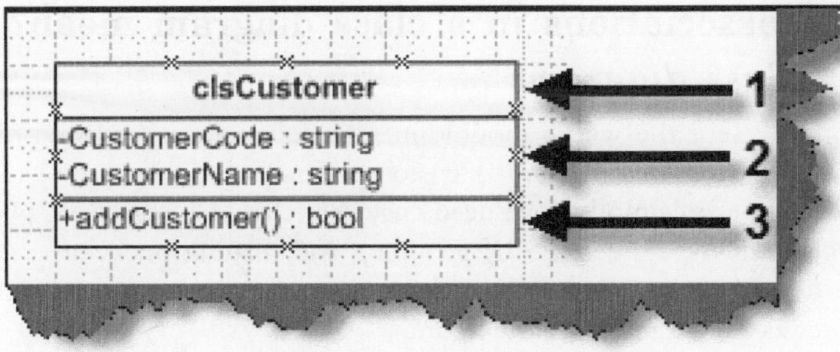

Figure: Three sections of the class

Now in the next section we will have a look on Association relationship between these classes.

(B) How do we represent private, public and protected in class diagrams?

In order to represent visibility for properties and methods in class diagram we need to place symbols next to each property and method as shown in figure 'Private, Public and Protected'. '+' indicates that it's public properties/methods. '-'indicates private properties which means it can not be accessed outside the class. '#' indicate protected/friend properties. Protected properties can only be seen within the component and not outside the component.

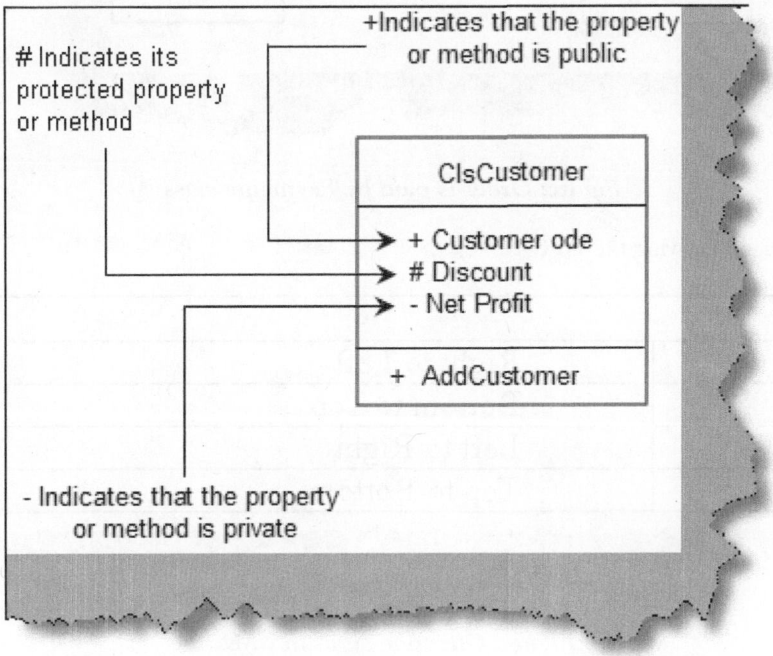

Figure: Private, public and protected

(I) What does associations in a class diagram mean?

Associations in Class diagrams

A single Class cannot represent the whole module in a project so we need one or more classes to represent a module. For instance, a module named 'customer detail' cannot be completed by the customer class alone , to complete the whole module we need customer class, address class, phone class in short there is relationship between the classes. So by grouping and relating between the classes we create module and these are termed as Association. In order to associate them we need to draw the arrowed lines between the classes as shown in the below figure.

In the figure 'Order is paid by payments class', we can see Order class and the Payment class and arrowed line showing relationship that the order class is paid using payment class in other words order class is going to be used by payment class to pay the order. The left to right marked arrow basically shows the flow that order class uses the payment class.

In case payment class uses the order class then the marked arrow should be right to left showing the direction of the flow.

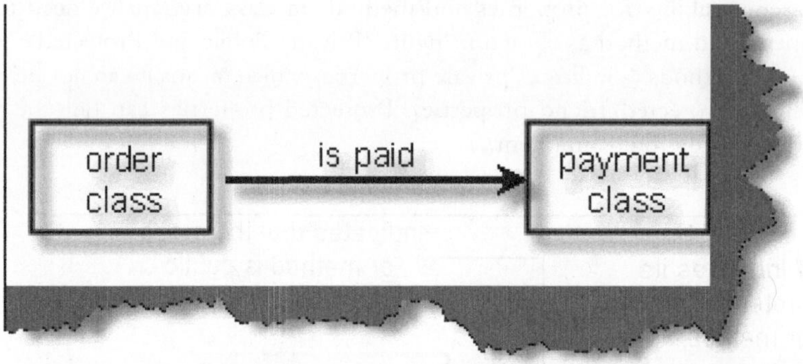

Figure: Order is paid by Payments class

There are four signs showing the flow:

<	Right to Left
^	Bottom to Top
>	Left to Right
v	Top to Bottom

Figure: Direction signs in UML

Multiplicity

Multiplicity can be termed as classes having multiple associations or one class can be linked to instances of many other classes. If you look at the below figure the customer class is basically associated with the address class and also observes the notations (*, 0 and 1).If you look at the right hand side the (1….*) notation indicates that at least one or many instance of the address class can be present in the customer class. Now towards left hand side we have (0….*) notation indicating that address class can exist without or many customer class can link him.

In order to represent multiplicity of classes we have to show notations like (1….*), (0….*) as shown in below figure.

> **Note:** *'*' means "many" where as '(0, 1)' means "(zero or at least one)" respectively.*

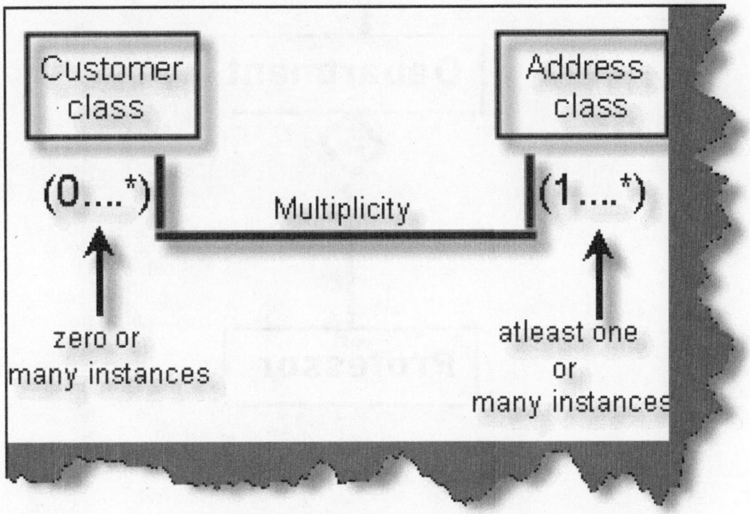

Figure: Multiplicity in Classes

(I) Can you explain aggregation and composition in class diagrams?

In this Association there are two types mainly Aggregation Association and Composition Association.

Aggregation Association signifies that the whole object can exist without the Aggregated

Object. For example in the below figure we have three classes university class, department class and the Professor Class. The university cannot exist without department which means that university will be closed as the department is closed. In other words lifetime of the university depend on the lifetime of department.

In the same figure we have defined second Association between the department and the Professor. In this case, if the professor leaves the department still the department continues in other words department is not dependent on the professor this is called as **Composition** Association.

Note: *The filled diamond represents the aggregation and the empty diamond represents the composition. You can see the figure below for more details.*

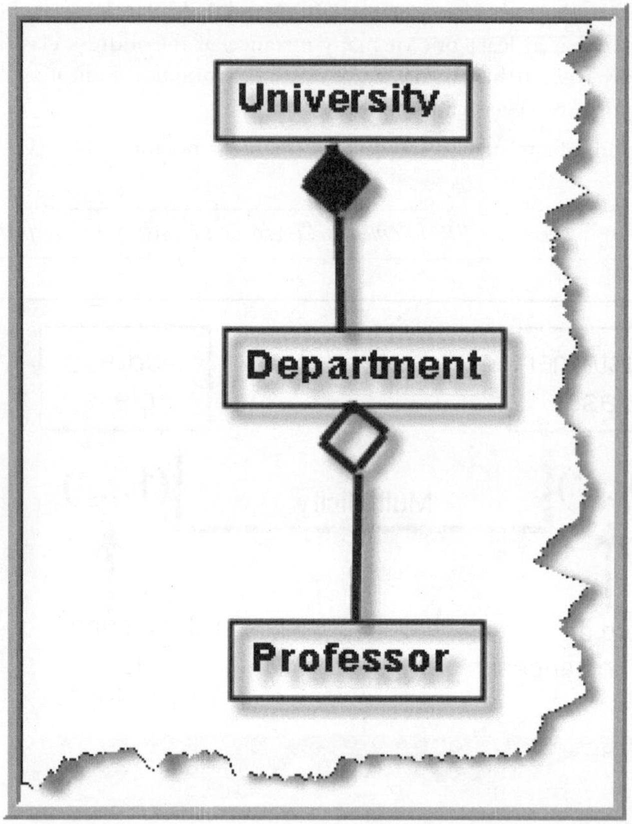

Figure: Aggregation and composition in action

(A) What are composite structure diagram and reflexive association in class diagrams?

Composite structure diagram

When we try to show Aggregation and Composition in a complete project the diagram becomes very complicated so in order to keep it simple we can use Composite structure diagram. In the below figure we have shown two diagrams one is normal diagram other is Composite structure diagram and the simplicity can easily be identified. In the composite diagram the aggregated classes are self contained in the main class which makes it simpler to read.

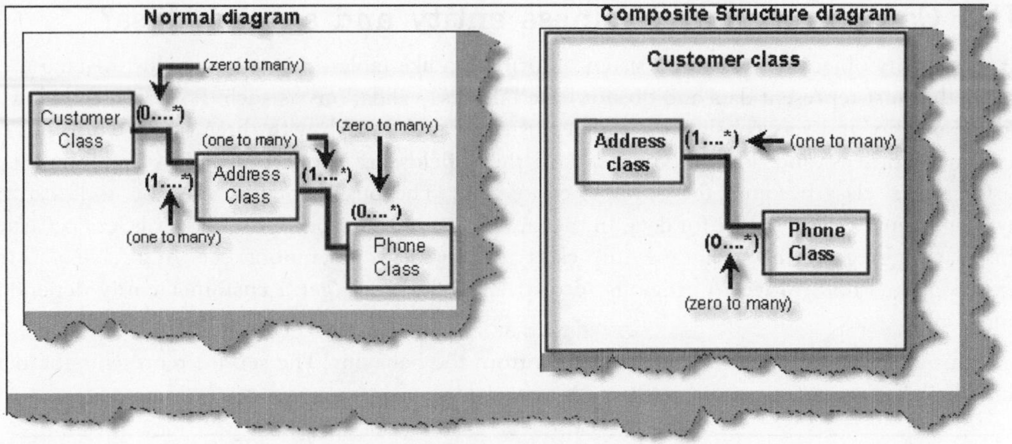

Figure: Composite Structure diagram

Reflexive associations

In many scenarios you need to show that two instances of the same class are associated with each other and this scenario is termed as Reflexive Association. For instance in the below figure shows Reflexive Association in the real project. Here you can see customer class has multiple address class and addresses can be a Head office, corporate office or Regional office. One of the address objects is Head office and we have linked the address object to show Reflexive Association relationship. This is the way we can read the diagram Regional address object is blocked by zero or one instance of Head office object.

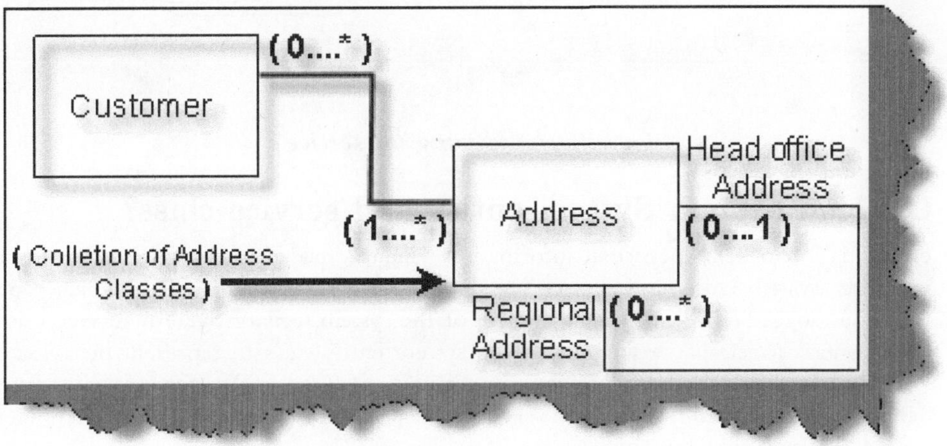

Figure: Reflexive association

(I) Can you explain business entity and service class?

Business entity objects represent persistent information like tables of a database. Just making my point clearer they just represent data and do not have business validations as such. For instance below figure 'Business entity and service' shows a simple customer table which with three fields 'Customer Code',' Customer Address' and 'Phone Number'. All these fields are properties in 'ClsCustomer' class. So 'ClsCustomer' class becomes the business entity class. The business entity class by itself can not do anything it's just a place holder for data. In the same figure we have one more class 'ClsServiceCustomer'. This class aggregates the business entity class and performs operations like 'Add',' Next' (Move to next record), 'Prev' (Move to previous record) and 'GetItem' (get a customer entity depending on condition).

With this approach we have separated the data from the behavior. The service represents the behavior while the business entity represents the persistent data.

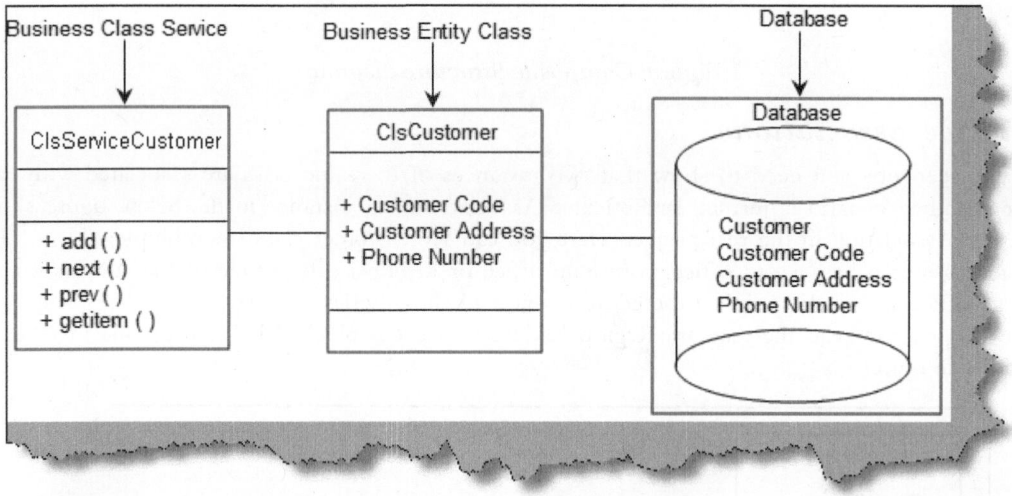

Figure:Business entity and service

(I) Can you explain System entity and service class?

System entity class represents persistent information which is related to the system. For instance in the below figure 'System entity and service class' we have a system entity class which represents information about 'loggedindate' and 'loggedintime' of the system registry. **System service** class come in two flavors one is it acts like a wrapper in the system entity class to represent behavior for the persistent system entity data. In the figure you can see how the 'ClsAudit' system entity is wrapped by the 'ClsAuditSytem' class which is the system service class. 'ClsAuditSystem' adds 'Audit' and 'GetAudit' behavior to the 'ClsAudit' system entity class.

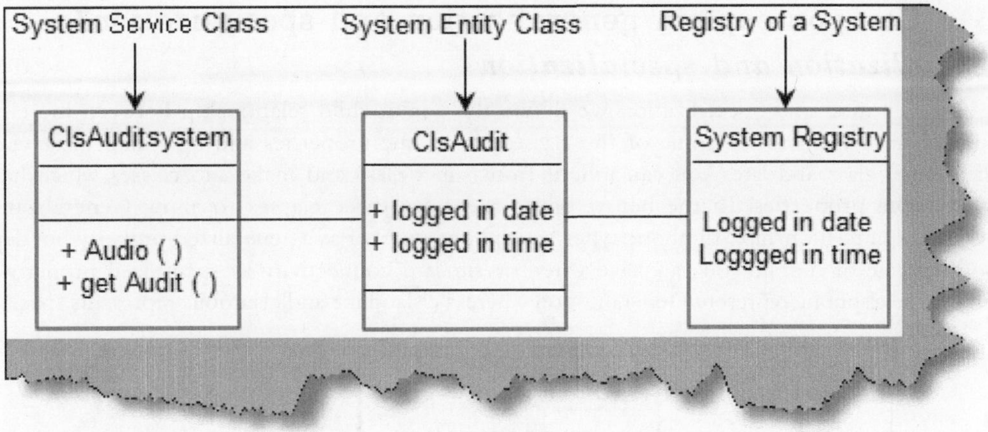

Figure: System entity and service class

The other flavor of the system service class is to operate on non-persistent information. The first flavor operated on persistent information. For instance the below figure 'Non-persistent information' shows how the class 'ClsPaymentService' class operates on the payment gateway to Check is the card exists , Is the card valid and how much is the amount in the card ?. All these information are non-persistent. By separating the logic of non-persistent data in to a system service class we bring high reusability in the project.

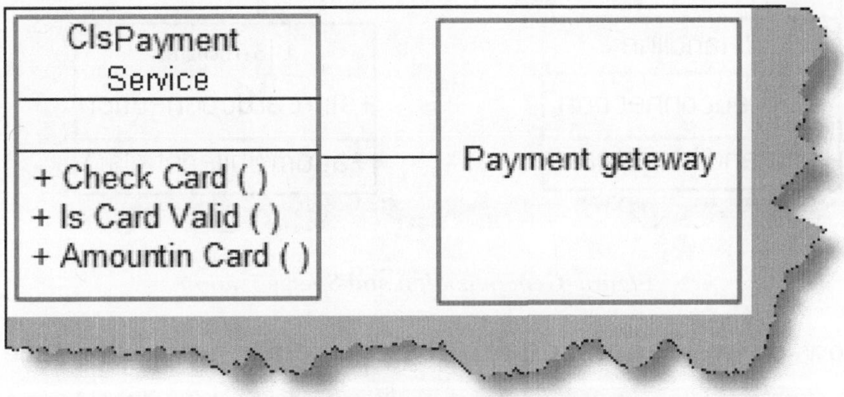

Figure: Non-persistent information

> **Note:** *The above question can be asked in interview from the perspective of how you have separated the behavior from the data. The question will normally come twisted like 'How did you separate the behavior from the data?'.*

(B) Can you explain generalization and specialization?

Generalization and specialization

In Generalization and Specialization we define the parent-child relationship between the classes. In many instance you will see some of the classes have same properties and operation these classes are called super class and later you can inherit from super class and make sub classes which have their own custom properties. In the below figure there are three classes to show Generalization and Specialization relationship. All phone types have phone number as a generalized property but depending upon landline or mobile you can have wired or simcard connectivity as specialized property. In this diagram the clsphone represent Generalization whereas clslandline and clsmobile represents specialization.

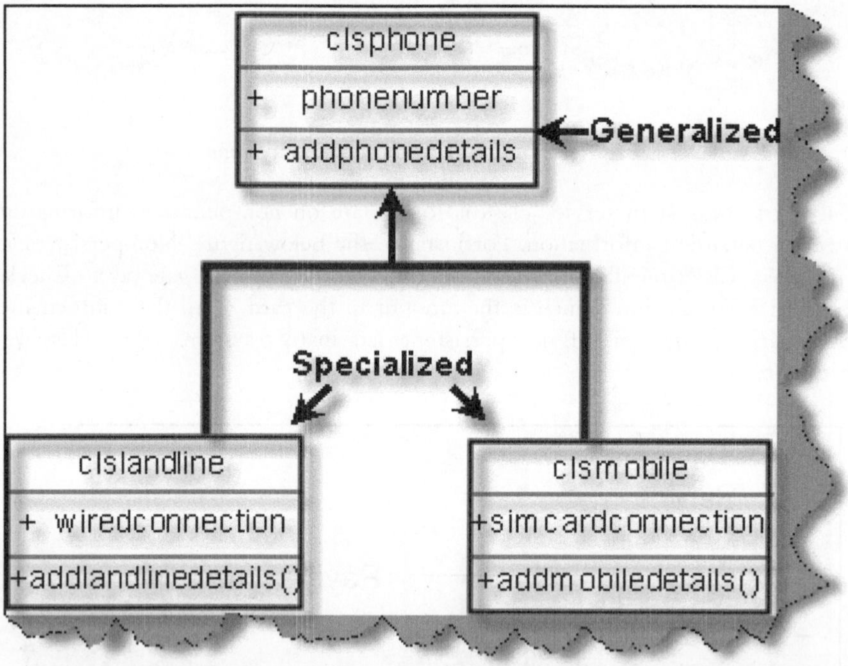

Figure: Generalization and Specialization

(B) How do we represent an abstract class and interface UML?

Interface is represented by <<type>> in the class diagram. Below figure 'Interface in action' shows we have defined an interface 'IContext'. Note the '<<type>>' represents an interface. If we want to show that the interface is used in a class we show the same with a line and a simple circle as shown in figure 'Interface in Action'.

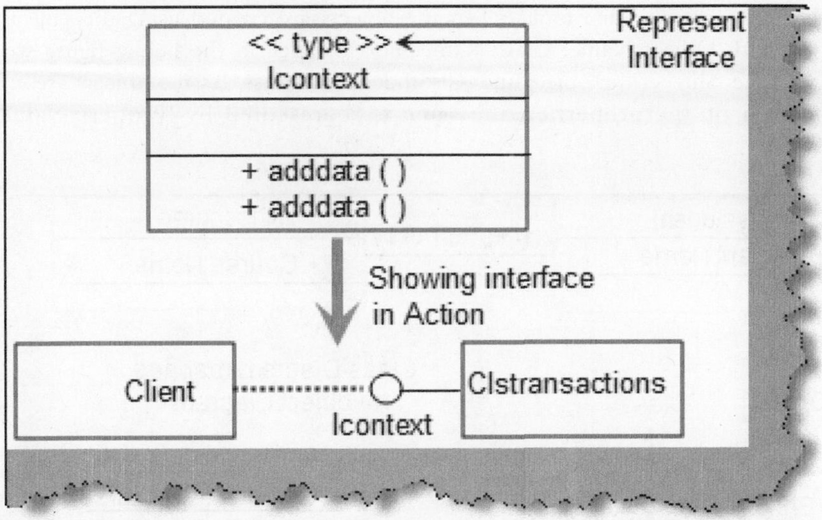

Figure: Interface in action

Abstract classes are represented by '{abstract}' as shown in figure 'Abstract classes in action'.

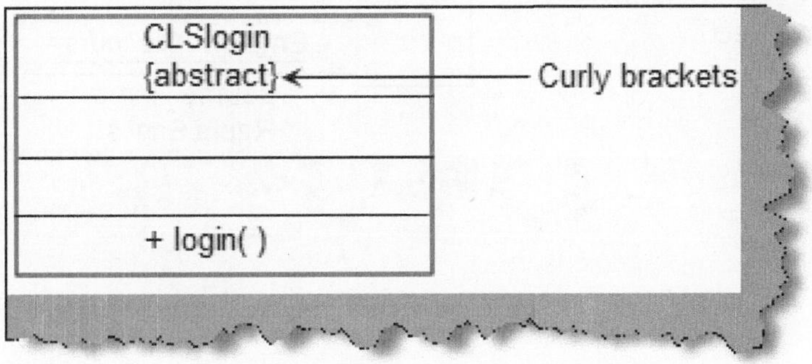

Figure: Abstract classes in action.

(B) How do we achieve generalization and specialization?

By using inheritance.

(I) Can you explain object diagrams in UML?

Class represents shows the static nature of the system. From the previous question you can easily judge that class diagrams shows the types and how they are linked. Classes come to live only when objects are created from them. Object diagram gives a pictorial representation of class diagram at any point of time. Below figure 'Object diagram' shows how a class looks in when actual objects are created. We have shown a simple student and course relationship in the object diagram. So a student can take multiple courses. The class diagram shows the same with the multiplicity relationship. We have also shown how the class diagram then looks when the objects are created using the object diagram. We represent object with Object Name: Class Name. For instance in the below figure we have shown 'Shiv : ClsStudent' i.e 'Shiv' is the object and 'ClsStudent' the class. As the objects are created we also need to show data of the properties, the same is represented by 'PropertyName=Value' i.e. 'StudentName=Shiv'.

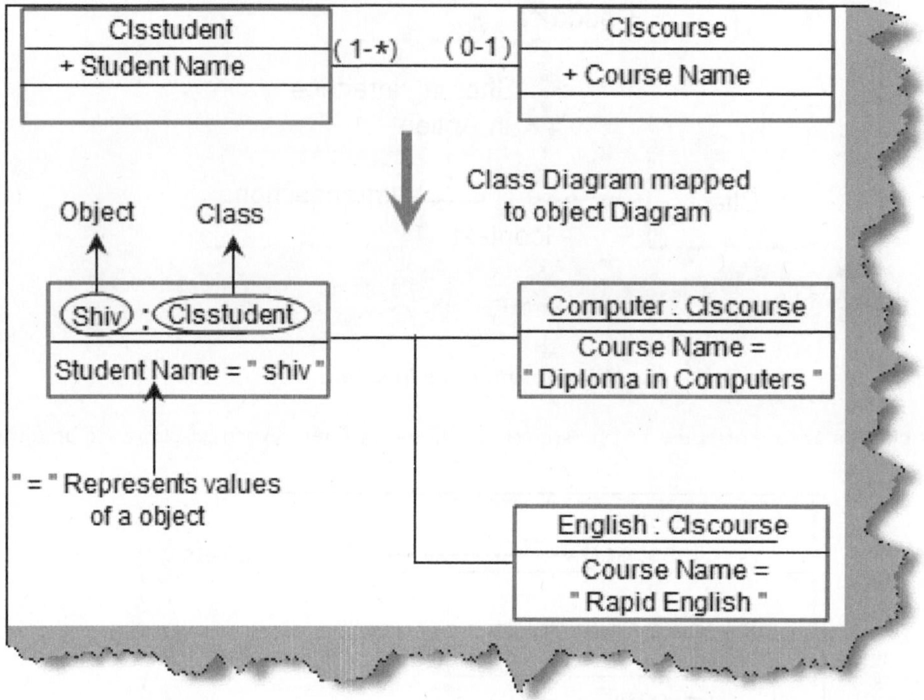

Figure: Object diagrams

The diagram also states that 'ClsStudent' can apply for many courses. The same is represented in object diagram by showing two objects one of the 'Computer' and the other of 'English'.

> **Note:** *Object diagrams should only be drawn to represent complicated relationship between objects. It's possible that it can also complicate your technical document as lot. So use it sparingly.*

(I) Can you explain sequence diagrams?

Sequence diagrams

Sequence diagram shows interaction between objects over a specific period time. Below figure 'Sequence diagram' shows how a sequence diagram looks like. In this sequence diagram we have four objects 'Customer','Product','Stock' and 'Payment'. The message flow is shown vertically in waterfall manner i.e. it starts from the top and flows to the bottom. Dashed lines represent the duration for which the object will be live. Horizontal rectangles on the dashed lines represent activation of the object. Messages sent from a object is represented by dark arrow and dark arrow head. Return message are represented by dotted arrow. So the figure shows the following sequence of interaction between the four objects:

- Customer object sends message to the product object to request if the product is available or not.
- Product object sends message to the stock object to see if the product exists in the stock.
- Stock object answers saying yes or No.
- Product object sends the message to the customer object.
- Customer object then sends a message to the payment object to pay money.
- Payment object then answers with a receipt to the customer object.

One of the points to be noted is product and stock object is not active when the payment activity occurs.

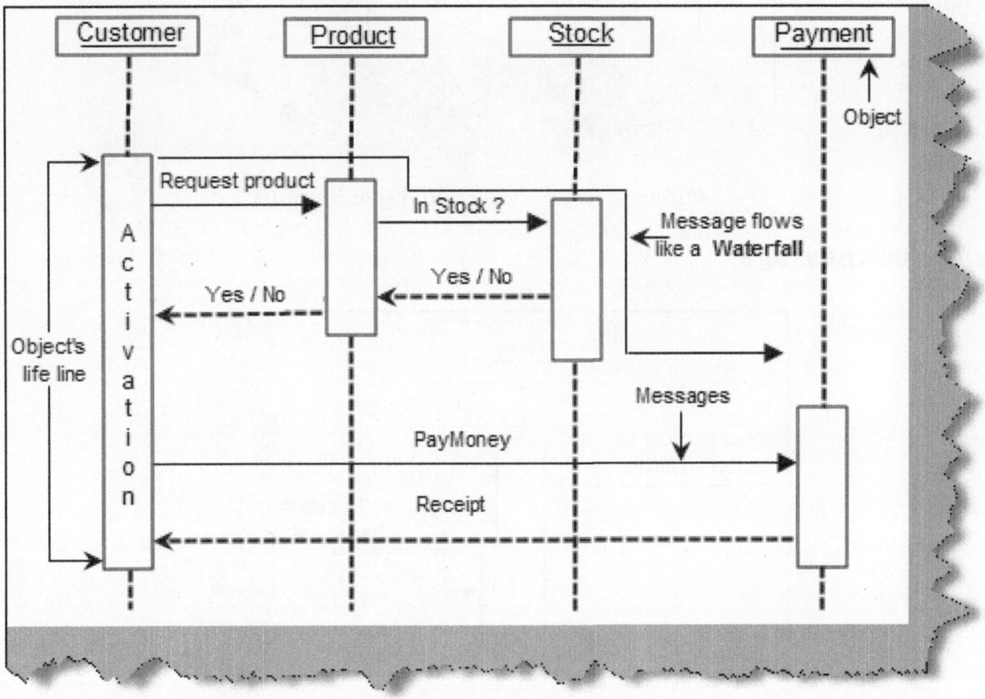

Figure: Sequence diagram

Messages in sequence diagrams

There are five different kinds of messages which can be represented by sequence diagram.

Synchronous and asynchronous messages

Synchronous messages are represented by a dark arrow head while asynchronous messages are shown by a thin arrow head as shown in figure 'Synchronous and Asynchronous'.

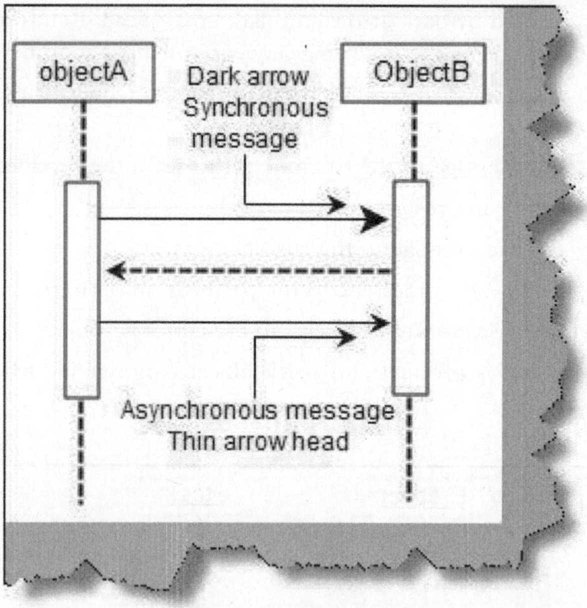

Figure: Synchronous and Asynchronous

Recursive message

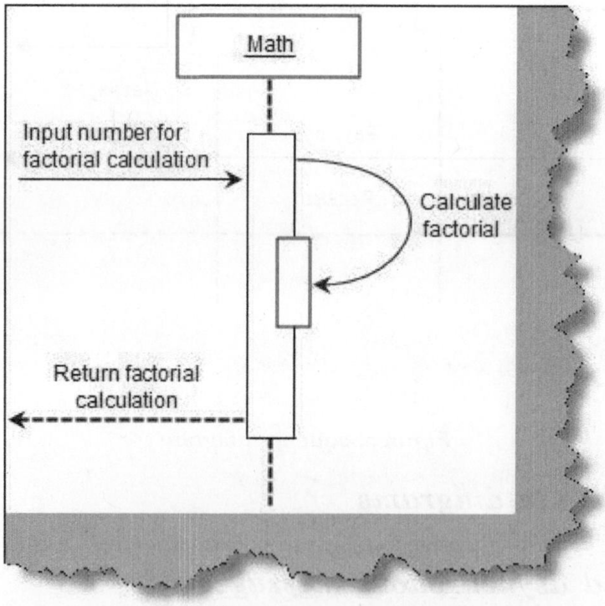

Figure: Recursive message

We have scenarios where we need to represent function and subroutines which are called recursively. Recursive means the method calling himself. Recursive messages are represented by small rectangle inside a big rectangle with an arrow going from the big rectangle to the small rectangle as shown in figure 'Recursive message'.

Message iteration

Message iteration represents loops during sequences of activity. Below figure 'message iteration' shows how 'order' calls the 'orderitem' objects in a loop to get cost. To represent loop we need to write 'For each <<object name>>'. In the below figure the object is the 'orderitem'. Also note the for each is put in a box to emphasize that it's a loop.

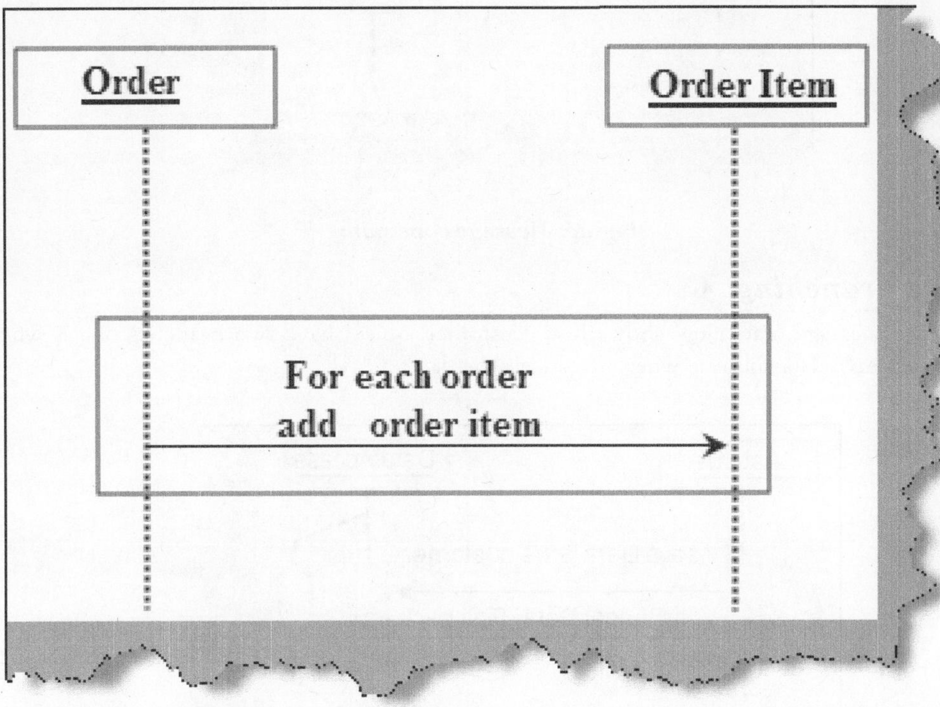

Figure: Message iteration

Message constraint

If we want to represent constraints it is put in a rectangle bracket as shown in figure 'message constraint'. In the below figure 'message constraint' the 'customer' object can call 'book tickets' only if the age of the customer is greater than 10.

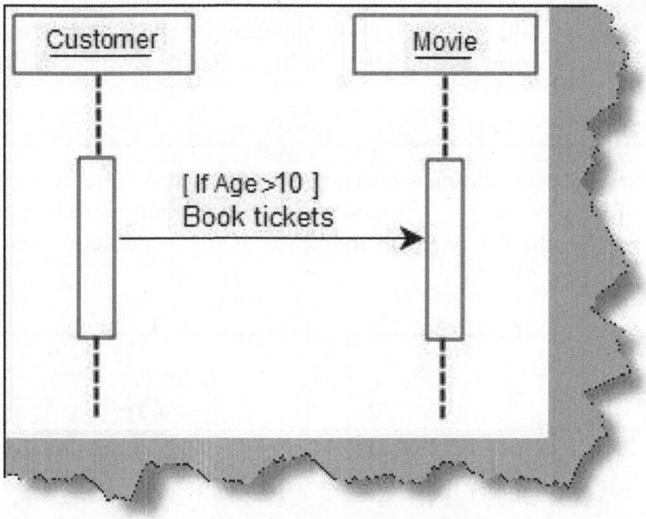

Figure: Message constraint

Message branching

Below figure 'message branching' shows how 'customer' object have two branches one is when the customer calls save data and one when he cancels the data.

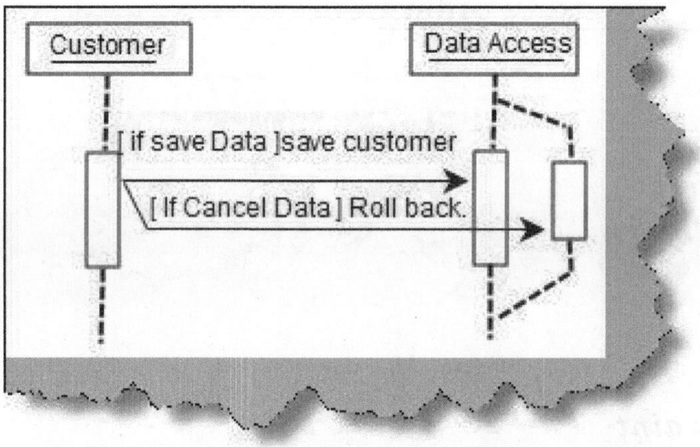

Figure: Message branching

Doing Sequence diagram practically

Let's take a small example to understand sequence diagram practically. Below is a simple voucher entry screen for accounts data entry. Following are the steps how the accountant will do data entry for the voucher:

- Accountant loads the voucher data entry screen. Voucher screen loads with debit account codes and credit account codes in the respective combo boxes.
- Accountant will then fill in all details of the voucher like voucher description, date, debit account code, credit account code, description, and amount and then click 'add voucher' button.
- Once 'add voucher' is clicked it will appear in the voucher screen below in a grid and the voucher entry screen will be cleared and waiting for new voucher to be added. During this step voucher is not added to database it's only in the collection.
- If there are more vouchers to be added the user again fills voucher and clicks 'add voucher'.
- Once all the vouchers are added he clicks 'submit voucher' which finally adds the group of vouchers to the database.

Below figure 'Voucher data entry screen' shows pictorially how the screen looks like.

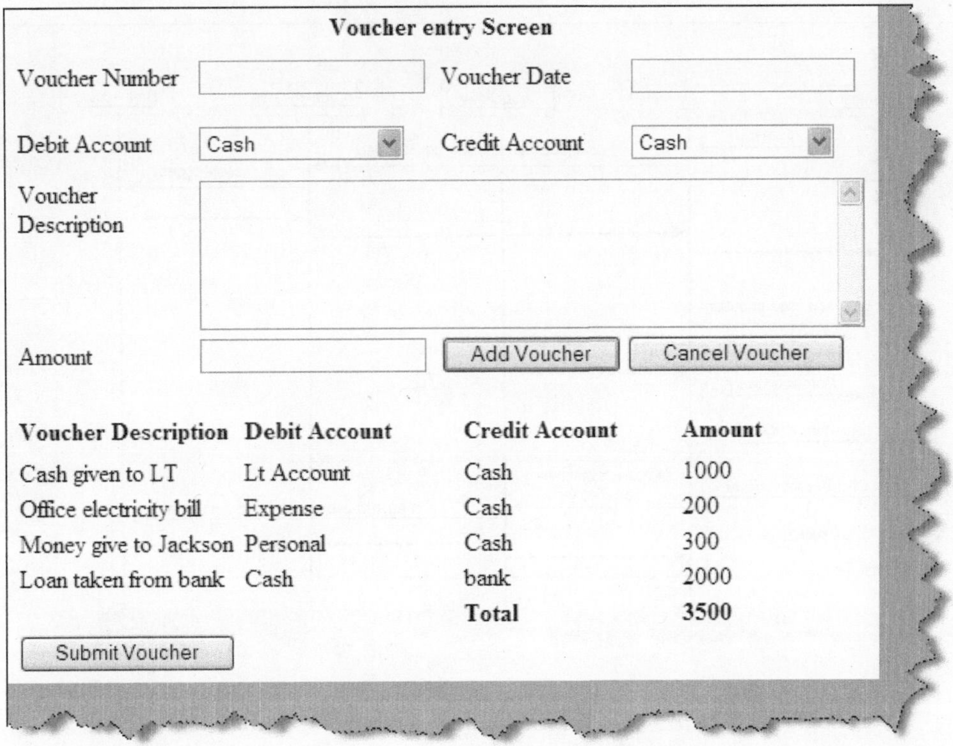

Figure: Voucher data entry screen

Figure 'Voucher data entry sequence diagram' shows how the sequence diagram looks like. Below diagram shows a full sequence diagram view of how the flow of the above screen will flow from the user interface to the data access layer. There are three main steps in the sequence diagram, let's understand the same step by step.

Step 1: The accountant loads the voucher data entry screen. You can see from the voucher data entry screen image we have two combo boxes debit and credit account codes which are loaded by the UI. So the UI calls the 'Account Master' to load the account code which in turn calls the data access layer to load the accounting codes.

Step 2: In this step the accountant starts filling the voucher information. The important point to be noted in this step is that after a voucher is added there is a conditional statement which says do we want to add a new voucher. If the accountant wants to add new voucher he again repeats step 2 sequence in the sequence diagram. One point to be noted is the vouchers are not added to database they are added in to the voucher collection.

Step 3: If there are no more vouchers the accountant clicks submit and finally adds the entire voucher in the database. We have used the loop of the sequence diagram to show how the whole voucher collection is added to the database.

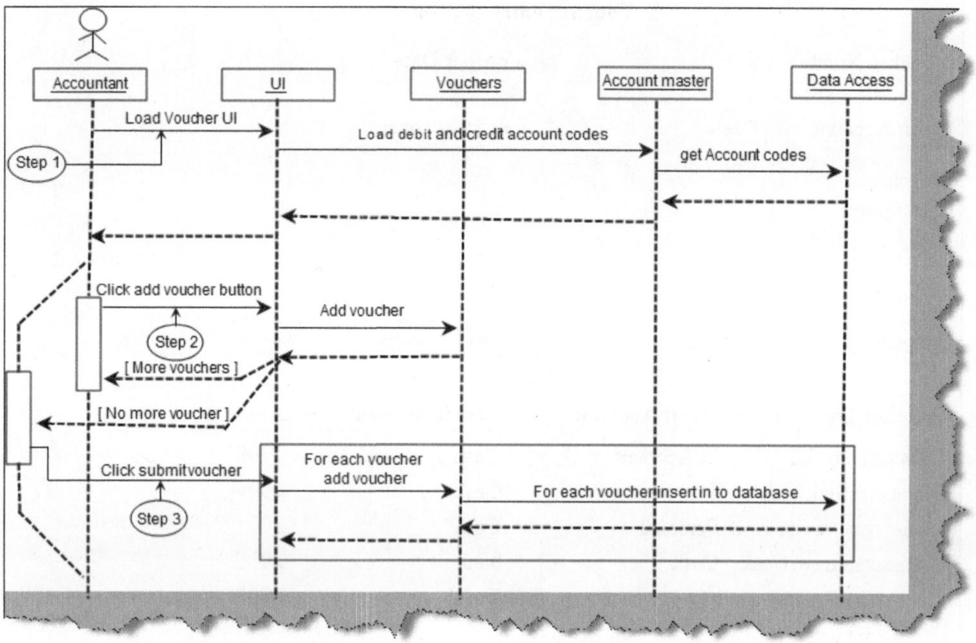

Figure: Voucher data entry sequence diagram

(I) Can you explain collaboration diagrams ?

Collaboration diagrams

Collaboration diagrams provide the same information as shown by sequence diagram but they show it in a different way. In sequence diagram we pay more attention to the time and sequence order, but in collaboration diagram we pay more emphasis on the interaction messages between the objects.

Figure 'Collaboration diagrams' shows how a collaboration diagram looks like. Below are some points you can easily pick up looking at the figure:

- Objects are represented in rectangle.
- Messages are represented by an arrow and sequence number. For instance in figure 'collaboration diagrams' we can see the 'order product' has a arrow which shows that the message is sent from the customer object to the product and '1' represents that it's the first messages.
- Conditional statements are denoted by square brackets '['.
- We can also group sequence numbers by grouping them using decimals. For instance 'Pay by master' and 'Pay by Visa' are all grouped in to message sequence number '3' ('Do payment'). So they are denoted by 3,3.1 and 3.2 respectively.

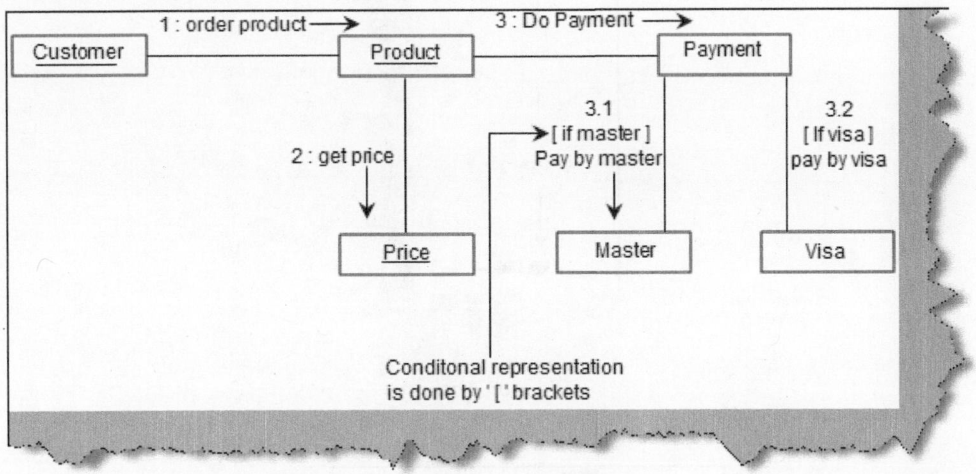

Figure: Collaboration diagrams

You can represent the for each loop using the 'for each' keyword as shown in below figure 'for each in collaboration'.

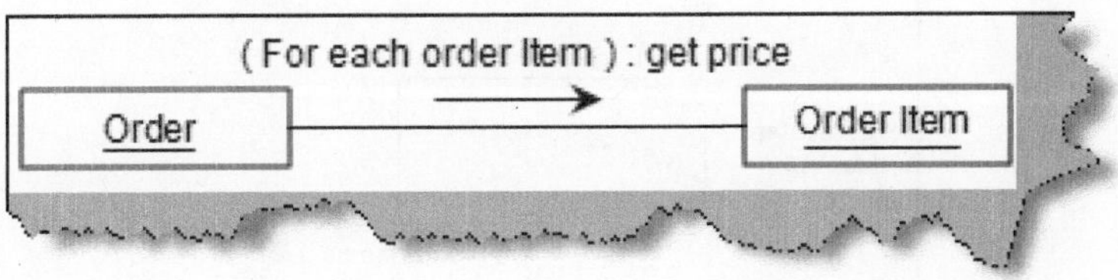

Figure: For each in collaboration

Note: *Try drawing a collaboration diagram for the same voucher data entry screen. Sequence and collaboration diagrams are also called as* **iteraction diagrams.**

(I) Can you explain activity diagrams?

Activity diagrams

Activity diagram are used to capture complicated process flows in a system. Below figure 'Activity' shows a simple activity diagram. Some of the points which you can easily note from the activity diagram figure are:

- Start of an activity is denoted by a dark circle.
- End of an activity is denoted by a dark circle inside a white circle.
- Activities are denoted by simple oval rectangles.

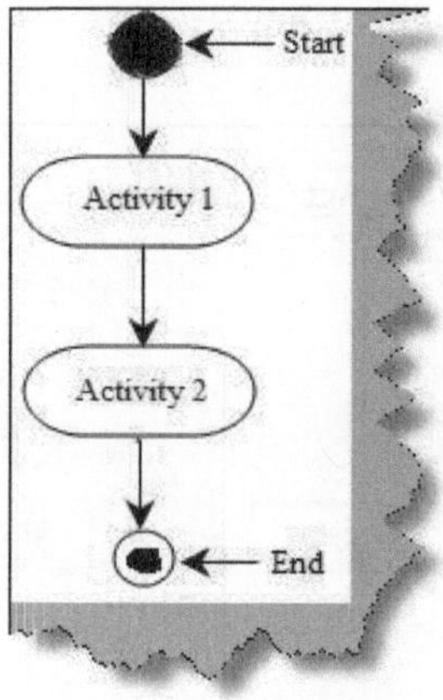

Figure: Activity

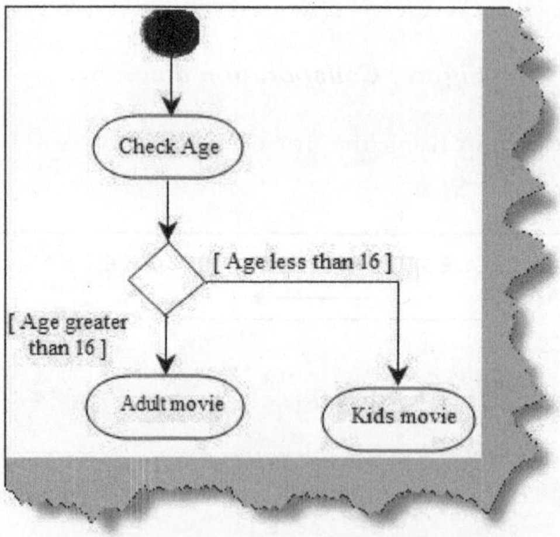

Figure: Decision in Activity Diagram

A decision in activity diagram is as shown figure 'Decision in Activity Diagram'. Figure shows the condition in a '[' (Square bracket). So the first activity is 'Check Age', if the age is greater than 16 then we can go for 'Adult Movie' activity or else we need to execute the 'Kids Movie' activity.

There are situations in project where we need to execute two parallel activities in a project. A solid bold line represents from where the activities will split and execute in parallel and then again a solid line is where the parallel activities will meet. For instance in the below figure 'Parallel Processing' we can see how 'Make lemon juice' and 'Make Ginger Juice' activities are executed in parallel.

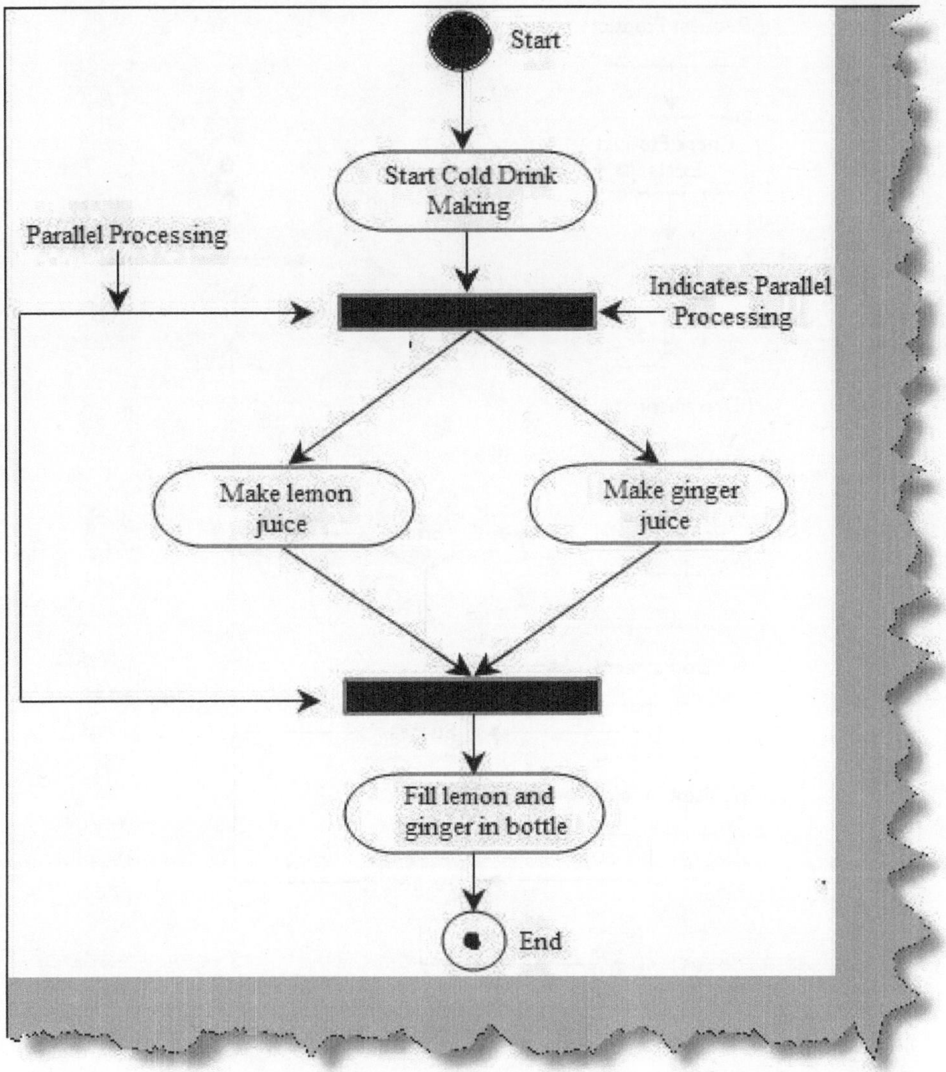

Figure: Parallel Processing

In big and complex activity diagrams it's very difficult to figure out which object is responsible for which activities. This problem is solved by 'Swimlanes'. Consider the below figure 'Without Swimlanes'. The whole activity diagram looks very complex and it's very difficult to figure out which object is responsible for which activity.

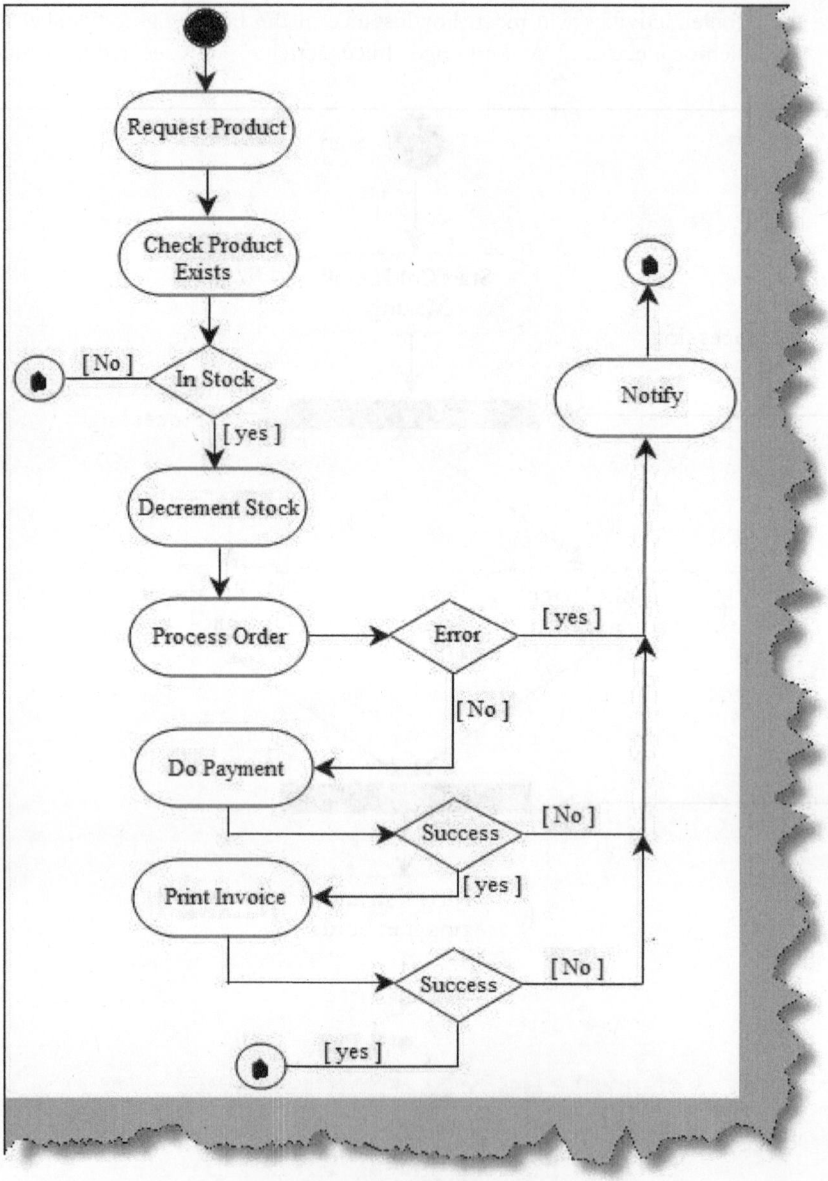

Figure: Without Swimlanes

Now see the below figure 'With Swimlanes' we have partitioned the activity to the respective objects like Customer, Stock, Order processing, Payment and Invoice. These partitions are termed as 'Swimlanes' , so if you feel that the activity diagram is complex think about using 'Swimlanes' it can really make your activity diagram readable.

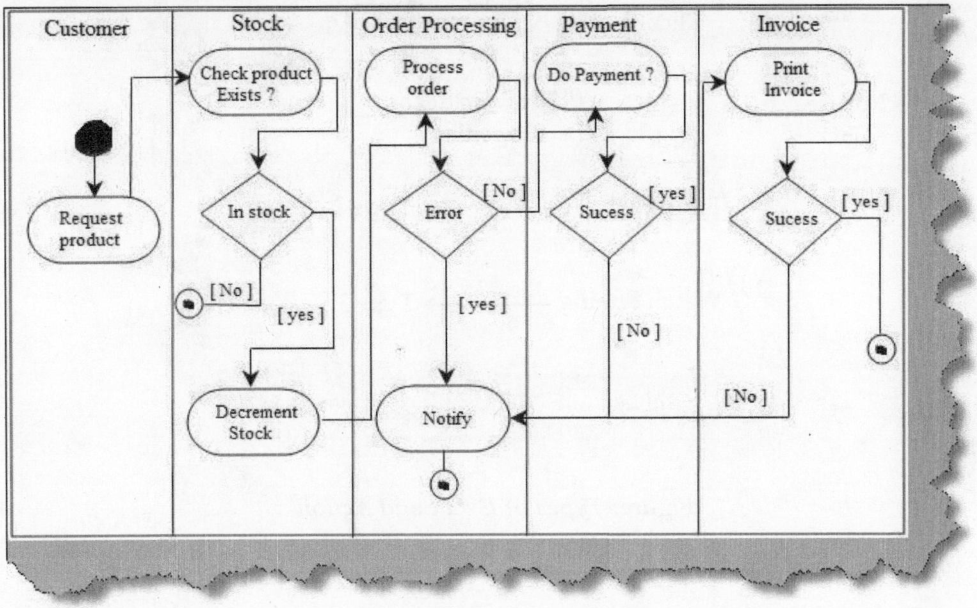

Figure: With Swimlanes

(I) What is state chart diagram?

State Chart Diagram

State diagram depicts different states that an object goes through during their life cycle. State diagram depicts how an object responds to events. We think state diagrams as optional and should be used if your project has scenarios where the object goes through lot of complicated states and transitions. If your project does not have such kind of scenarios then sequence, collaboration or activity would be sufficient to meet your needs. So all objects have states and an object moves from one state to other state when there is some event or transition.

There are three important things when we consider state of an object event, guard and action. Let's first define these three things: .

Action: Action triggers an object state from one state to another.

Event: Event triggers the action.

Guard: Guard is condition on which it evaluates which action to be triggered.

These three things are principle component of state chart diagrams. Below figure 'Types of event and action' shows how they are represented in state chart diagrams.

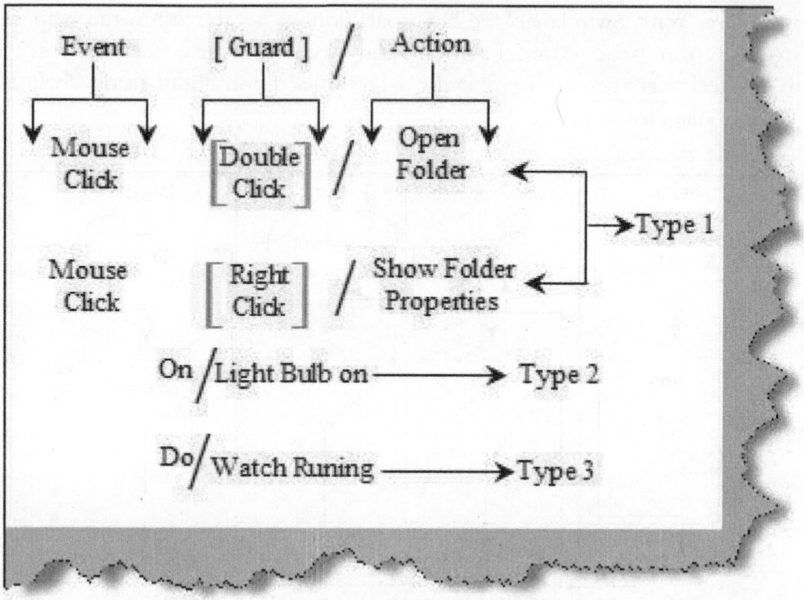

Figure: Types of Event and Action

There are three ways by which we can represent the same.

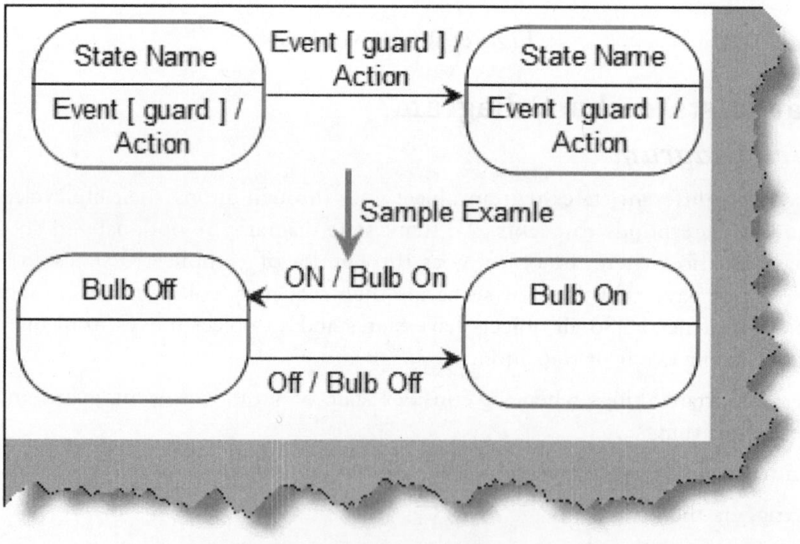

Figure: State example

Type 1: This methodology of writing is used when we need to map an event with action using a guard. For instance in the above figure 'Types of Event and Action' shows the event → mouse click, guard → double click and the resulting action → open folder.

Type 2: The guard is optional. For instance sometimes we only have events and actions, i.e. with out the guard. For instance when the even 'On' happens the action is that 'Light Bulb is on'.

Type 3: This type of representation shows an infinite loop for an action. For instance the 'Watch will be running' infinitely during a state, as shown in figure 'Type of Event and Action'.

Now that we know how to write event, actions and guard, let's see how state diagram looks like. Figure 'State example' shows how a state looks like. It's an oval rectangle as shown below. In order to show a transition we need to show an arrow from one state to other state as shown in figure 'State example'.

Below figure 'Sample state chart' shows a simple state chart diagram. Some points which are immediately visible from the diagrams are as follows:

- A dark black arrow indicates start of a state chart diagram.
- A dark circle with a white circle outside indicates end of a state chart diagram.
- Circular rectangle indicates state while arrows indicate events / transitions.

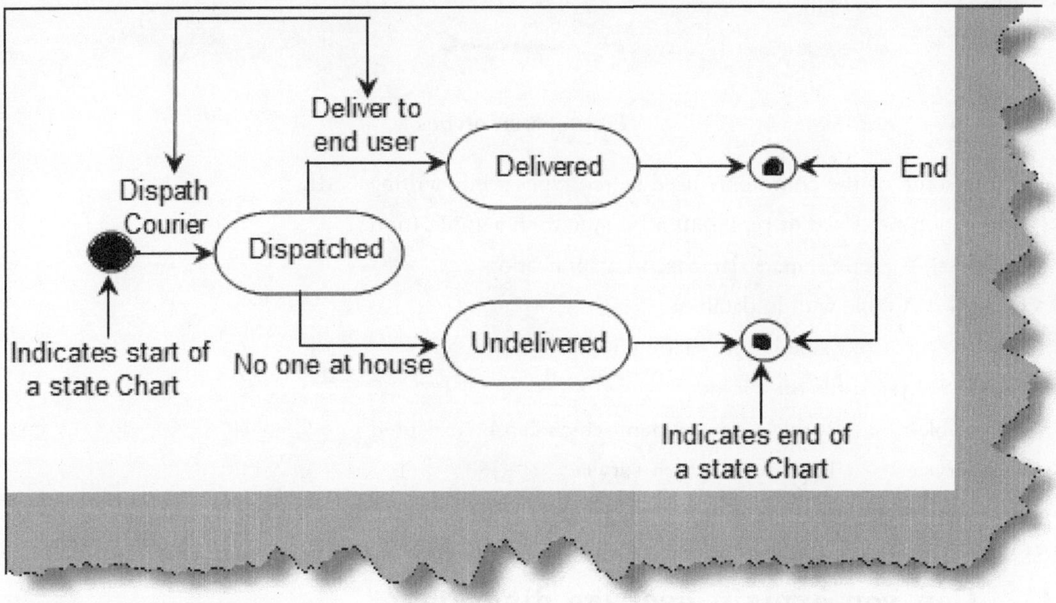

Figure: Sample state chart

(I) Can you explain stereotypes in UML?

Stereotypes are a way to define variations on existing UML model. This variation is brought in to place to extend UML in a consistent manner. They are displayed in double less than and double greater than sign with a simple text as shown below. The below figure shows at the left hand side a class diagram with out stereo types while the right hand side shows with stereo types. You can easily make out how the class diagram is readable with stereo types. For instance the 'Customer()' can be mistaken for a method but we have clarified that it's a constructor by using stereo types.

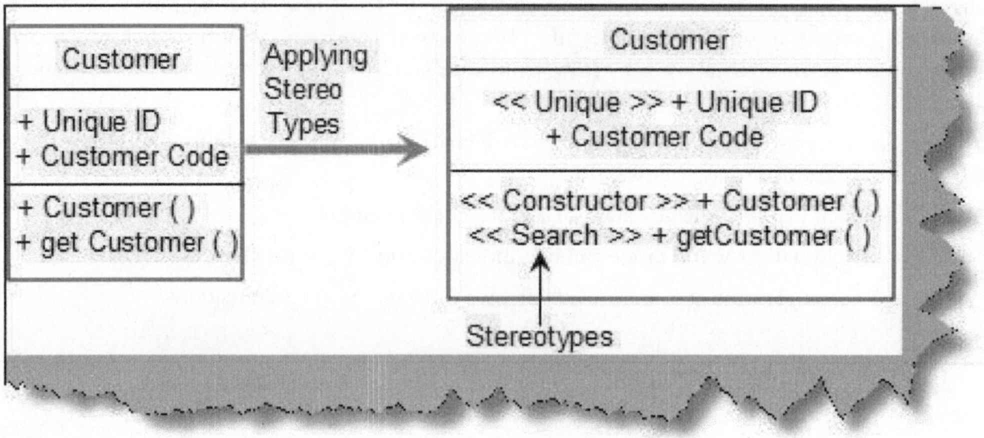

Figure: Stereotypes

Below are some of the commonly used stereo types while writing UML.

<<Application>>: Used to represent a UI system in a application.

<<Database>> : represents a database in a application.

<<Table>> : A table with in database.

<<Library>> : A reusable library or function.

<<File>> : Physical file on a folder.

<<Executable>> : A software component which can be executed.

<<Web services>> : Represents a web service.

<<JDBC>> : Java database connectivity , a JAVA API to connect to database.

<<ODBC>> : Open database connectivity , a Microsoft API to connect to database.

(I) Can you explain package diagrams?

Packages are like folders in a system which allows you to logically group UML diagrams. They make complex UML diagram readable. In actual projects they are used to logically group use cases and classes. So we can say there are two types of package diagrams one is class package diagram and other is use case package diagram. Package diagram depict a high level of overview for class and use cases.

Class package diagram: Class package diagram are used to logical group classes. You can think that package technically map to 'Package' in JAVA and 'Namespaces' in C# and VB.NET. Packages are denoted by small rectangle on a big rectangle as shown in figure 'Package diagram'. One of the points to be noted is the stereotypes. We have numbered the figure so that we can understand it better.

1 – We are using the MVC (Model View controller) framework. So we have denoted this package using the << Framework >> stereo type. Refer the commonly used stereo type table discussed in the previous sections.

2 and 3 – 'Book tickets' is the second package which inherits from the MVC model. The stereo type is '<<application>>' which means it's a user interface.

4 – A simple line shows a link between two classes stating that one class package uses the other class package.

5 – This package is collection of the booking engine library.

6 – The final package is the database.

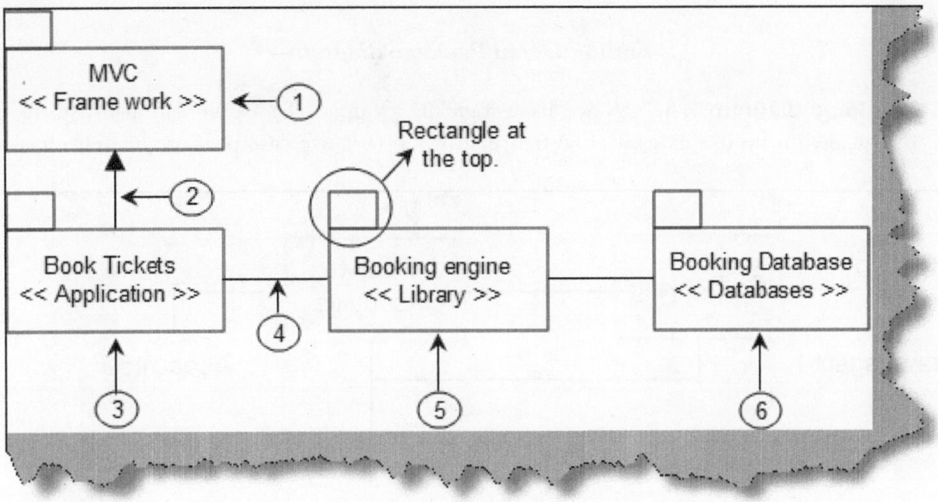

Figure: Package diagram

As said before packages are nothing but collection of logical classes or any UML entity. We have shown the detail of the above package diagram. We should restrict from using package diagram for showing the in depth architecture as it can become very complicated. For instance the below diagram 'Detail Package diagram' shows how complicated it can look if use the package diagram to show in depth architecture. To avoid complication its good to only draw an over all diagram as shown in 'Package diagram'.

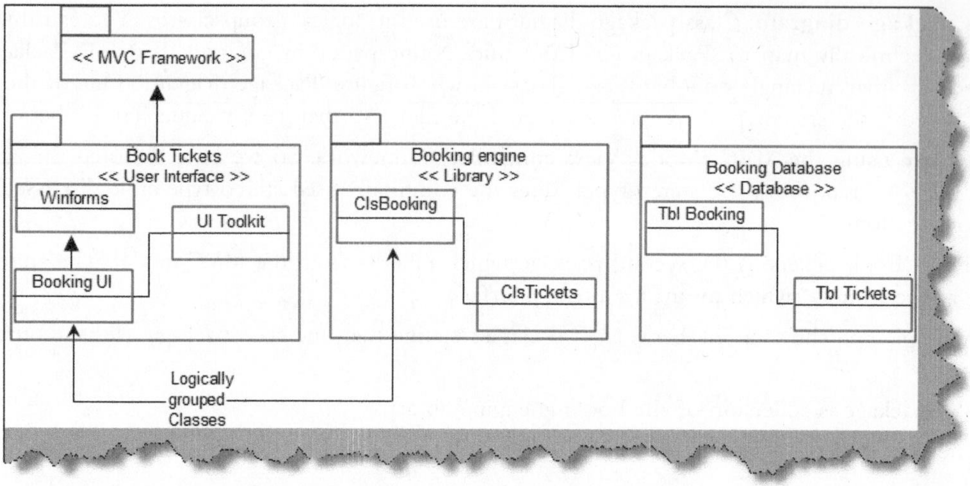

Figure: Detail Package diagram

Use case package diagram: The way we have logically grouped classes we can also use the package diagram to logically group use cases. Below figure shows how a use case package diagram looks like.

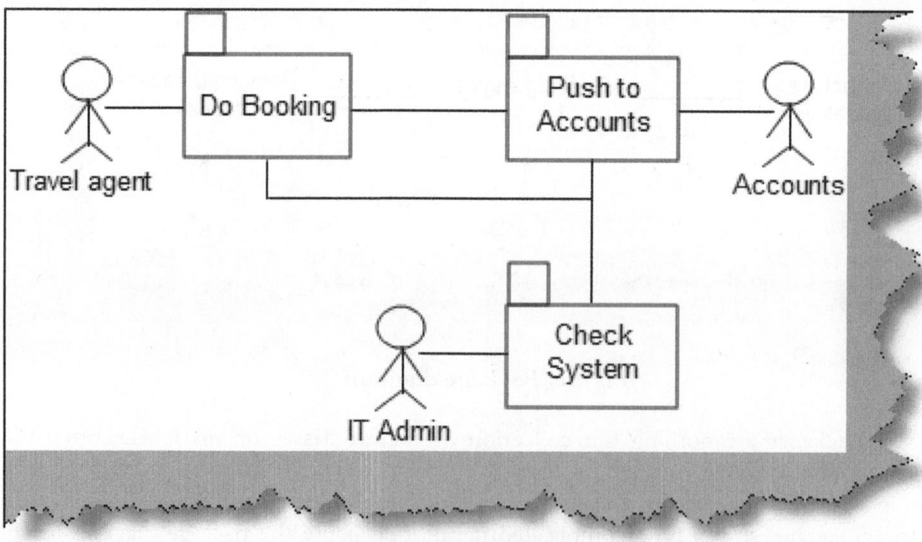

Figure: Use Case Package

(B) Can you explain component diagrams?

Component diagrams achieve the same objective like package diagrams. They show the dependencies among software components. Below figure 'Component diagram' shows a sample component diagram for simple data entry application which uses a web service to interact with the database. We have numbered the steps to understand the details of the component diagram.

1 – Two rectangles are shown to represent a component of a system.

2 – Stereo types are used to denote what kind of system it represents.

3 – A line with a circle denotes an interface by which the external world can interact with the component. For instance in the figure we have represented a 'Customer Web service' which can is interacted by using XML.

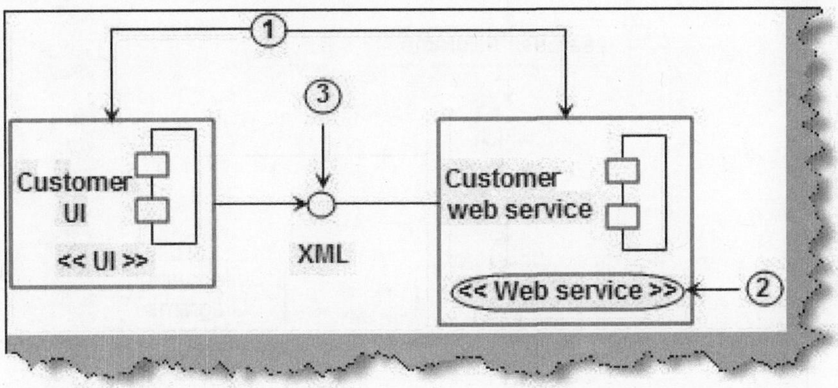

Figure: Component Diagram

(B) Can you explain deployment diagrams?

Deployment diagrams represents an overall static view of how software and hardware nodes in the application. They show what the hardware is and which components are installed on which hardware. In deployment diagram we represent the hardware with a solid box and simple underlined text description showing which hardware is it. You can have more than one component on a single hardware. So the browser is an application UI which resides on the workstation computer and the database and web server resides on the web server hardware. Deployment diagram can be more complex with firewalls, payment gateways, PDA devices, VPN etc.

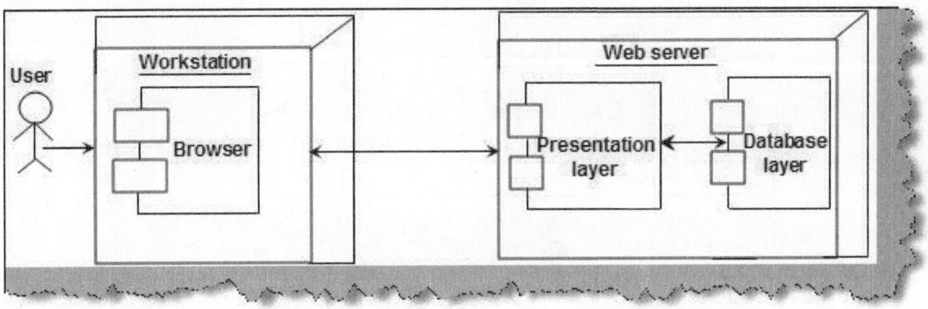

Figure: Deployment diagram

(I) Can you explain how UML flows in actual project?

In actual projects we do not draw all the diagrams. Every UML diagram is made for a purpose. It completely depends on what's the nature of the project. In short you should ask yourself questions like, is this diagram important, what's my need etc. So below is a flow which you can follow in your project, again as we said it depends on what kind of scenario you want to depict.

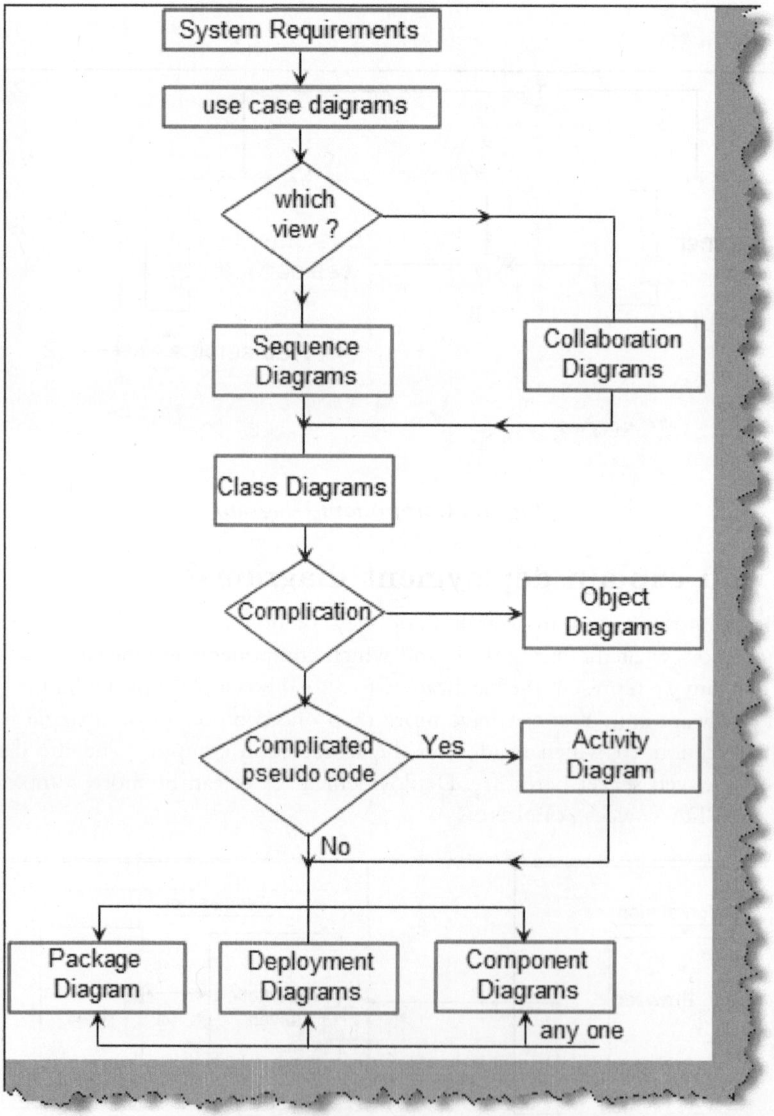

Figure: UML flow in actual projects

- The first step is to derive use cases from the requirement documents.
- Once use cases are derived we need to decide the messages which will flow in the system. This can be done using interaction diagrams. If you need to know the object creation life times we use the sequence diagram and if we want to concentrate on the messages we use the collaboration diagrams. So depending on scenario we need to make a choice which diagram we need to draw.
- Now that we are clear about messages we can draw class diagrams to depict the static part of the project i.e. classes.
- If we find any complicated class relationships we draw object diagrams.
- If we need to depict any complicated code we need to represent same with a activity diagram.
- Finally to give an overview of the project we can use package diagram, component or deployment diagram. As said before we can use combination of component and deployment diagram to give a overview of the architecture.

Note: *Never say in a interview that we have used all UML diagrams in the technical document. It can give a very bad impression. As said every UML diagram is drawn according to the scenario of the project.*

4

Design Patterns

(B) What are design patterns?

Design patterns are documented tried and tested solutions for recurring problems in a given context. So basically you have a problem context and the proposed solution for the same. Design patterns existed in some or other form right from the inception stage of software development. Let's say if you want to implement a sorting algorithm the first thing comes to mind is bubble sort. So the problem is sorting and solution is bubble sort. Same holds true for design patterns.

(I) Which are the three main categories of design patterns?

There are three basic classifications of patterns Creational, Structural, and Behavioral patterns.

Creational Patterns

- **Abstract Factory:** Creates an instance of several families of classes
- **Builder:** Separates object construction from its representation
- **Factory Method:** Creates an instance of several derived classes
- **Prototype:** A fully initialized instance to be copied or cloned
- **Singleton:** A class in which only a single instance can exist

> **Note:** *The best way to remember Creational pattern is by ABFPS (Abraham Became First President of States).*

Structural Patterns

- **Adapter:** Match interfaces of different classes.
- **Bridge:** Separates an object's abstraction from its implementation.
- **Composite:** A tree structure of simple and composite objects.
- **Decorator:** Add responsibilities to objects dynamically.
- **Façade:** A single class that represents an entire subsystem.
- **Flyweight:** A fine-grained instance used for efficient sharing.
- **Proxy:** An object representing another object.

> **Note:** *To remember structural pattern best is (ABCDFFP)*

Behavioral Patterns

- **Mediator:**Defines simplified communication between classes.
- **Memento:**Capture and restore an object's internal state.
- **Interpreter:** A way to include language elements in a program.
- **Iterator:**Sequentially access the elements of a collection.
- **Chain of Resp:** A way of passing a request between a chain of objects.
- **Command:**Encapsulate a command request as an object.
- **State:**Alter an object's behavior when its state changes.
- **Strategy:**Encapsulates an algorithm inside a class.
- **Observer:** A way of notifying change to a number of classes.
- **Template Method:**Defer the exact steps of an algorithm to a subclass.
- **Visitor:**Defines a new operation to a class without change.

Note: *Just remember Music....... 2 MICS On TV (MMIICCSSOTV).*

Note: *In the further section we will be covering all the above design patterns in a more detail manner.*

(A) Can you explain factory pattern?

Factory pattern is one of the types of creational patterns. You can make out from the name factory itself it's meant to construct and create something. In software architecture world factory pattern is meant to centralize creation of objects. Below is a code snippet of a client which has different types of invoices. These invoices are created depending on the invoice type specified by the client. There are two issues with the code below:

- First we have lots of 'new' keyword scattered in the client. In other ways the client is loaded with lot of object creational activities which can make the client logic very complicated.
- Second issue is that the client needs to be aware of all types of invoices. So if we are adding one more invoice class type called as 'InvoiceWithFooter' we need to reference the new class in the client and recompile the client also.

```
if (intInvoiceType == 1)
{
   objinv = new clsInvoiceWithHeader();
}
else if (intInvoiceType == 2)
{
    objinv = new clsInvoiceWithOutHeaders();
}
```

Figure: Different types of invoice

Taking these issues as our base we will now look in to how factory pattern can help us solve the same. Below figure 'Factory Pattern' shows two concrete classes 'ClsInvoiceWithHeader' and 'ClsInvoiceWithOutHeader'.

The **first issue** was that these classes are in direct contact with client which leads to lot of 'new' keyword scattered in the client code. This is removed by introducing a new class 'ClsFactoryInvoice' which does all the creation of objects.

The **second issue** was that the client code is aware of both the concrete classes i.e. 'ClsInvoiceWithHeader' and 'ClsInvoiceWithOutHeader'. This leads to recompiling of the client code when we add new invoice types. For instance if we add 'ClsInvoiceWithFooter' client code needs to be changed and recompiled accordingly. To remove this issue we have introduced a common interface 'IInvoice'. Both the concrete classes 'ClsInvoiceWithHeader' and 'ClsInvoiceWithOutHeader' inherit and implement the 'IInvoice' interface.

The client references only the 'IInvoice' interface which results in zero connection between client and the concrete classes ('ClsInvoiceWithHeader' and 'ClsInvoiceWithOutHeader'). So now if we add new concrete invoice class we do not need to change any thing at the client side.

In one line the creation of objects is taken care by 'ClsFactoryInvoice' and the client disconnection from the concrete classes is taken care by 'IInvoice' interface.

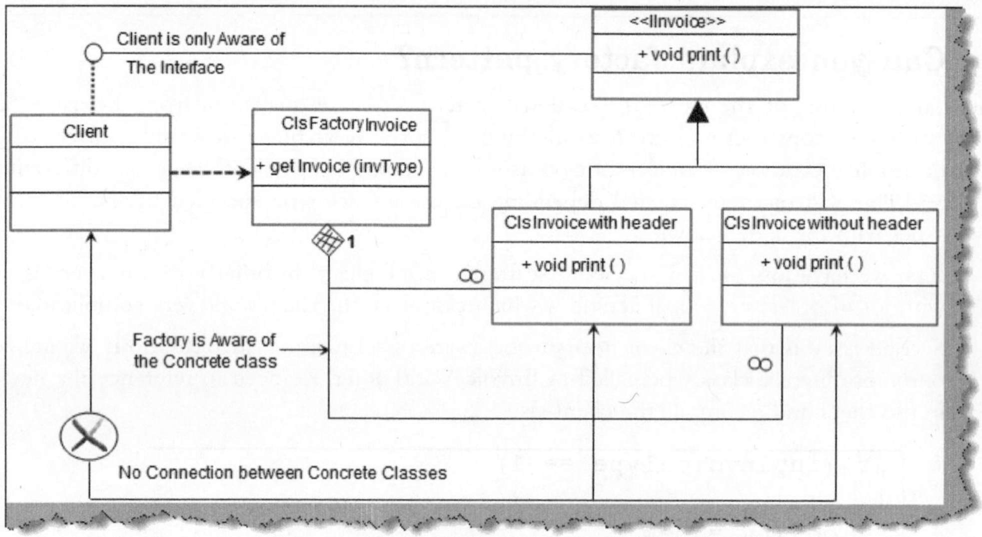

Figure: Factory pattern

Below are the code snippets of how actually factory pattern can be implemented in C#. In order to avoid recompiling the client we have introduced the invoice interface 'IInvoice'. Both the concrete classes 'ClsInvoiceWithOutHeaders' and 'ClsInvoiceWithHeader' inherit and implement the 'IInvoice' interface.

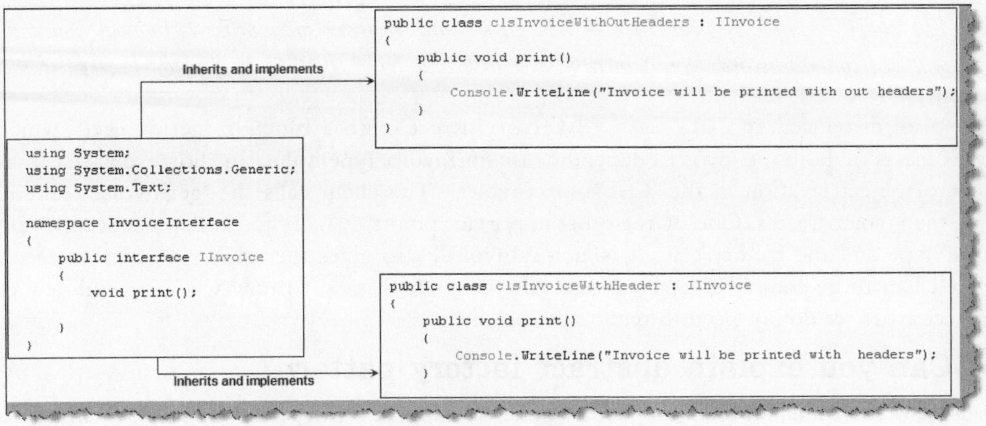

Figure: Interface and concrete classes

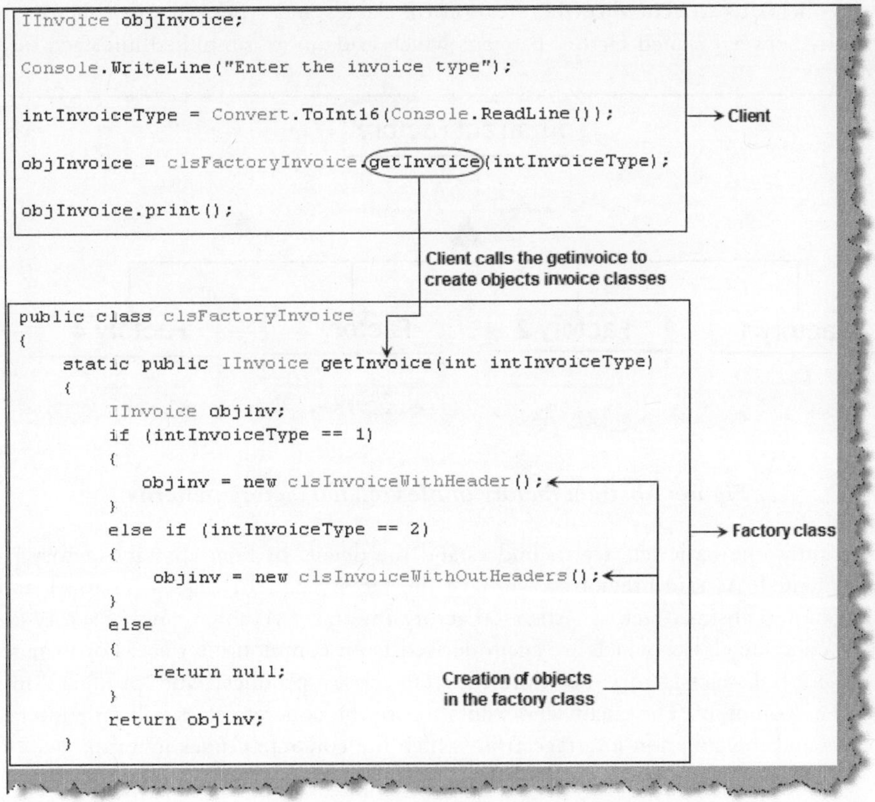

Figure: Factory class which generates objects

> **Note:** *The above example is given in C# . Even if you are from some other technology you can still map the concept accordingly. You can get source code from the CD in 'FactoryPattern' folder.*

We have also introduced an extra class 'ClsFactoryInvoice' with a function 'getInvoice()' which will generate objects of both the invoices depending on 'intInvoiceType' value. In short we have centralized the logic of object creation in the 'ClsFactoryInvoice'. The client calls the 'getInvoice' function to generate the invoice classes. One of the most important points to be noted is that client only refers to 'IInvoice' type and the factory class 'ClsFactoryInvoice' also gives the same type of reference. This helps the client to be complete detached from the concrete classes, so now when we add new classes and invoice types we do not need to recompile the client.

(I) Can you explain abstract factory pattern?

Abstract factory expands on the basic factory pattern. Abstract factory helps us to unite similar factory pattern classes in to one unified interface. So basically all the common factory patterns now inherit from a common abstract factory class which unifies them in a common class. All other things related to factory pattern remain same as discussed in the previous question.

A factory class helps us to centralize the creation of classes and types. Abstract factory helps us to bring uniformity between related factory patterns which leads more simplified interface for the client.

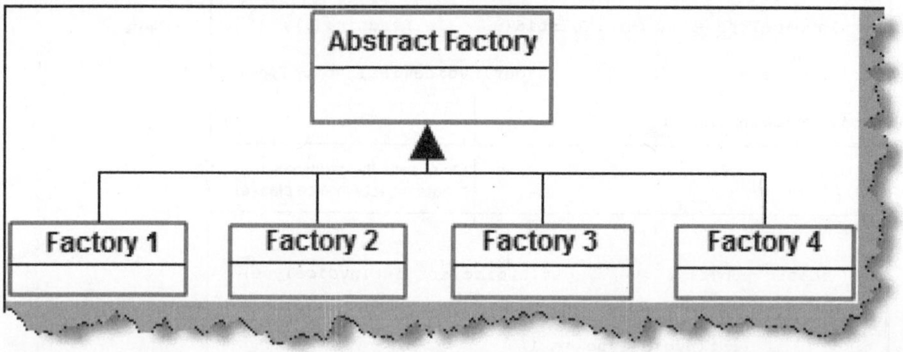

Figure: Abstract factory unifies related factory patterns

Now that we know the basic lets try to understand the details of how abstract factory patterns are actually implemented. As said previously we have the factory pattern classes (factory1 and factory2) tied up to a common abstract factory (AbstractFactory Interface) via inheritance. Factory classes stand on the top of concrete classes which are again derived from common interface. For instance in figure 'Implementation of abstract factory' both the concrete classes 'product1' and 'product2' inherits from one interface i.e. 'common'. The client who wants to use the concrete class will only interact with the abstract factory and the common interface from which the concrete classes inherit.

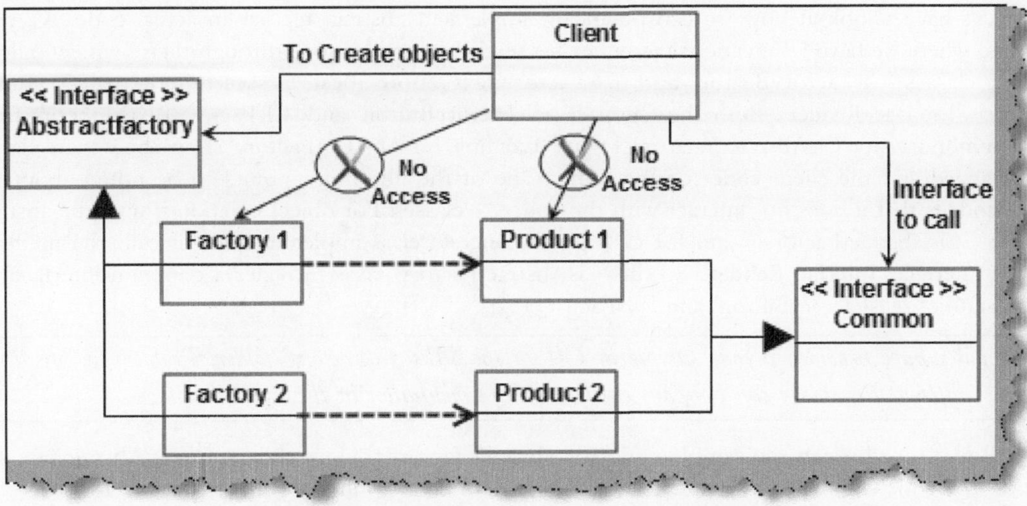

Figure: Implementation of abstract factory

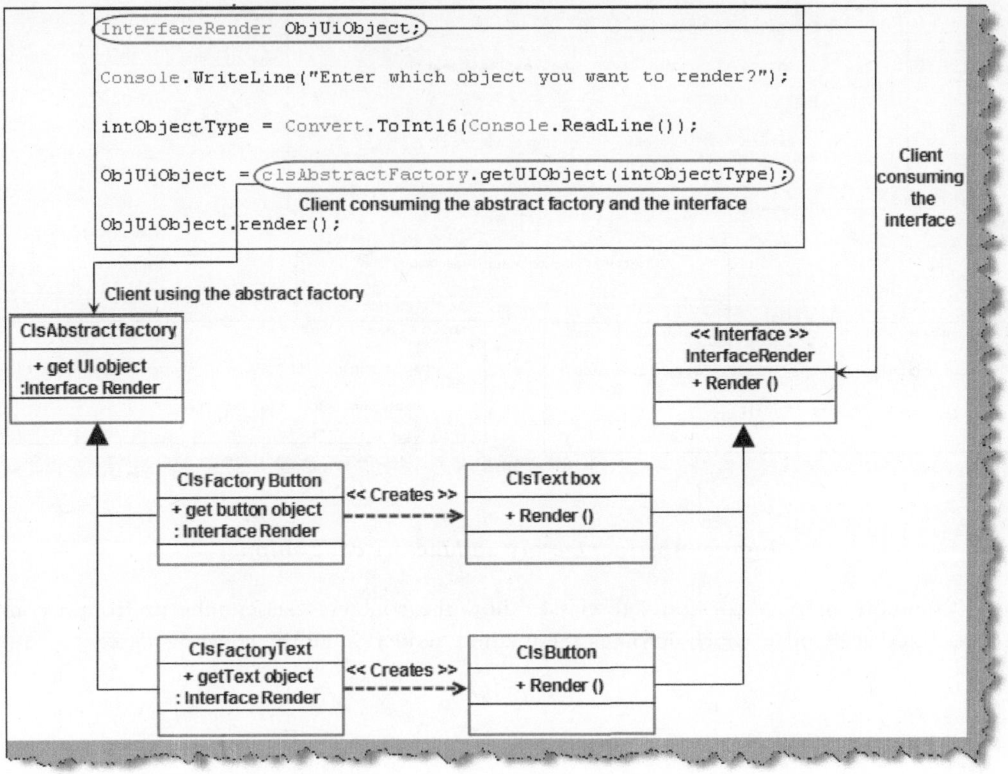

Figure: Example for abstract factory

Now let's have a look at how we can practically implement abstract factory in actual code. We have scenario where we have UI creational activities for textboxes and buttons through their own centralized factory classes 'ClsFactoryButton' and 'ClsFactoryText'. Both these classes inherit from common interface 'InterfaceRender'. Both the factories 'ClsFactoryButton' and 'ClsFactoryText' inherits from the common factory 'ClsAbstractFactory'. Figure 'Example for AbstractFactory' shows how these classes are arranged and the client code for the same. One of the important points to be noted about the client code is that it does not interact with the concrete classes. For object creation it uses the abstract factory (ClsAbstractFactory) and for calling the concrete class implementation it calls the methods via the interface 'InterfaceRender'. So the 'ClsAbstractFactory' class provides a common interface for both factories 'ClsFactoryButton' and 'ClsFactoryText'.

> **Note:** *We have provided a code sample in C# in the 'AbstractFactory' folder. People who are from different technology can compare easily the implementation in their own language.*

We will just run through the sample code for abstract factory. Below code snippet 'Abstract factory and factory code snippet' shows how the factory pattern classes inherit from abstract factory.

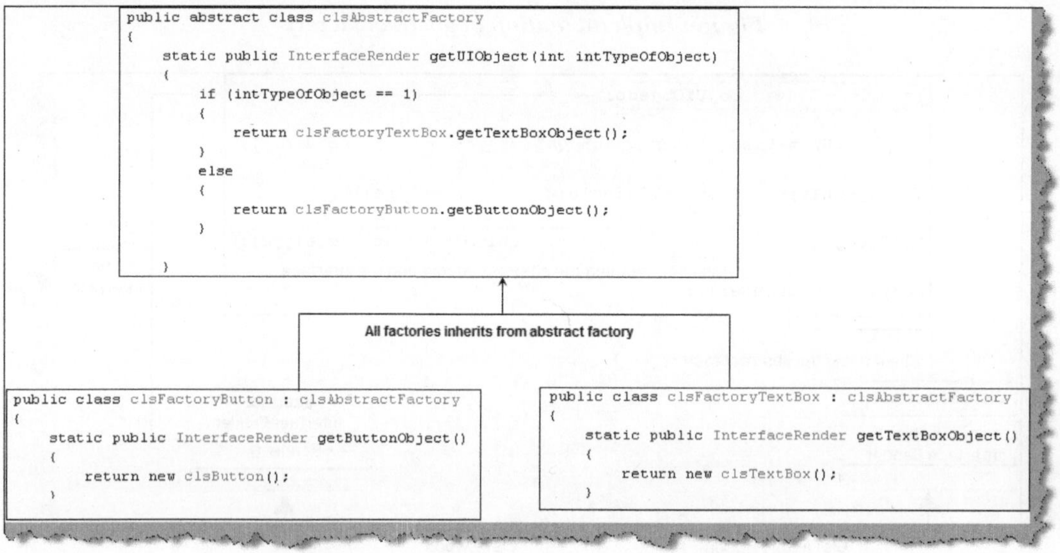

Figure: Abstract factory and factory code snippet

Figure 'Common Interface for concrete classes' how the concrete classes inherits from a common interface 'InterFaceRender' which enforces the method 'render' in all the concrete classes.

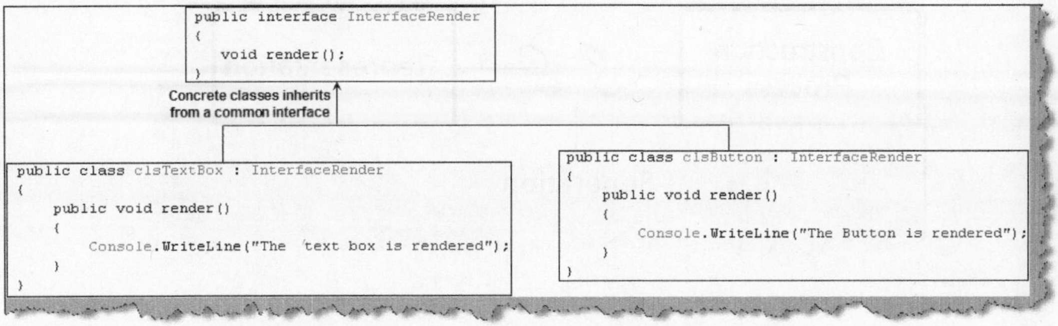

Figure: Common interface for concrete classes

The final thing is the client code which uses the interface 'InterfaceRender' and abstract factory 'ClsAbstractFactory' to call and create the objects. One of the important points about the code is that it is completely isolated from the concrete classes. Due to this any changes in concrete classes like adding and removing concrete classes does not need client level changes.

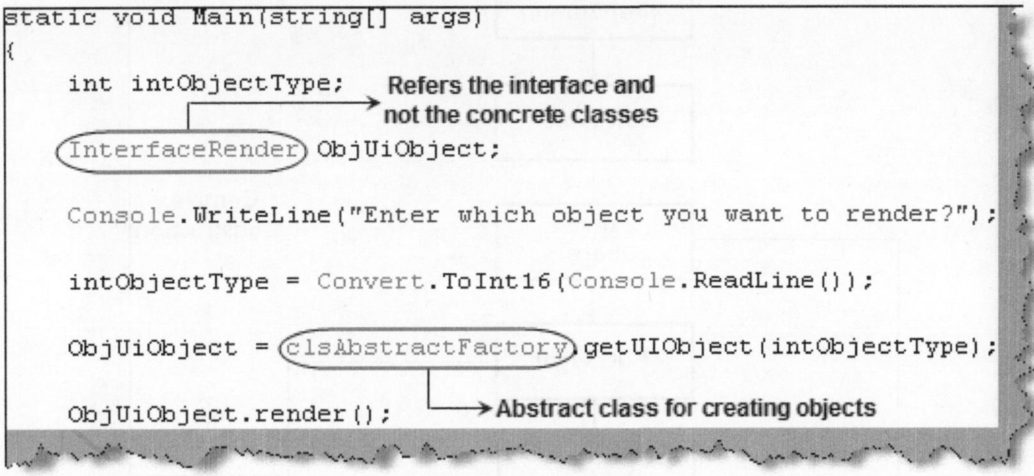

Figure: Client, interface and abstract factory

(I) Can you explain builder pattern?

Builder falls under the type of creational pattern category. Builder pattern helps us to separate the construction of a complex object from its representation so that the same construction process can create different representations. Builder pattern is useful when the construction of the object is very complex. The main objective is to separate the construction of objects and their representations. If we are able to separate the construction and representation, we can then get many representations from the same construction.

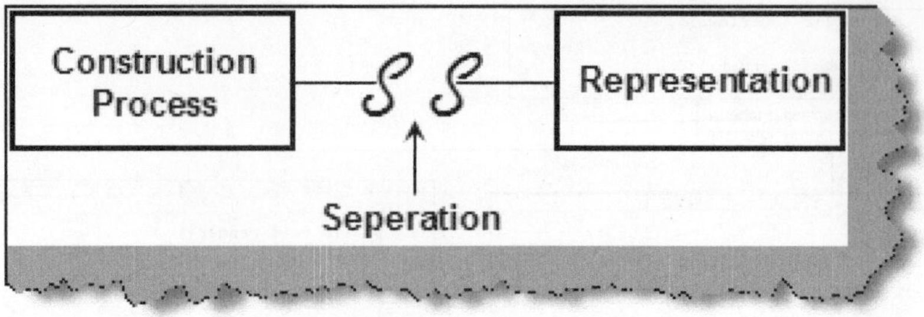

Figure: Builder concept

To understand what we mean by construction and representation lets take the example of the below 'Tea preparation' sequence.

You can see from the figure 'Tea preparation' from the same preparation steps we can get three representation of tea's (i.e. Tea with out sugar, tea with sugar / milk and tea with out milk).

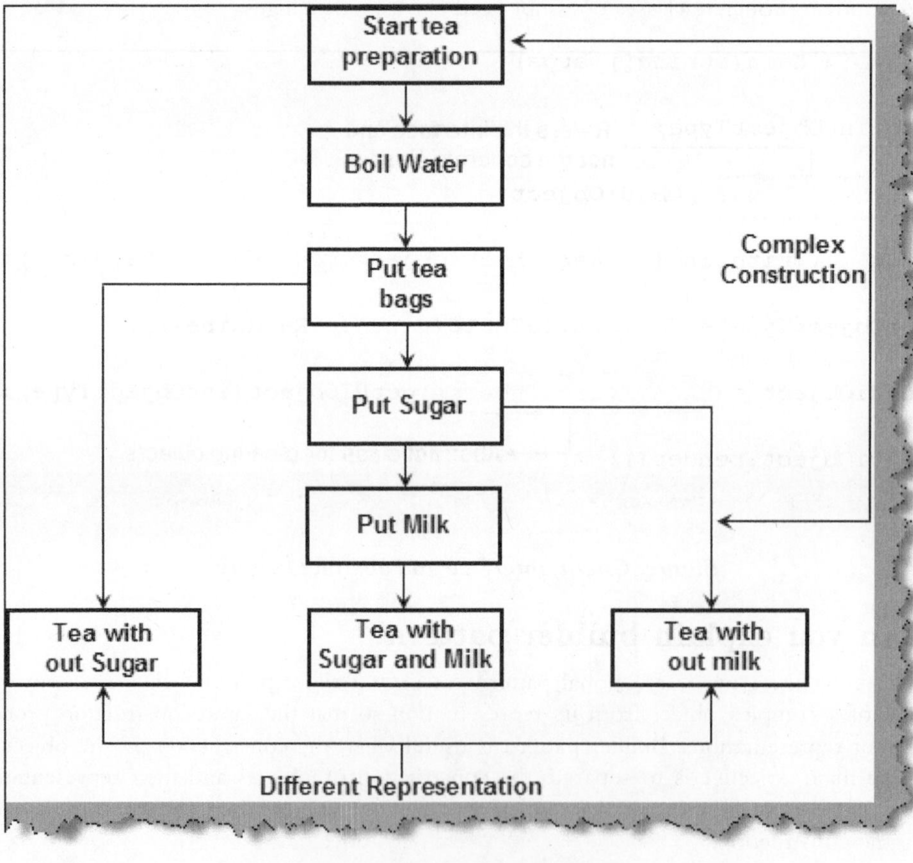

Figure: Tea preparation

Now let's take a real time example in software world to see how builder can separate the complex creation and its representation. Consider we have application where we need the same report to be displayed in either 'PDF' or 'EXCEL' format. Figure 'Request a report' shows the series of steps to achieve the same. Depending on report type a new report is created, report type is set, headers and footers of the report are set and finally we get the report for display.

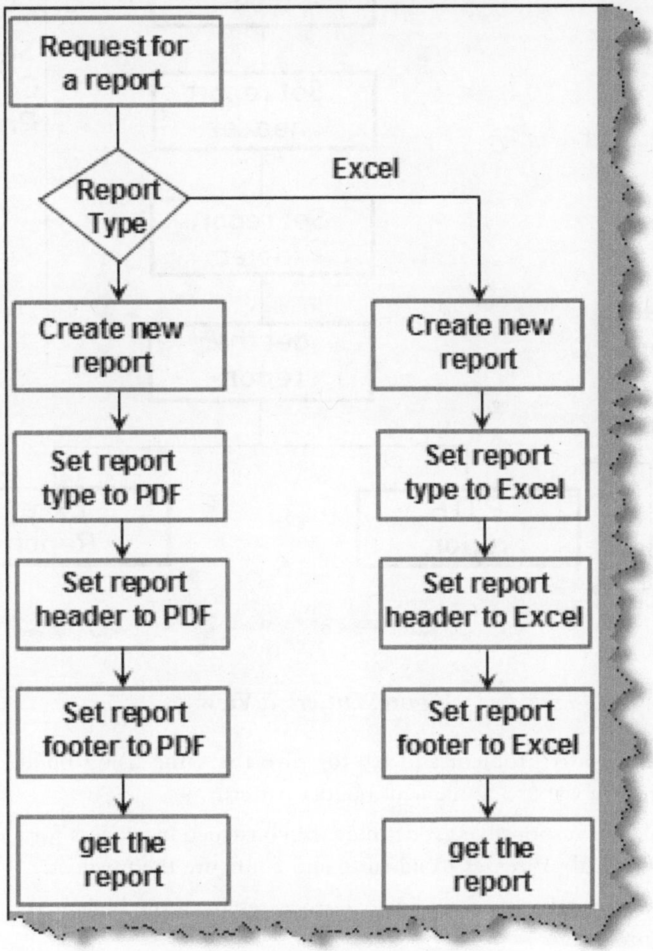

Figure: Request a report

Now let's take a different view of the problem as shown in figure 'Different View'. The same flow defined in 'Request a report' is now analyzed in representations and common construction. The construction process is same for both the types of reports but they result in different representations.

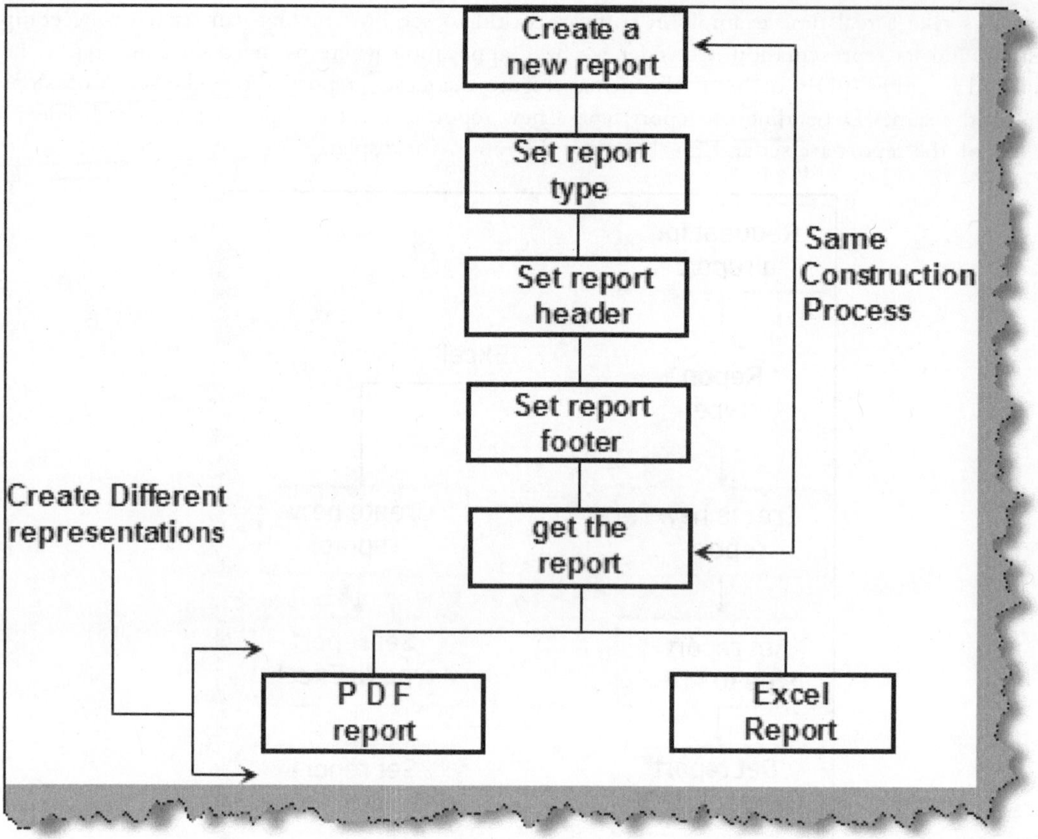

Figure: Different View

We will take the same report problem and try to solve the same using builder patterns. There are three main parts when you want to implement builder patterns.

- **Builder**: Builder is responsible for defining the construction process for individual parts. Builder has those individual processes to initialize and configure the product.
- **Director**: Director takes those individual processes from the builder and defines the sequence to build the product.
- **Product**: Product is the final object which is produced from the builder and director coordination.

First let's have a look at the builder class hierarchy. We have a abstract class called as 'ReportBuilder' from which custom builders like 'ReportPDF' builder and 'ReportEXCEL' builder will be built.

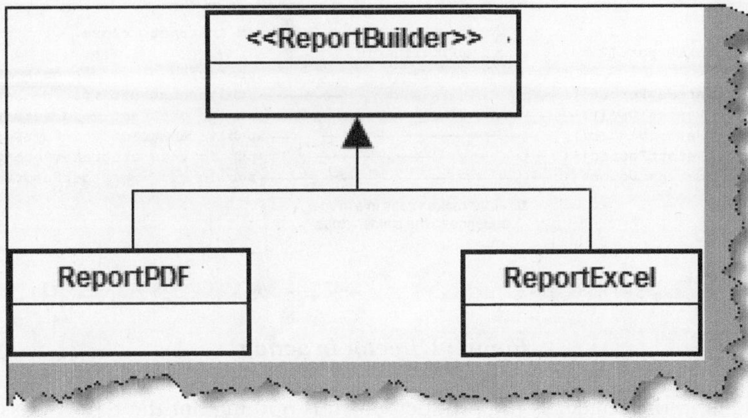

Figure: Builder class hierarchy

Figure 'Builder classes in actual code' shows the methods of the classes. To generate report we need to first Create a new report, set the report type (to EXCEL or PDF) , set report headers , set the report footers and finally get the report. We have defined two custom builders one for 'PDF' (ReportPDF) and other for 'EXCEL' (ReportExcel). These two custom builders define there own process according to the report type.

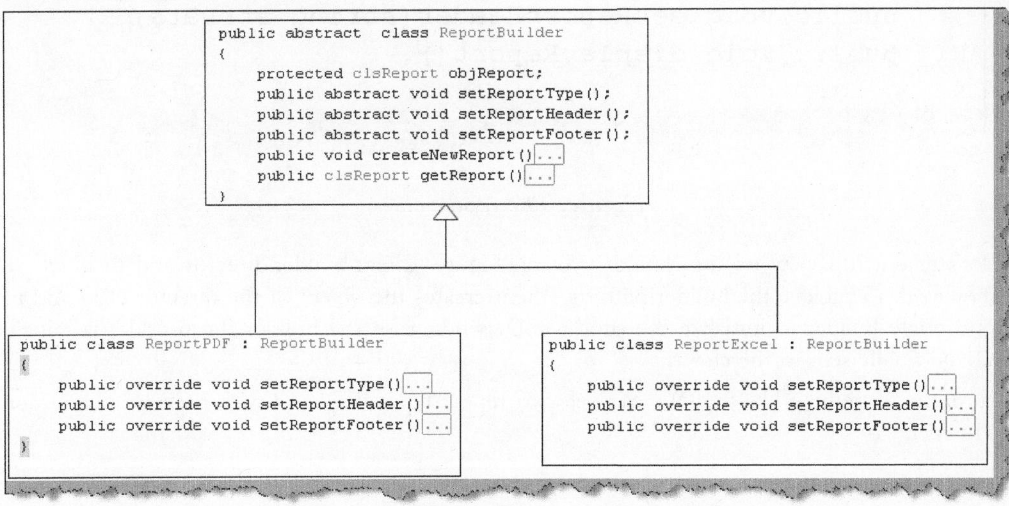

Figure: Builder classes in actual code

Now let's understand how director will work. Class 'clsDirector' takes the builder and calls the individual method process in a sequential manner. So director is like a driver who takes all the individual processes and calls them in sequential manner to generate the final product, which is the report in this case. Figure 'Director in action' shows how the method 'MakeReport' calls the individual process to generate the report product by PDF or EXCEL.

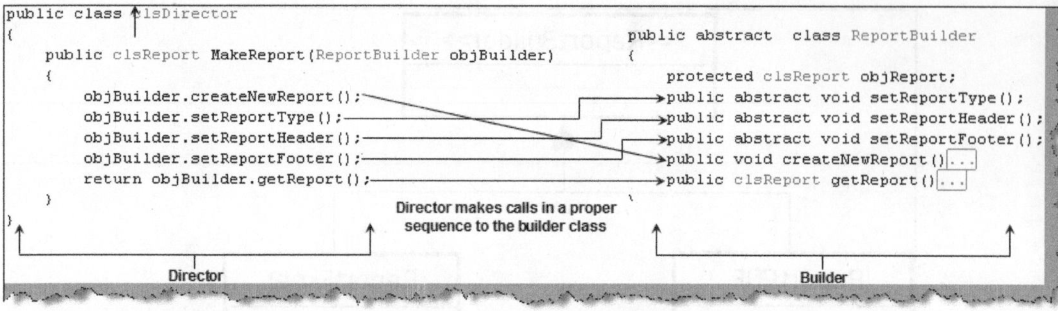

Figure: Director in action

The third component in the builder is the product which is nothing but the report class in this case.

```
public class clsReport
{
    public string strReportType;
    private ArrayList objHeader = new ArrayList();
    private ArrayList objFooter = new ArrayList();
    public void setReportFooter(string strData)...
    public void setReportHeader(string strData)...
    public void displayReport()...
}
```

Figure: The report class

Now let's take a top view of the builder project. Figure 'Client,builder,director and product' shows how they work to achieve the builder pattern. Client creates the object of the director class and passes the appropriate builder to initialize the product. Depending on the builder the product is initialized/ created and finally sent to the client.

The output is something like this. We can see two report types displayed with their headers according to the builder.

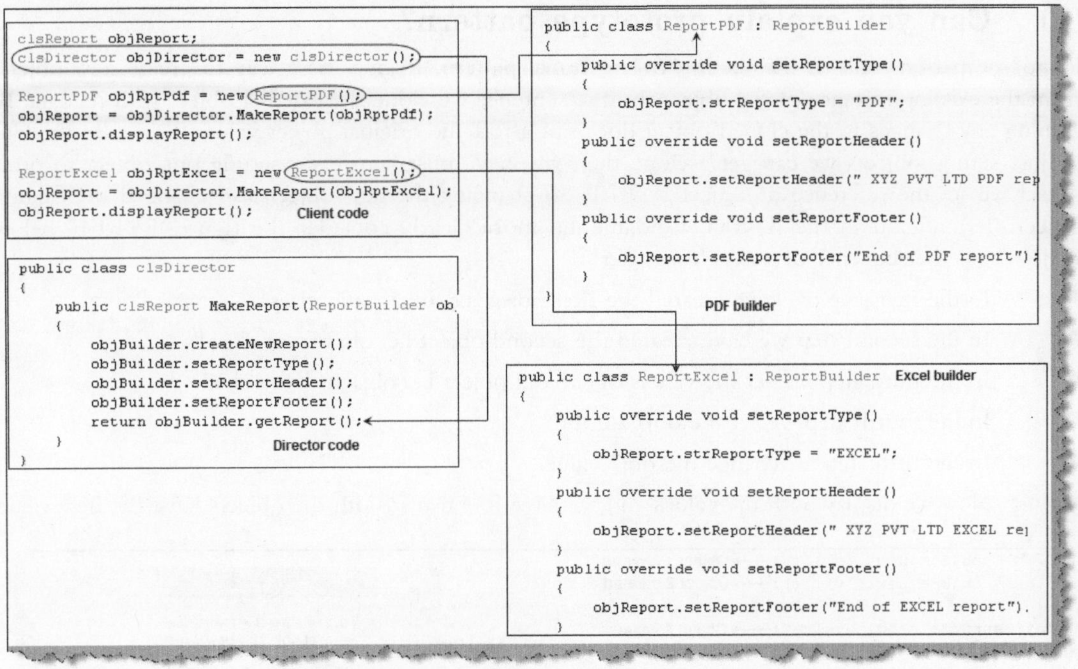

Figure: Client, builder, director and product

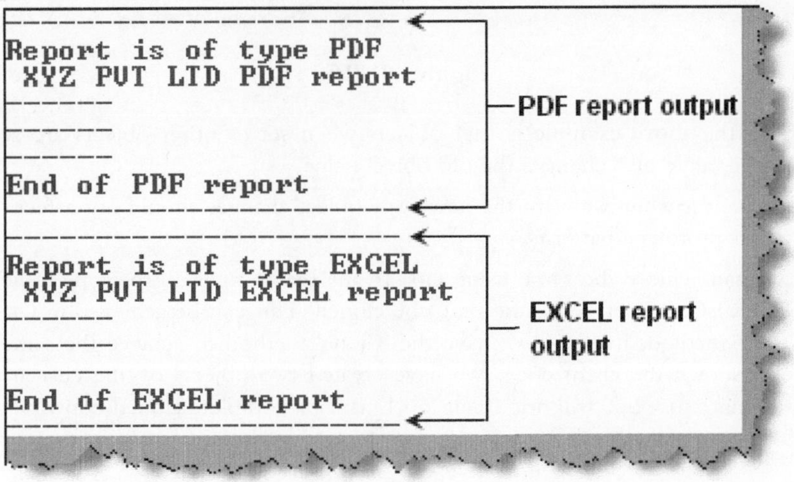

Figure: Final output of builder

Note: *In CD we have provided the above code in C# in 'BuilderPattern' folder.*

(I) Can you explain prototype pattern?

Prototype pattern falls in the section of creational pattern. It gives us a way to create new objects from the existing instance of the object. In one sentence we clone the existing object with its data. By cloning any changes to the cloned object does not affect the original object value. If you are thinking by just setting objects we can get a clone then you have mistaken it. By setting one object to other object we set the reference of object BYREF. So changing the new object also changed the original object. To understand the BYREF fundamental more clearly consider the figure 'BYREF' below. Following is the sequence of the below code:

- In the first step we have created the first object i.e. obj1 from class1.
- In the second step we have created the second object i.e. obj2 from class1.
- In the third step we set the values of the old object i.e. obj1 to 'old value'.
- In the fourth step we set the obj1 to obj2.
- In the fifth step we change the obj2 value.
- Now we display both the values and we have found that both the objects have the new value.

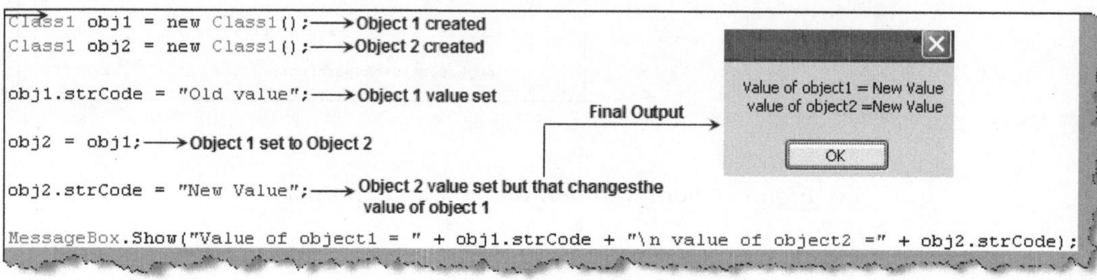

Figure: BYREf

The conclusion of the above example is that objects when set to other objects are set BYREF. So changing new object values also changes the old object value.

There are many instances when we want the new copy object changes should not affect the old object. The answer to this is prototype patterns.

Lets look how we can achieve the same using C#. In the below figure 'Prototype in action' we have the customer class 'ClsCustomer' which needs to be cloned. This can be achieved in C# my using the 'MemberWiseClone' method. In JAVA we have the 'Clone' method to achieve the same. In the same code we have also shown the client code. We have created two objects of the customer class 'obj1' and 'obj2'. Any changes to 'obj2' will not affect 'obj1' as it's a complete cloned copy.

> **Note:** *You can get the above sample in the CD in 'Prototype' folder. In C# we use the 'MemberWiseClone' function while in JAVA we have the 'Clone' function to achieve the same.*

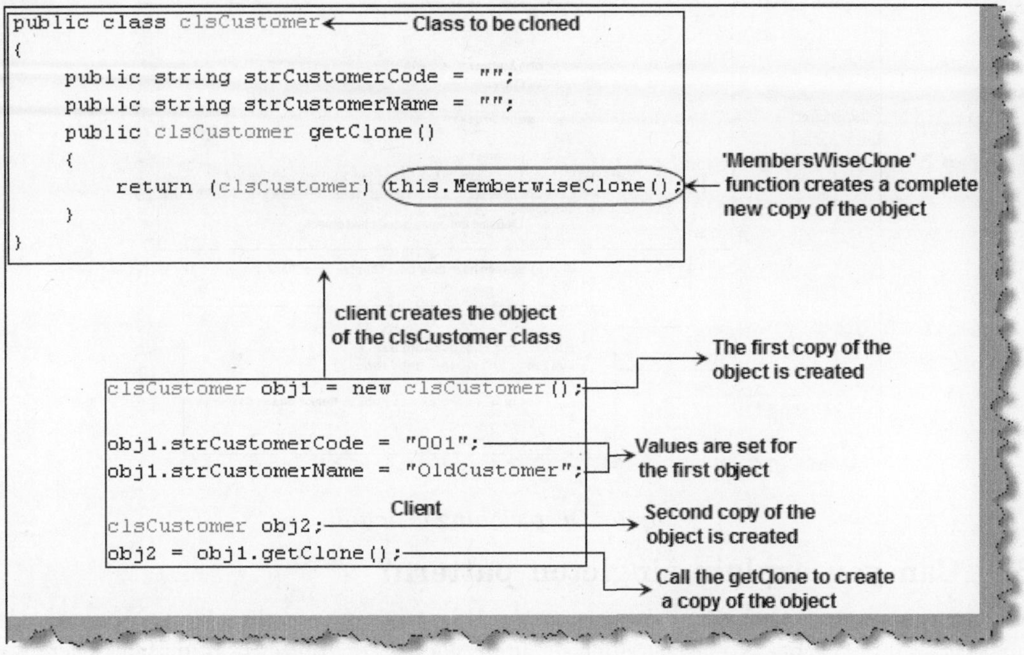

Figure: Prototype in action

(A) Can you explain shallow copy and deep copy in prototype patterns?

There are two types of cloning for prototype patterns. One is the shallow cloning which you have just read in the first question. In shallow copy only that object is cloned, any objects containing in that object is not cloned. For instance consider the figure 'Deep cloning in action' we have a customer class and we have an address class aggregated inside the customer class. 'MemberWiseClone' will only clone the customer class 'ClsCustomer' but not the 'ClsAddress' class. So we added the 'MemberWiseClone' function in the address class also. Now when we call the 'getClone' function we call the parent cloning function and also the child cloning function, which leads to cloning of the complete object. When the parent objects are cloned with their containing objects it's called as **deep cloning** and when only the parent is clones its termed as **shallow cloning**.

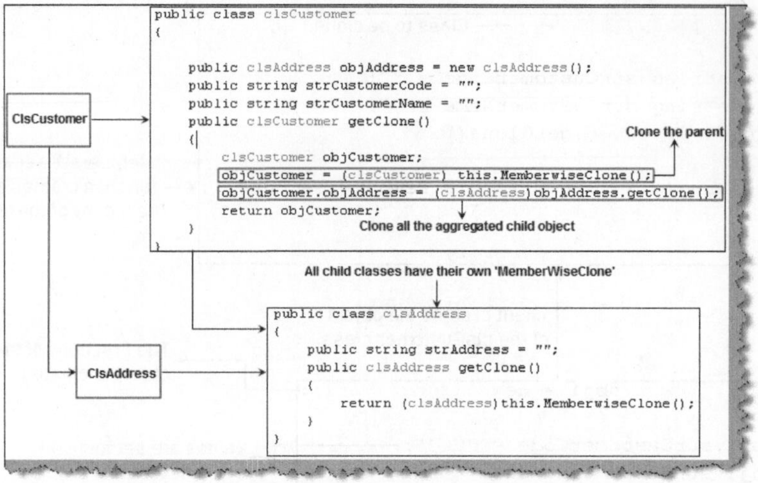

Figure: Deep cloning in action

(B) Can you explain singleton pattern?

There are situations in a project where we want only one instance of the object to be created and shared between the clients. No client can create an instance of the object from outside. There is only one instance of the class which is shared across the clients. Below are the steps to make a singleton pattern:

- Define the constructor as private.
- Define the instances and methods as static.

Below is a code snippet of a singleton in C#. We have defined the constructor as private, defined all the instance and methods using the **static** keyword as shown in the below code snippet figure 'Singleton in action'. The static keyword ensures that you only one instance of the object is created and you can all the methods of the class with out creating the object. As we have made the constructor private, we need to call the class directly.

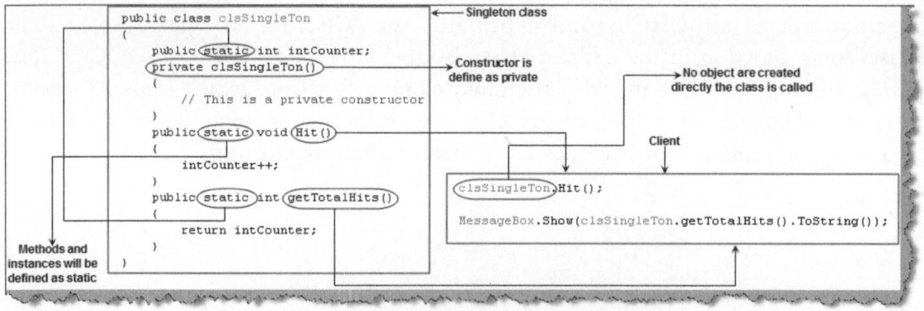

Figure: Singleton in action

> **Note:** *In JAVA to create singleton classes we use the STATIC keyword , so its same as in C#. You can get a sample C# code for singleton in the 'singleton' folder.*

(A) Can you explain command patterns?

Command pattern allows a request to exist as an object. Ok let's understand what it means. Consider the figure 'Menu and Commands' we have different actions depending on which menu is clicked. So depending on which menu is clicked we have passed a string which will have the action text in the action string. Depending on the action string we will execute the action. The bad thing about the code is it has lot of 'IF' condition which makes the coding more cryptic.

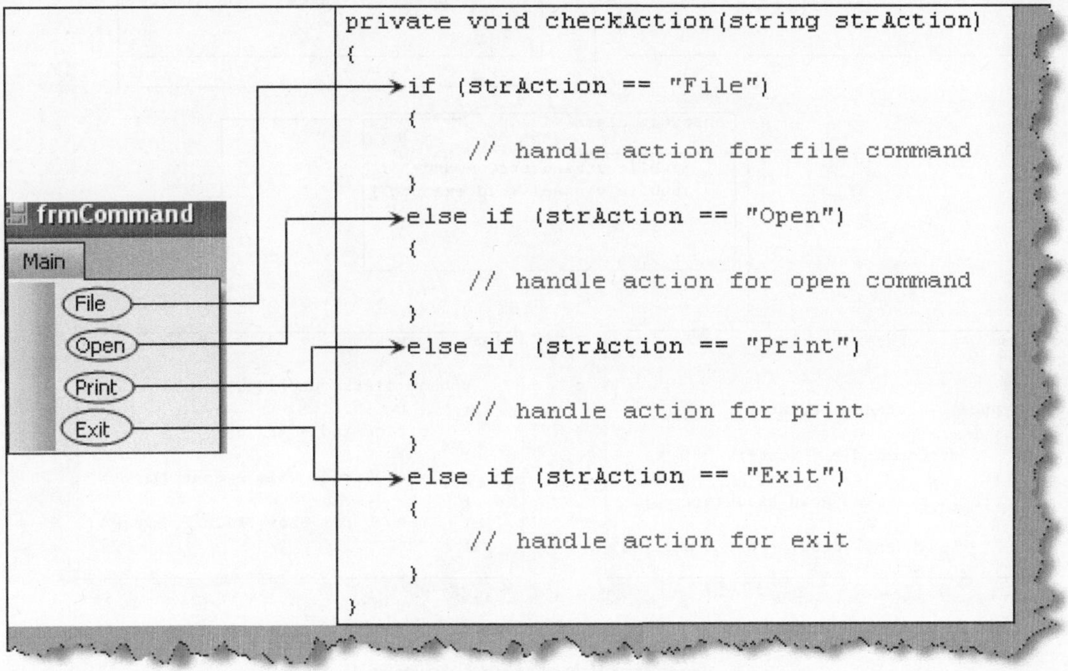

Figure: Menu and Commands

Command pattern moves the above action in to objects. These objects when executed actually execute the command.

As said previously every command is an object. We first prepare individual classes for every action i.e. exit, open, file and print. Al l the above actions are wrapped in to classes, like Exit action is wrapped in 'clsExecuteExit' , open action is wrapped in 'clsExecuteOpen', print action is wrapped in 'clsExecutePrint' and so on. All these classes are inherited from a common interface 'IExecute'.

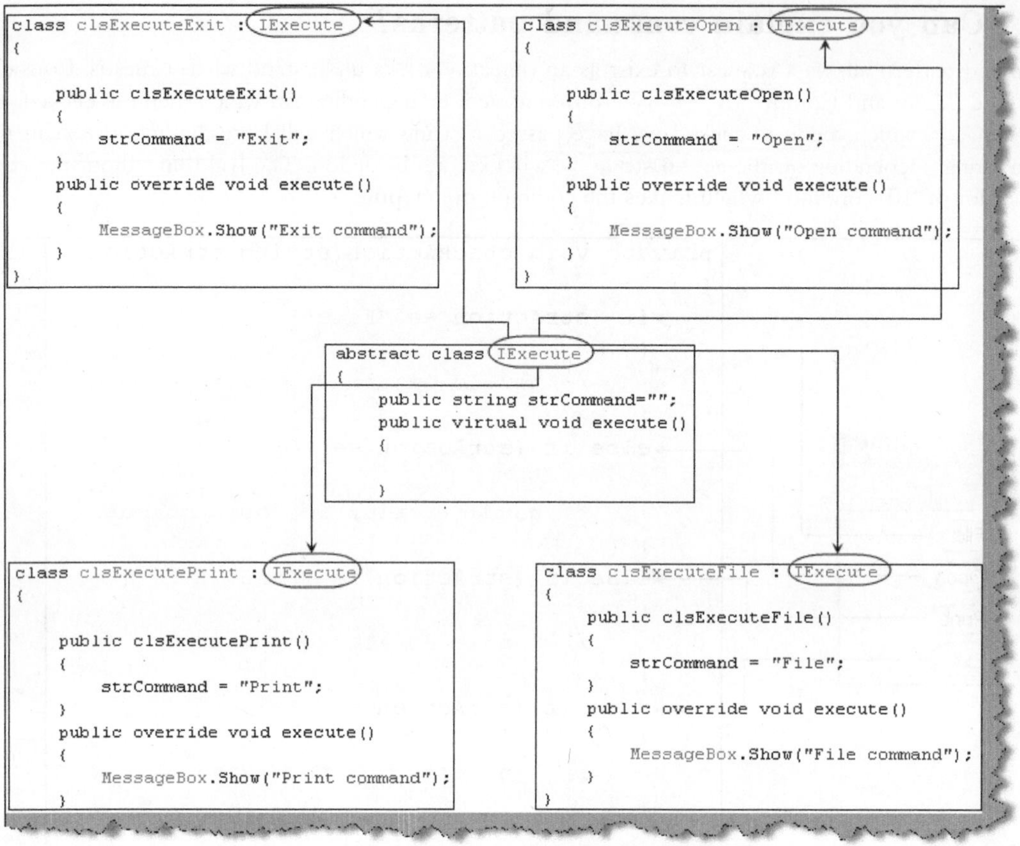

Figure: Objects and Command

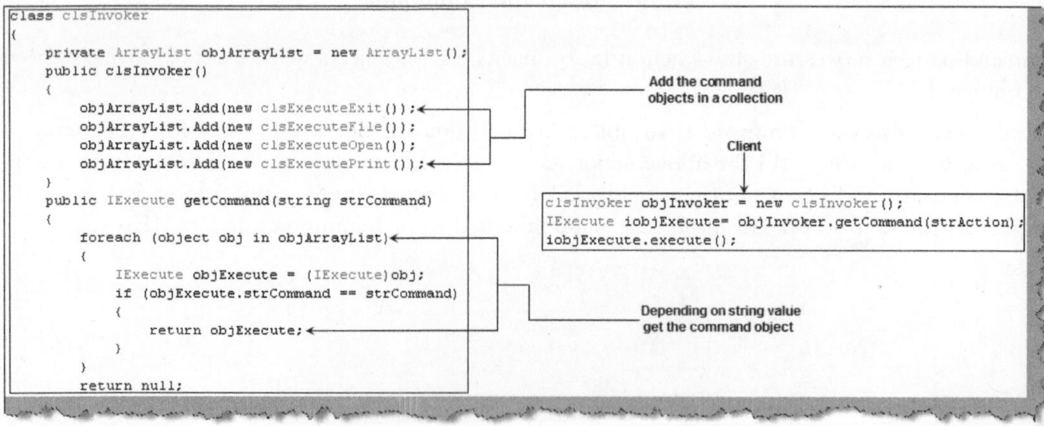

Figure: Invoker and the clean client

Using all the action classes we can now make the invoker. The main work of invoker is to map the action with the classes which have the action.

So we have added all the actions in one collection i.e. the arraylist. We have exposed a method 'getCommand' which takes a string and gives back the abstract object 'IExecute'. The client code is now neat and clean. All the 'IF' conditions are now moved to the 'clsInvoker' class.

Note: *You can find a sample code for C# code in command pattern in 'Command' folder.*

(I) What is Interpreter pattern?

Interpreter pattern allows us to interpret grammar in to code solutions. Ok, what does that mean?. Grammars are mapped to classes to arrive to a solution. In one line interpreter pattern gives us the solution of how to write an interpreter which can read a grammar and execute the same in the code. For instance below is a simple example where we can give the date format grammar and the interpreter will convert the same in to code solutions and give the desired output.

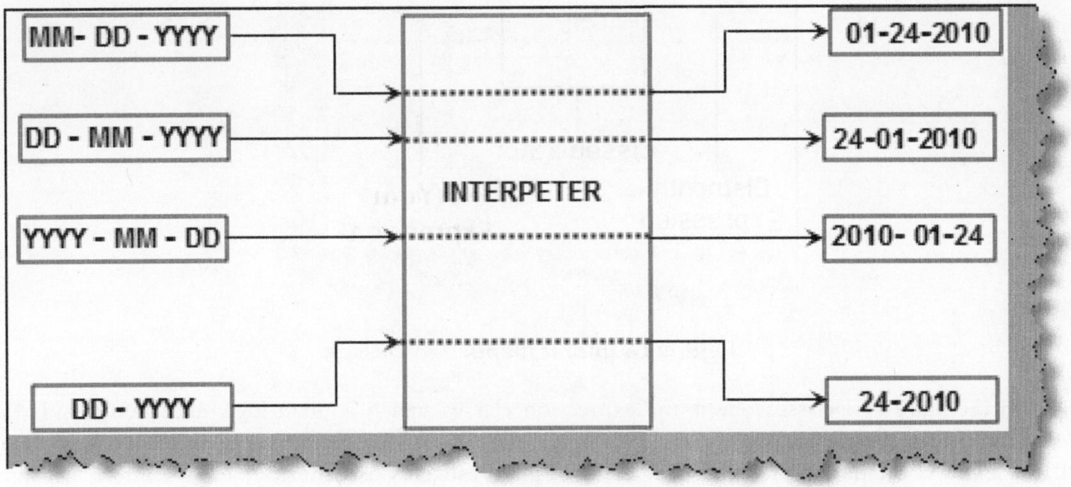

Figure: Date Grammar

Let's make an interpreter for date formats as shown in figure 'Date Grammar'. Before we start lets understand the different components of interpreter pattern and then we will map the same to make the date grammar. Context contains the data and the logic part contains the logic which will convert the context to readable format.

Let's understand what is the grammar in the date format is. To define any grammar we should first break grammar in small logical components. Figure 'Grammar mapped to classes' show how different components are identified and then mapped to classes which will have the logic to implement only that portion of the grammar. So we have broken the date format in to four components Month, Day, Year and the separator. For all these four components we will define separate classes which will contain the logic as shown in figure 'Grammar mapped to classes'. So we will be creating different classes for the various components of the date format.

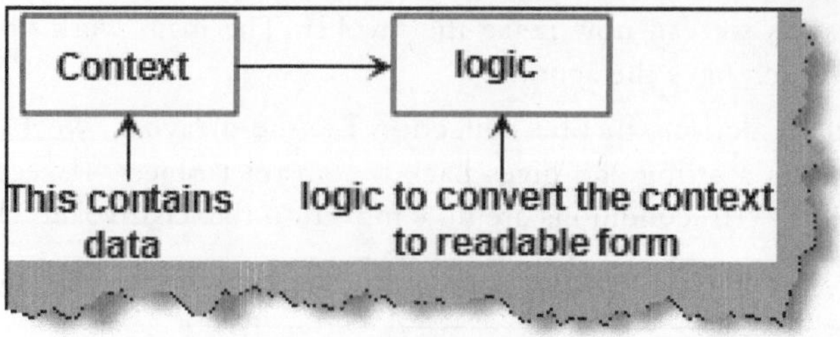

Figure: Context and Logic

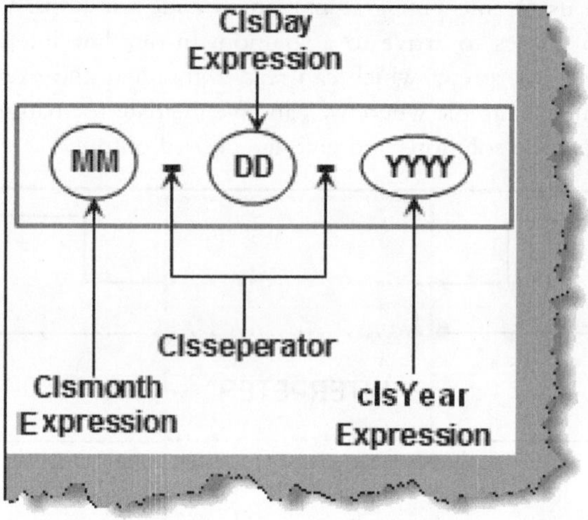

Figure: Grammar mapped to classes

As said there are two classes one is the expression classes which contain logic and the other is the context class which contain data as shown in figure 'Expression and Context classes'. We have defined all the expression parsing in different classes, all these classes inherit from common interface 'ClsAbstractExpression' with a method 'Evaluate'. The 'Evaluate' method takes a context class which has the data; this method parses data according to the expression logic. For instance 'ClsYearExpression' replaces the 'YYYY' with the year value,"ClsMonthExpression' replaces the 'MM' with month and so on.

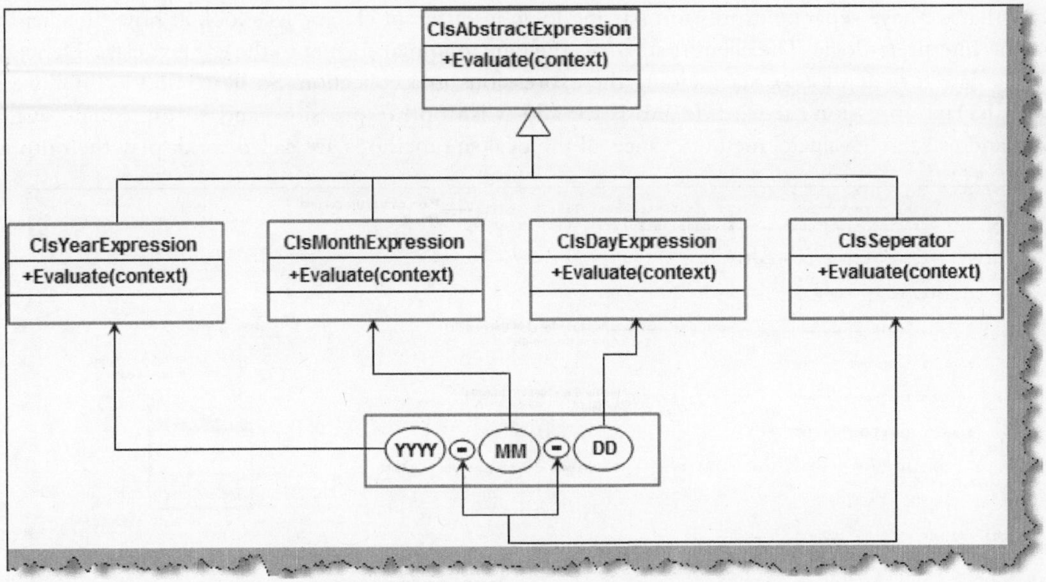

Figure: Class diagram for interpreter

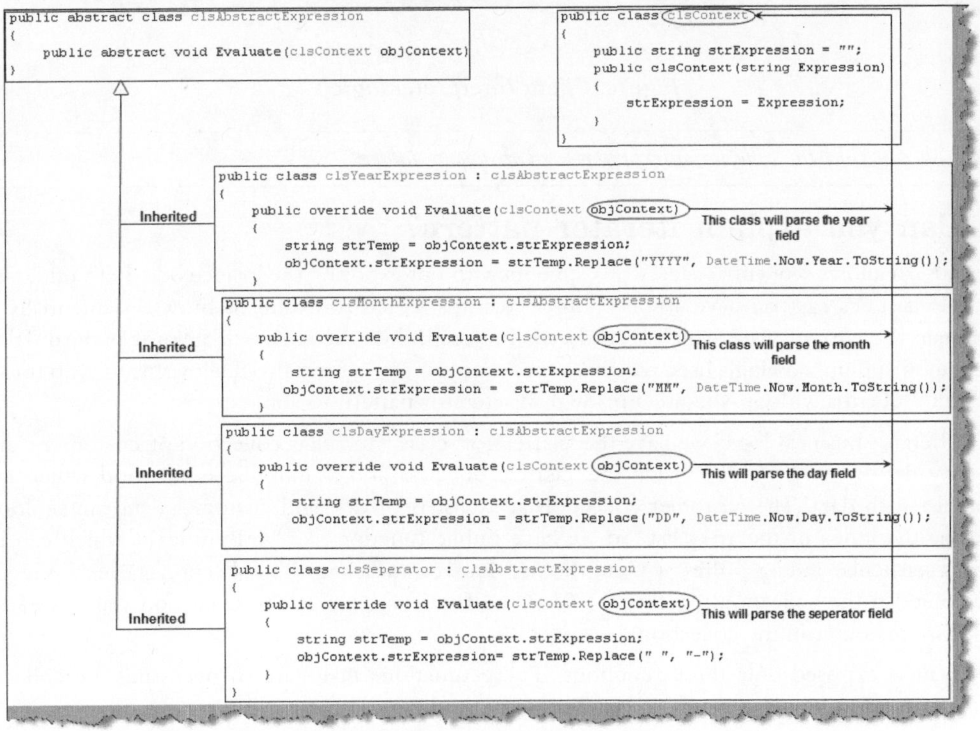

Figure: Expression and Context classes

Now that we have separate expression parsing logic in different classes, let's look at how the client will use the Interpreter logic. The client first passes the date grammar format to the context class. Depending on the date format we now start adding the expressions in a collection. So if we find a 'DD" we add the 'ClsDayExpression', if we find 'MM' we add 'ClsMonthExpression' and so on. Finally we just loop and call the 'Evaluate' method. Once all the evaluate methods are called we display the output.

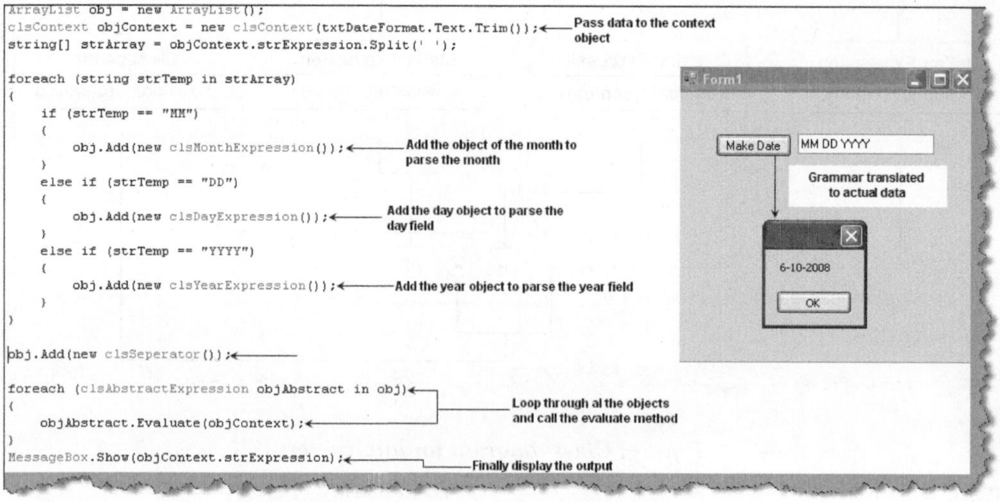

Figure: Client Interpreter logic

> **Note:** *You can find the code for interpreter in 'Interpeter' folder.*

(B) Can you explain iterator pattern?

Iterator pattern allows sequential access of elements with out exposing the inside code. Let's understand what it means. Let's say you have a collection of records which you want to browse sequentially and also maintain the current place which recordset is browsed, then the answer is iterator pattern. It's the most common and unknowingly used pattern. Whenever you use a 'foreach' (It allows us to loop through a collection sequentially) loop you are already using iterator pattern to some extent.

In figure 'Iterator business logic' we have the 'clsIterator' class which has collection of customer classes. So we have defined an array list inside the 'clsIterator' class and a 'FillObjects' method which loads the array list with data. The customer collection array list is private and customer data can be looked up by using the index of the array list. So we have public function like 'getByIndex' (which can look up using a particular index) , 'Prev' (Gets the previous customer in the collection , 'Next' (Gets the next customer in the collection), 'getFirst' (Gets the first customer in the collection) and 'getLast' (Gets the last customer in the collection).

So the client is exposed only these functions. These functions take care of accessing the collection sequentially and also it remembers which index is accessed.

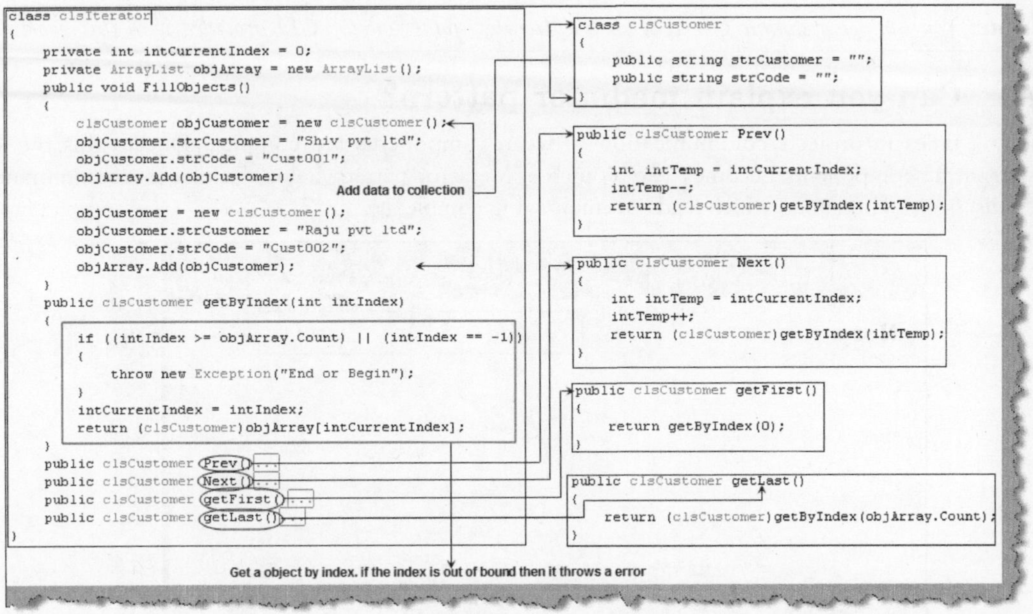

Figure: Iterator business logic

Below figures 'Client Iterator Logic' shows how the 'ObjIterator' object which is created from class 'clsIterator' is used to display next, previous, last, first and customer by index.

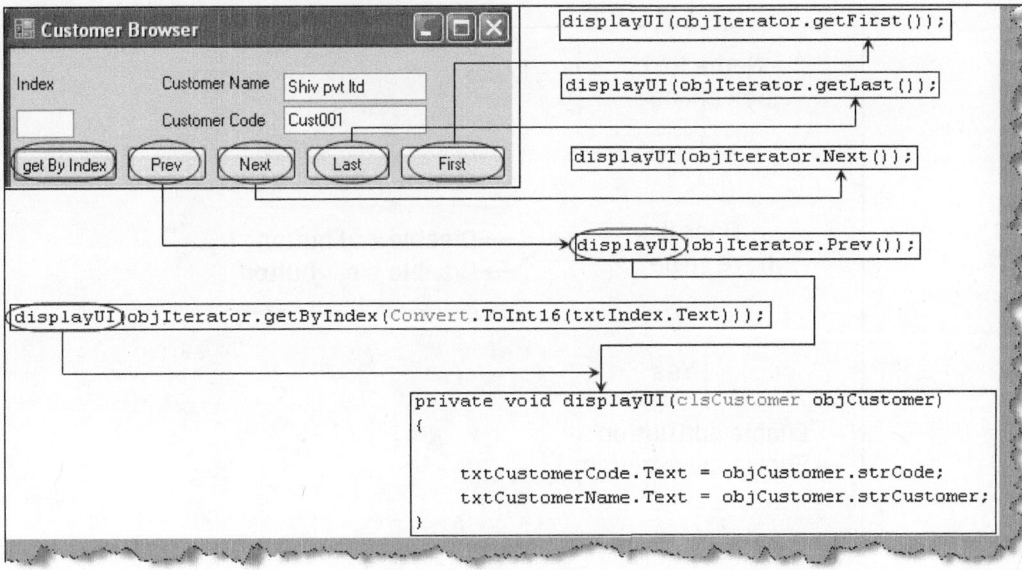

Figure: Client Iterator logic

> **Note:** *You can get a sample C# code in the 'Iterator' folder of the CD provided with this book.*

(A) Can you explain mediator pattern?

Many a times in projects communication between components are complex. Due to this the logic between the components becomes very complex. Mediator pattern helps the objects to communicate in a disassociated manner, which leads to minimizing complexity.

Figure: Mediator sample example

Let's consider the figure 'Mediator sample example' which depicts a true scenario of the need of mediator pattern. It's a very user-friendly user interface. It has three typical scenarios.

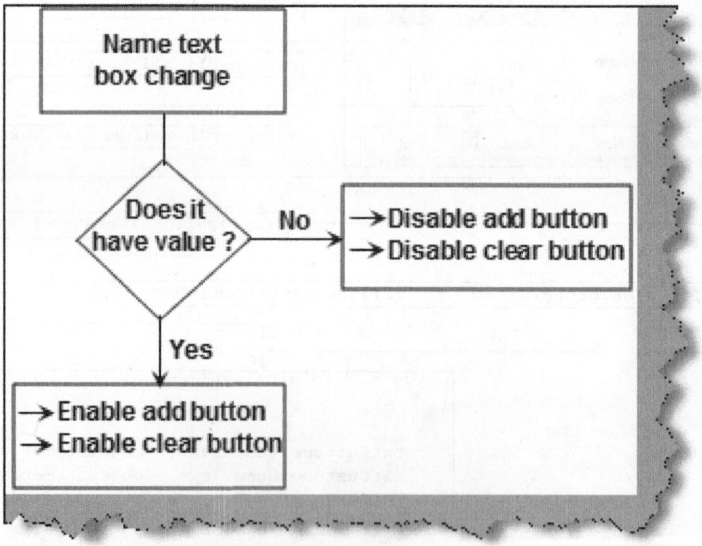

Figure: Scenario 1

Scenario 1: When a user writes in the text box it should enable the add and the clear button. In case there is nothing in the text box it should disable the add and the clear button.

Scenario 2: When the user clicks on the add button the data should get entered in the list box. Once the data is entered in the list box it should clear the text box and disable the add and clear button.

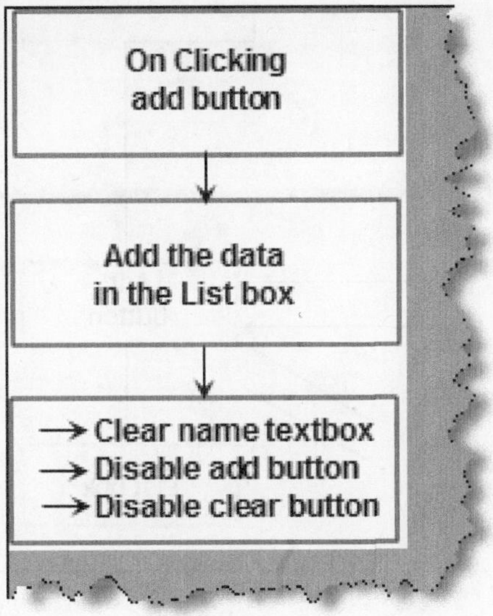

Figure: Scenario 2

Scenario 3: If the user click the clear button it should clear the name text box and disable the add and clear button.

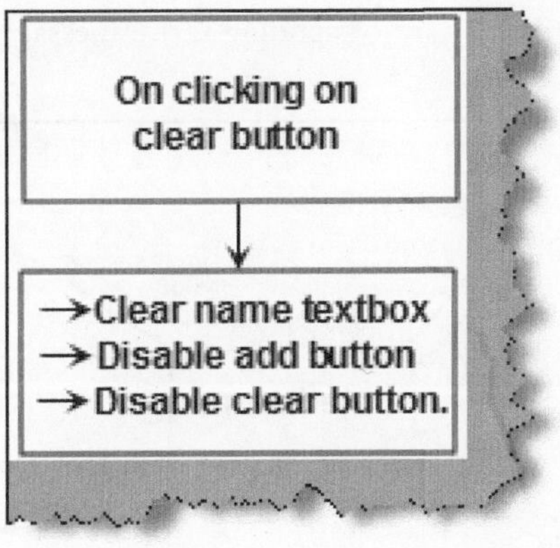

Figure: Scenario 3

Now looking at the above scenarios for the UI we can conclude how complex the interaction will be in between these UI's. Below figure 'Complex interactions between components' depicts the logical complexity.

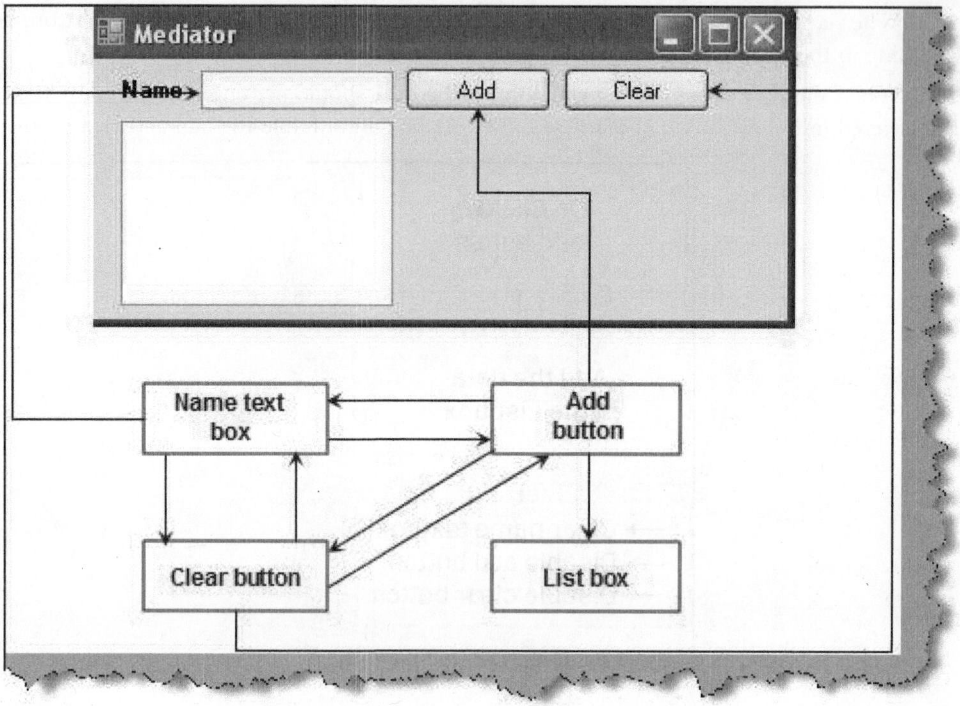

Figure: Complex interactions between components

Ok now let me give you a nice picture as shown below 'Simplifying using mediator'. Rather than components communicating directly with each other if they communicate to centralized component like mediator and then mediator takes care of sending those messages to other components, logic will be neat and clean.

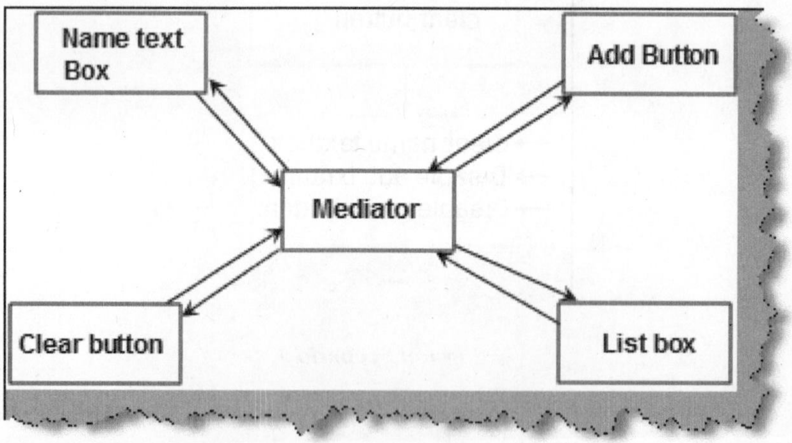

Figure: Simplifying using mediator

Now let's look at how the code will look. We will be using C# but you can easily replicate the thought to JAVA or any other language of your choice. Below figure 'Mediator class' shows the complete code overview of what the mediator class will look like.

The first thing the mediator class does is takes the references of the classes which have the complex communication. So here we have exposed three overloaded methods by name 'Register'. 'Register' method takes the text box object and the button objects. The interaction scenarios are centralized in 'ClickAddButton','TextChange' and 'ClickClearButton' methods. These methods will take care of the enable and disable of UI components according to scenarios.

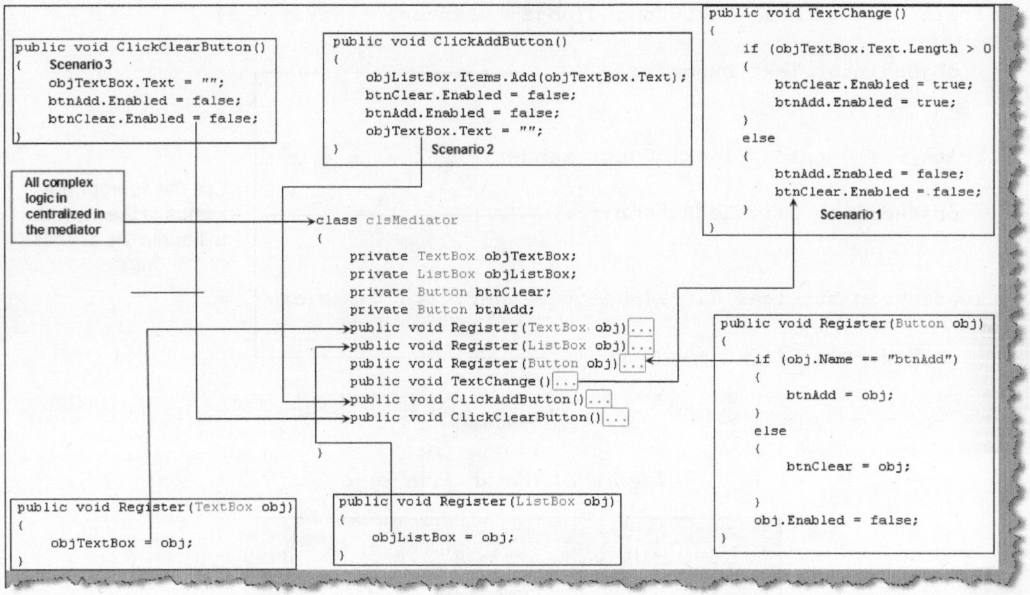

Figure: Mediator class

The client logic is pretty neat and cool now. In the constructor we first register all the components with complex interactions with the mediator. Now for every scenario we just call the mediator methods. In short when there is a text change we can the 'TextChange' method of the mediator, when the user clicks add we call the 'ClickAddButton' and for clear click we call the 'ClickClearButton'.

Note: *You can get the C# code for the above mediator example in the 'mediator' folder.*

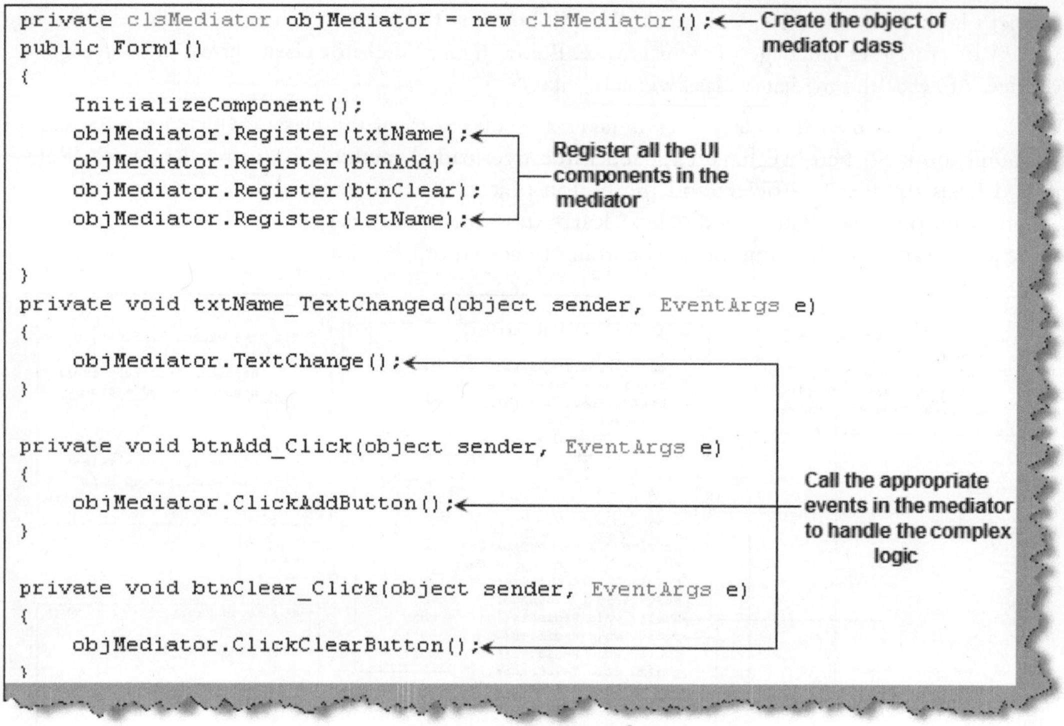

Figure: Mediator client logic

Figure: Memento practical example

(I) Can you explain memento pattern?

Memento pattern is the way to capture objects internal state with out violating encapsulation. Memento pattern helps us to store a snapshot which can be reverted at any moment of time by the object. Let's understand what it means in practical sense. Consider figure 'Memento practical example', it shows a customer screen. Let's say if the user starts editing a customer record and he makes some changes.

Later he feels that he has done something wrong and he wants to revert back to the original data. This is where memento comes in to play. It will help us store a copy of data and in case the user presses cancel the object restores to its original state.

Let's try to complete the same example in C# for the customer UI which we had just gone through. Below is the customer class 'clsCustomer' which has the aggregated memento class 'clsCustomerMemento' which will hold the snapshot of the data. The memento class 'clsCustomerMemento' is the exact replica (excluding methods) of the customer class 'clsCustomer'. When the customer class 'clsCustomer' gets initialized the memento class also gets initialized. When the customer class data is changed the memento class snapshot is not changed. The 'Revert' method sets back the memento data to the main class.

```
class clsCustomer
{
    private string strCustomerName = "";
    private string strCustomerCode = "";
    private string strAddress = "";
    private clsCustomerMemento objMemento = new clsCustomerMemento();
    public string CustomerCode...
    public string CustomerName...
    public string Address...
    public  clsCustomer()
    {
        strCustomerName = "Shiv";
        strCustomerCode = "Cust001";
        strAddress = "Mumbai";
        objMemento = new clsCustomerMemento(strCustomerName, strCustomerCode, strAddress);
    }
    public void Revert()
    {
        strCustomerName = objMemento.strCustomerName;
        strCustomerCode = objMemento.strCustomerCode;
        strAddress = objMemento.strAddress;
    }
}
```

Serves as temprorary placeholder for the class data

The memento class also has a snapshot of the data

Takes the data from the memento and reverts the data of the main class

```
class clsCustomerMemento
{
    public string strCustomerName = "";
    public string strCustomerCode = "";
    public string strAddress = "";
    public clsCustomerMemento()
    {

    }
    public  clsCustomerMemento(string strCustName, string strCustCode, string strAdd)
    {
        strCustomerName = strCustName;
        strCustomerCode = strCustCode;
        strAddress = strAdd;
    }
}
```

Memento class is the exact replica of the main class.This class the memento class to the hold data

Figure: Customer class for memento

The client code is pretty simple. We create the customer class. In case we have issues we click the cancel button which in turn calls the 'revert' method and reverts the changed data back to the memento snapshot data. Figure 'Memento client code' shows the same in a pictorial format.

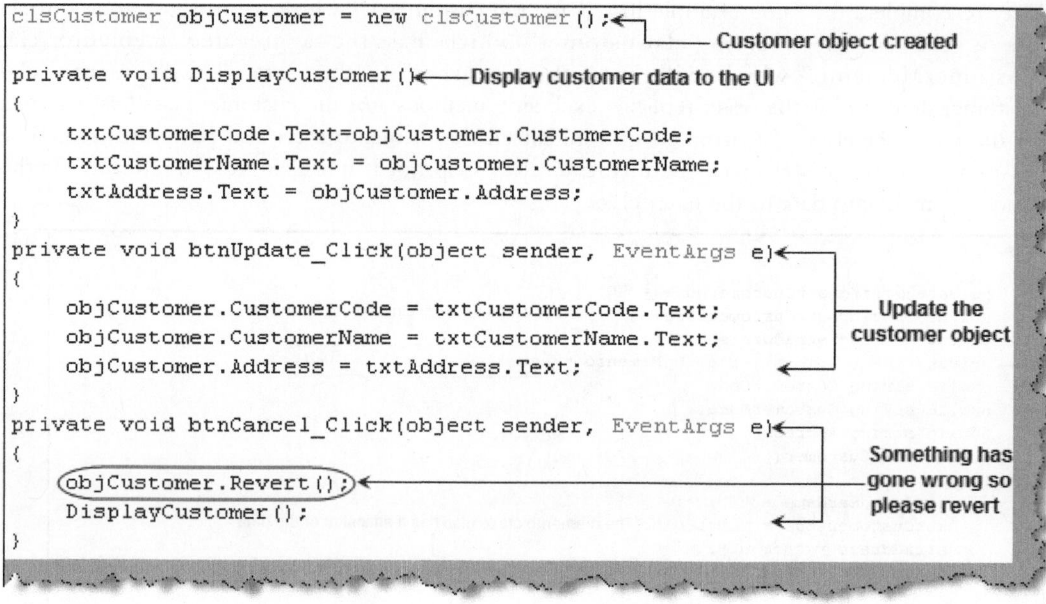

Figure: Memento client code

Note: *A sample code in C# for memento is available in the memento folder of the CD.*

(B) Can you explain observer pattern?

Observer pattern helps us to communicate between parent class and its associated or dependent classes. There are two important concepts in observer pattern 'Subject' and 'Observers'. The subject sends notifications while observers receive notifications if they are registered with the subject. Below figure 'Subject and observers' shows how the application (subject) sends notification to all observers (email, event log and SMS). You can map this example to publisher and subscriber model. The publisher is the application and subscribers are email, event log and sms.

Let's try to code the same example which we have defined in the previous section. First let's have a look at the subscribers / notification classes. Figure 'Subscriber classes' shows the same in a pictorial format. So we have a common interface for all subscribers i.e. 'INotification' which has a 'notify' method. This interface 'INotification' is implemented by all concrete notification classes. All concrete notification classes define their own notification methodology. For the current scenario we have just displayed a print saying the particular notification is executed.

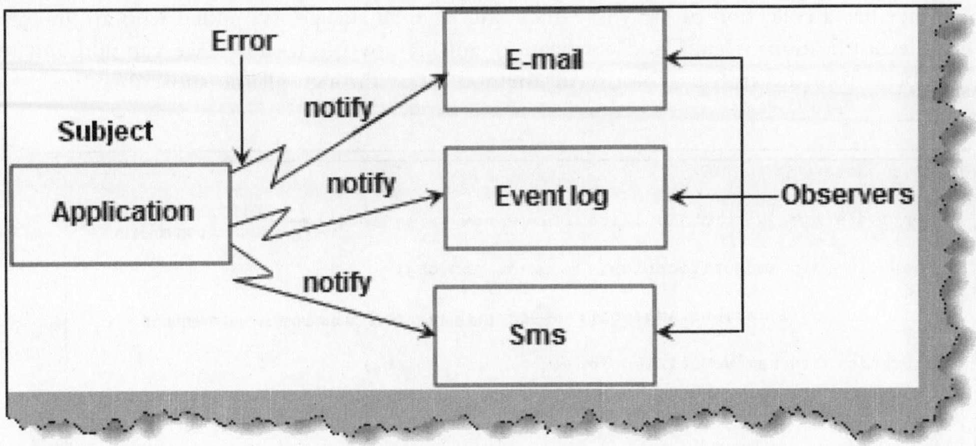

Figure: Subject and Observers

```
public interface INotification
{
    void Notify();
}
public class clsEmailNotification : INotification
{
    public void Notify()
    {
        System.Console.WriteLine("Email notification code executed");
    }
}
public class clsEventNotifcation : INotification
{
    public void Notify()
    {
        System.Console.WriteLine("Event log notification code executed");
    }
}
public class clsSMSNotification : INotification
{
    public void Notify()
    {
        System.Console.WriteLine("SMS notification code executed");
    }
}
```

Interface

Inherited

Figure: Subscriber classes

As said previously there are two sections in an observer pattern one is the observer/subscriber which we have covered in the previous section and second is the publisher or the subject.

The publisher has a collection of arraylist which will have all subscribers added who are interested in receiving the notifications. Using 'addNotification' and 'removeNotification' we can add and remove the subscribers from the arraylist. 'NotifyAll' method loops through all the subscribers and send the notification.

```
public class clsNotifier
{
    private ArrayList objNotifications = new ArrayList();  ← Will contain all the notification objects

    public void addNotification(INotification obj)
    {
        objNotifications.Add(obj);  ← Add the subscribers i.e email,sms and eventlogs
    }
    public void removeNotification(INotification obj)
    {
        objNotifications.Remove(obj);  ← Remove the notifications
    }
    public void NotifyAll()
    {
        foreach (INotification objNotification in objNotifications)
        {
            objNotification.Notify();  ← Notify all the subscribers which are registered
        }
    }
}
```

Figure: Publisher/Subject classes

```
// This application takes customer code and if
// the customer code length is above 20 it notifies
// the error to all the subscribers
string strCustomerCode = "";

// Notifier/Subject to notify all the observers
clsNotifier objNotifier = new clsNotifier();  ← Create a object of notifier

// Add subjects/subscribers which needs to be notified
clsEmailNotification objEmailNotification = new clsEmailNotification();
clsEventNotifcation objEventNotification = new clsEventNotifcation();
objNotifier.addNotification(objEmailNotification);
objNotifier.addNotification(objEventNotification);
        ← Create the object and add the subscribers to the notifiers

// create a error by entering length more than 10 characters
Console.WriteLine("Enter Customer Code");
strCustomerCode = Console.ReadLine();

// if the length is more than 10 characters notify all subjects/subscribers
if (strCustomerCode.Length > 10)
{
    objNotifier.NotifyAll();
}
        ← If the customer length is more than 20 characters then send notificationsto all thesubscribers/observers

Console.ReadLine();
```

Figure: Observer client code

Now that we have an idea about the publisher and subscriber classes lets code the client and see observer in action. Below is a code for observer client snippet. So first we create the object of the notifier which has collection of subscriber objects. We add all the subscribers who are needed to be notified in the collection.

Now if the customer code length is above 10 characters then notify all the subscribers about the same.

Note: *You can get the C# code snippet for observer pattern from the CD in 'Observer' folder.*

(I) Can you explain state pattern?

State pattern allows an object to change its behavior depending on the current values of the object. Consider the figure 'State pattern example'. It's an example of a bulb operation. If the state of the bulb is off and you press the switch the bulb will turn off. If the state of bulb is on and you press the switch the bulb will be off. So in short depending on the state the behavior changes.

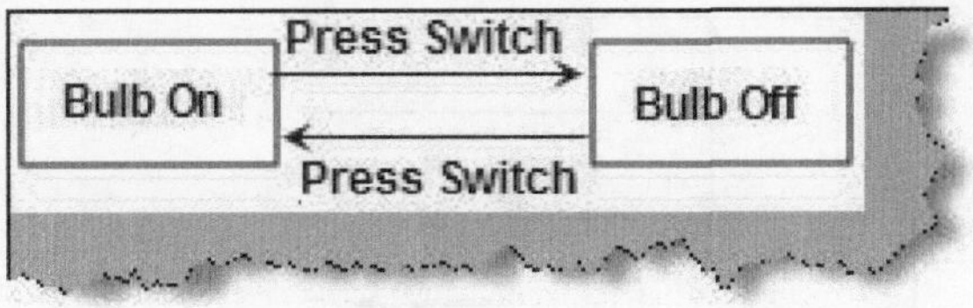

Figure: State pattern example

Now let's try to implement the same bulb sample in C#. Figure 'State pattern in action' shows both the class and the client code. We have made a class called as 'clsState' which has an enum with two state constants 'On' and 'Off'. We have defined a method 'PressSwitch' which toggles its state depending on the current state. In the right hand side of the same figure we have defined a client which consumes the 'clsState' class and calls the 'PressSwitch()' method. We have displayed the current status on the textbox using the 'getStatus' function.

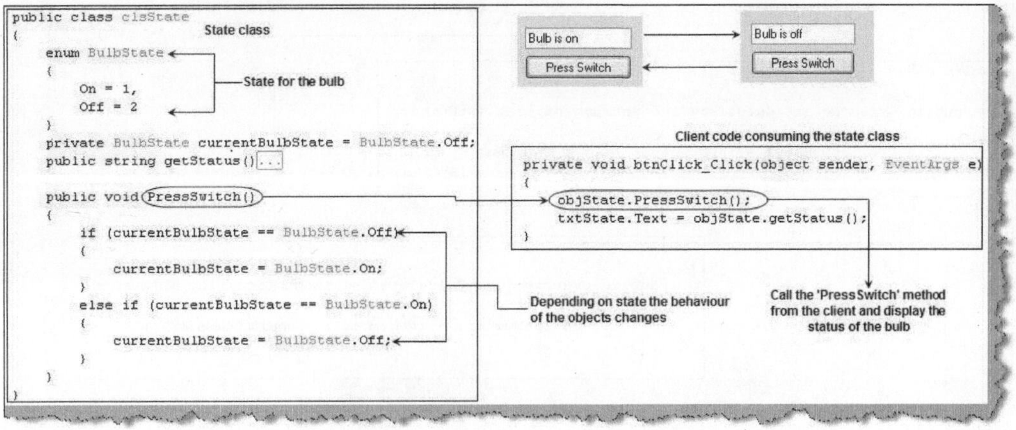

Figure: State pattern in action

When we click the press switch it toggles to the opposite state of what we have currently.

(I) Can you explain strategy pattern?

Strategy pattern are algorithms inside a class which can be interchanged depending on the class used. This pattern is useful when you want to decide on runtime which algorithm to be used.

Let's try to see an example of how strategy pattern works practically. Let's take an example of a math's calculation where we have strategies like add and substract. Figure 'Strategy in action' shows the same in a pictorial format. It takes two numbers and the depending on the strategy it gives out results. So if it's an addition strategy it will add the numbers, if it's a substraction strategy it will give the substracted results. These strategies are nothing but algorithms. Strategy pattern are nothing but encapsulation of algorithms inside classes.

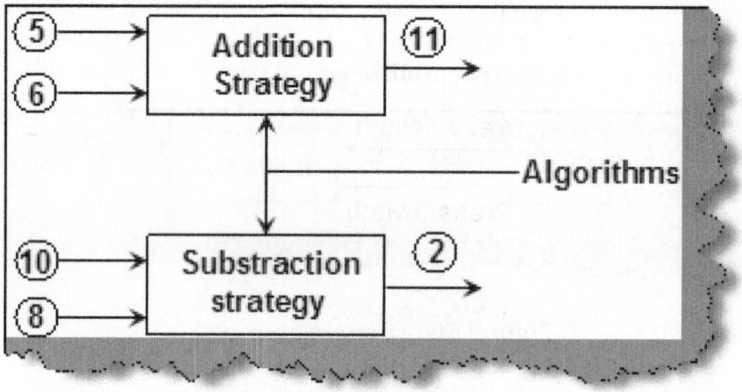

Figure: Strategy in action

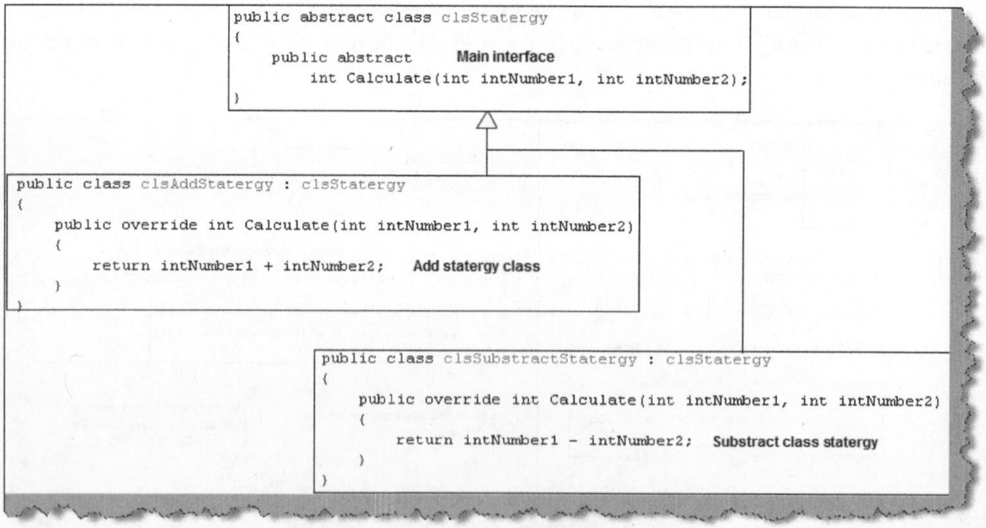

Figure: Algorithms encapsulated

So the first thing we need to look in to is how these algorithms can be encapsulated inside the classes. Below figure 'Algorithm encapsulated' shows how the 'add' is encapsulated in the 'clsAddStatergy' class and 'substract' in the 'clsSubstractStatergy' class. Both these classes inherit from 'clsStratergy' defining a 'calculate' method for its child classes.

Now we define a wrapper class called as 'clsMaths' which has a reference to the 'clsStatergy' class. This class has a 'setStatergy' method which sets the strategy to be used.

```
public class clsMaths
{
    public int intNumber1 = 0;
    public int intNumber2 = 0;
    private clsStatergy objStatergy;
    public void setStatergy(clsStatergy obj)
    {
        objStatergy = obj;
    }
    public int Calculate()
    {
        return objStatergy.Calculate(intNumber1, intNumber2);
    }
}
```

```
public abstract class clsStatergy
{
    public abstract
        int Calculate(int intNumber1, int intNumber2);
}
```

Figure: Strategy and the wrapper class

```
private void btnAdd_Click(object sender, EventArgs e)
{
    // create the new maths object
    clsMaths objMaths = new clsMaths();  <-- Create the maths object
    // set number1 value and number2 value
    objMaths.intNumber1 = Convert.ToInt16(txtNumber1.Text);  <-- Set number 1
    objMaths.intNumber2 = Convert.ToInt16(txtNumber2.Text);  <-- Set number 2
    // set the statergy currently we have set it to add
    objMaths.setStatergy(new clsAddStatergy());  <-- Set the statergy to add class
    // call the calculate method
    txtResults.Text = objMaths.Calculate().ToString();  <-- Finally call the calculate method
}

private void btSubstract_Click(object sender, EventArgs e)
{
    // create the new maths object
    clsMaths objMaths = new clsMaths();
    // set number1 and number2 value
    objMaths.intNumber1 = Convert.ToInt16(txtNumber1.Text);
    objMaths.intNumber2 = Convert.ToInt16(txtNumber2.Text);
    // we have set the statergy to subtract
    objMaths.setStatergy(new clsSubstractStatergy());  <-- Here we have set the statergy to substract
    // call the calculate method
    txtResults.Text = objMaths.Calculate().ToString();
}
```

Figure: Strategy client code

Below figure 'Strategy client code' shows how the wrapper class is used and the strategy object is set on runtime using the 'setStatergy' method.

(A) Can you explain visitor pattern?

Visitor pattern allows us to change the class logic with out changing the actual class. Its way of separating the logic and algorithm from the current data structure. Due to this you can add new logic to the current data structure with out altering the structure. Second you can alter the structure with out touching the logic.

Consider the below figure 'Logic and data structure' where we have a customer data structure. Every customer object has multiple address objects and every address object had multiple phone objects. This data structure needs to be displayed in two different formats one is simple string and second XML. So we have written two classes one is the string logic class and other is the XML logic class. These two classes traverse through the object structure and give the respective outputs. In short the visitor contains the logic.

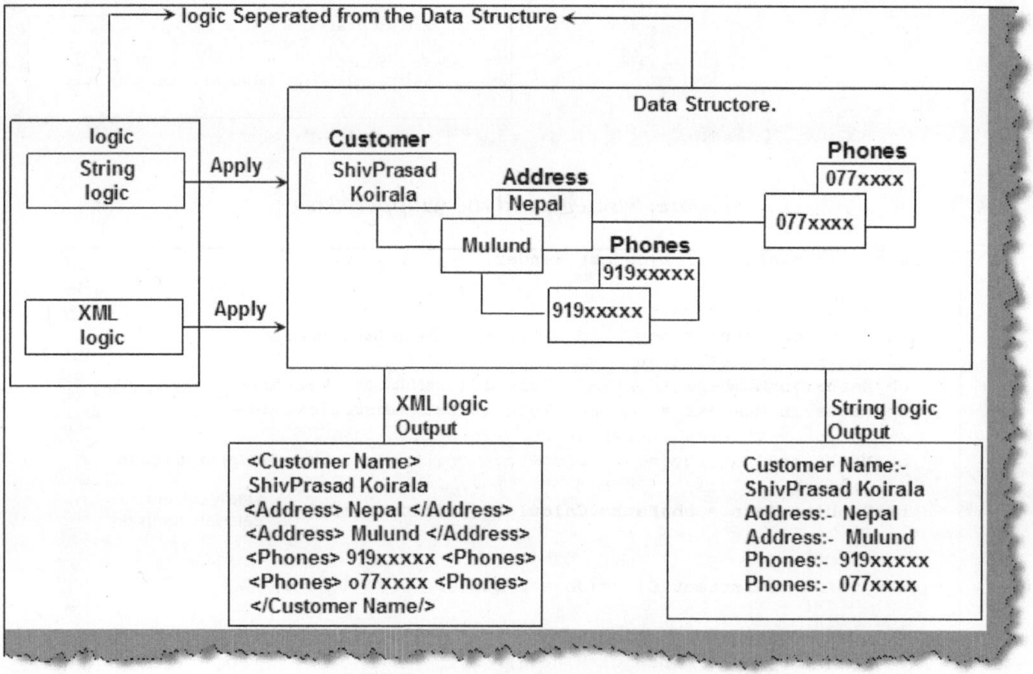

Figure: Logic and data structure

Let's take the above customer sample and try to implement the same in C#. If you are from other programming you should be able to map the same accordingly. We have created two visitor classes one which will be used to parse for the string logic and other for XML. Both these classes have a visit method which takes each object and parses them accordingly. In order to maintain consistency we have implemented them from a common interface 'IVisitor'.

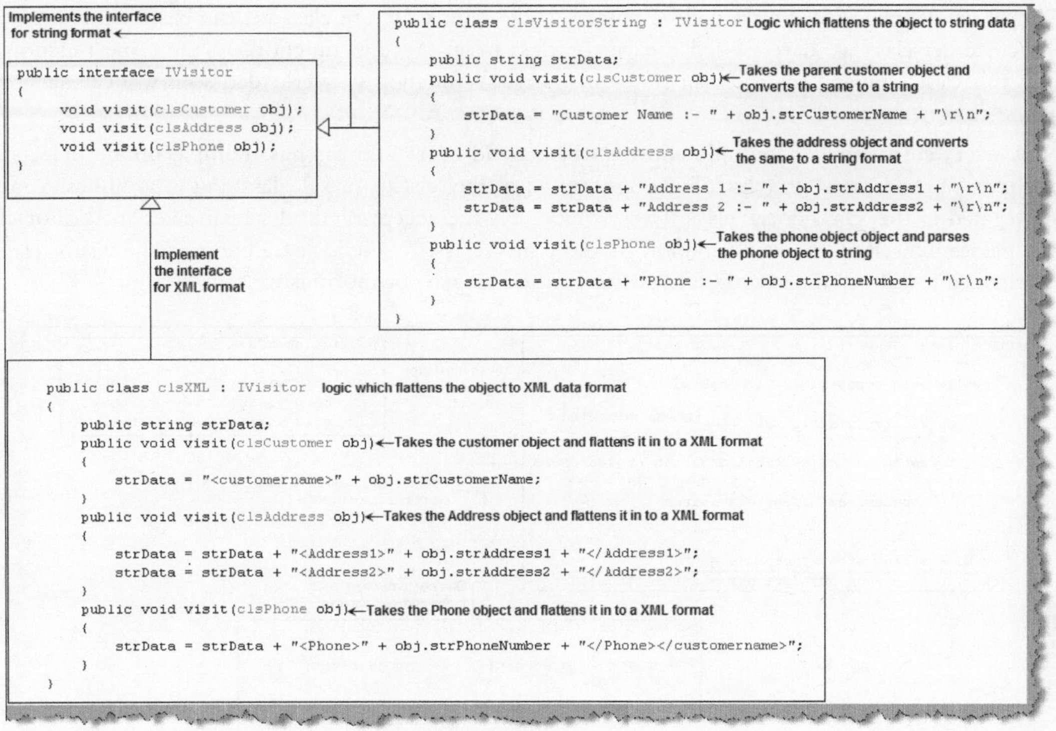

Figure: Visitor class

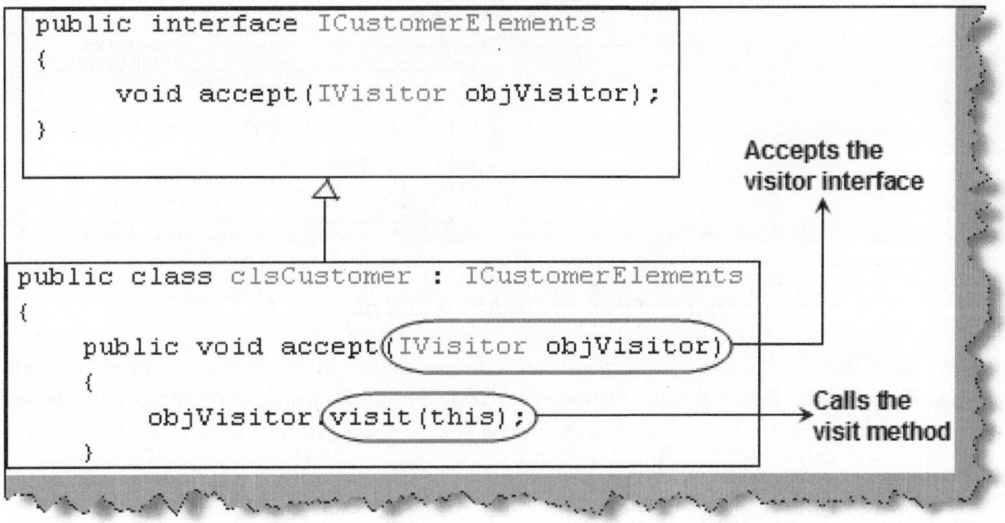

Figure: Visitor passed to data structure class

The above defined visitor class will be passed to the data structure class i.e. the customer class. So in the customer class we have passed the visitor class in an 'Accept' function. In the same function we pass this class type and call the visit function. The visit function is overloaded so it will call according to the class type passed.

Now every customer has multiple address objects and every address has multiple phone objects. So we have 'objAddresses' arraylist object aggregated in the 'clsCustomer' class and 'objPhones' arraylist aggregated in the 'clsAddress' class. Every object has the accept method which takes the visitor class and passes himself in the visit function of the visitor class. As the visit function of the visitor class is overloaded it will call the appropriate visitor method as per polymorphism.

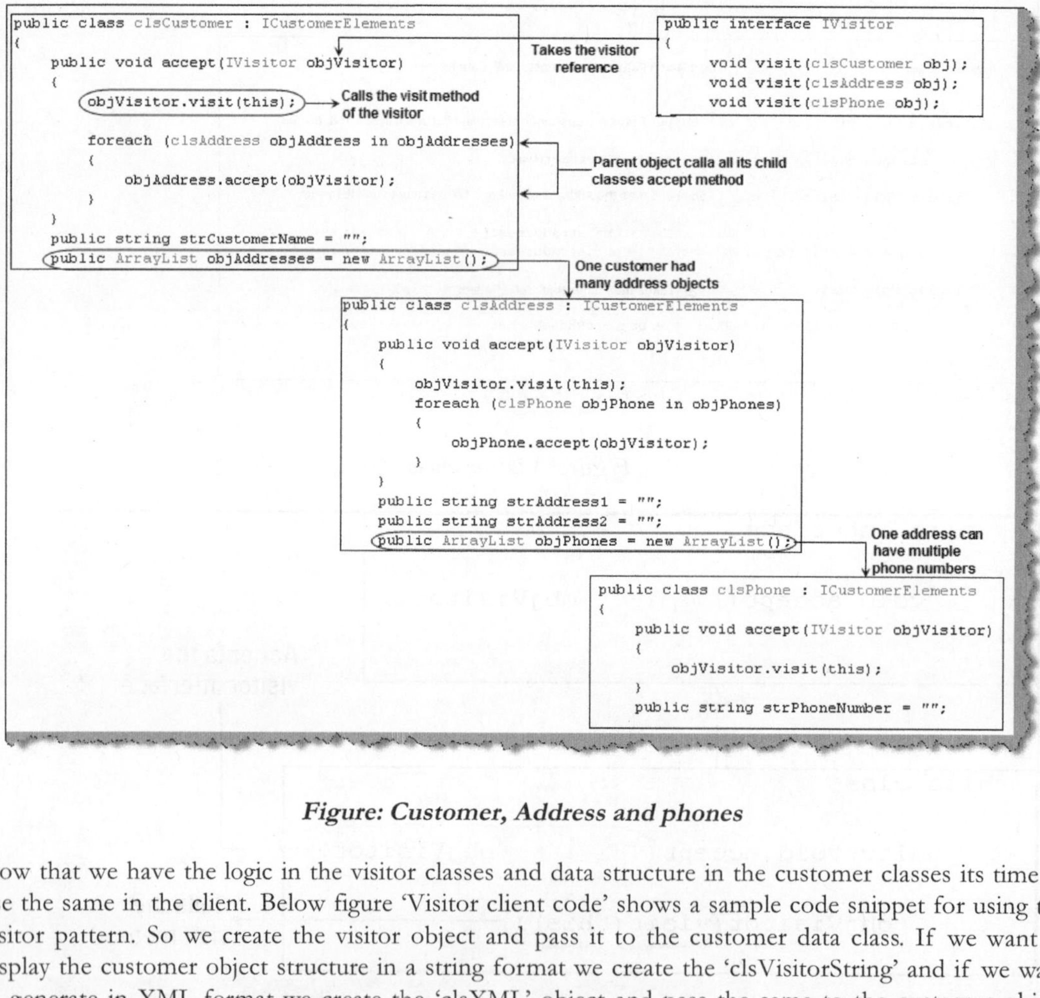

Figure: Customer, Address and phones

Now that we have the logic in the visitor classes and data structure in the customer classes its time to use the same in the client. Below figure 'Visitor client code' shows a sample code snippet for using the visitor pattern. So we create the visitor object and pass it to the customer data class. If we want to display the customer object structure in a string format we create the 'clsVisitorString' and if we want to generate in XML format we create the 'clsXML' object and pass the same to the customer object data structure. You can easily see how the logic is now separated from the data structure.

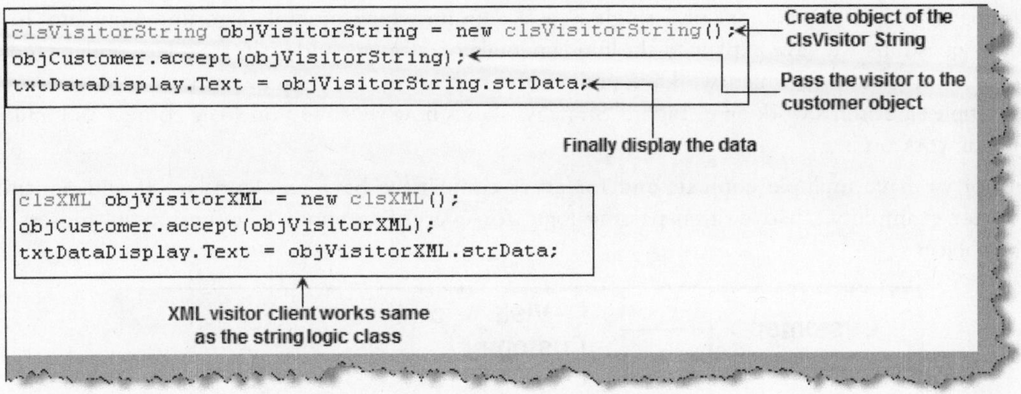

Figure: Visitor client code

> **Note:** *You can find a sample of the same in C# in the visitor folder of the CD. If you belong to some other programming domain you can map the same as the code is very generic.*

(A) What the difference between visitor and strategy pattern?

Visitor and strategy look very much similar as they deal with encapsulating complex logic from data. We can say visitor is more general form of strategy.

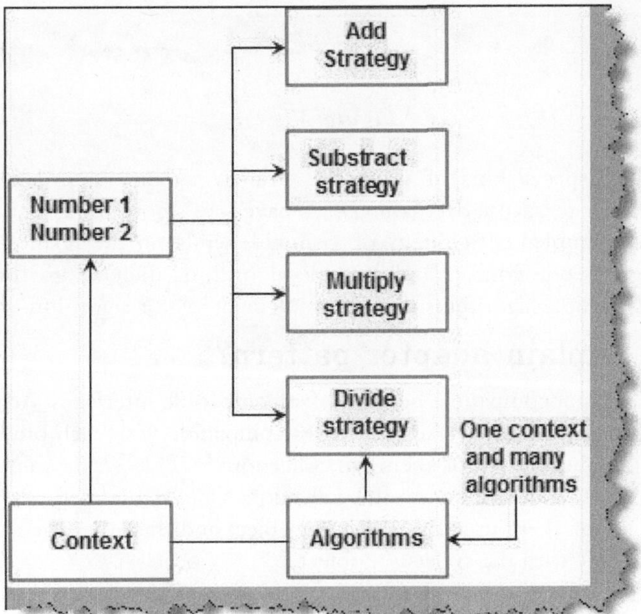

Figure: Strategy

In strategy we have one context or a single logical data on which multiple algorithms operate. In the previous questions we have explained the fundamentals of strategy and visitor. So let's understand the same by using examples which we have understood previously. In strategy we have a single context and multiple algorithms work on it. Figure 'Strategy' shows how we have a one data context and multiple algorithm work on it.

In visitor we have multiple contexts and for every context we have an algorithm. If you remember the visitor example we had written parsing logic for every data context i.e. customer, address and phones object.

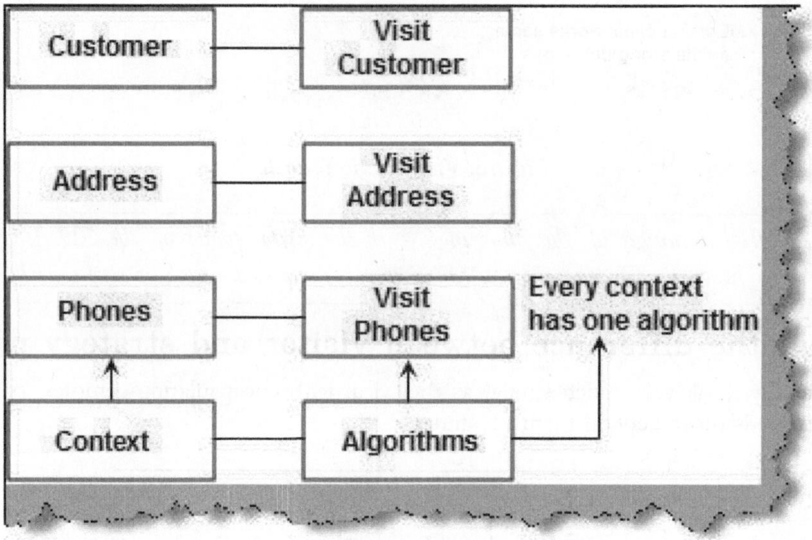

Figure: Visitor

So in short strategy is a special kind of visitor. In strategy we have one data context and multiple algorithms while in visitor for every data context we have one algorithm associated. The basic criteria of choosing whether to implement strategy or visitor depends on the relationship between context and algorithm. If there is one context and multiple algorithms then we go for strategy. If we have multiple contexts and multiple algorithms then we implement visitor algorithm.

(A) Can you explain adapter pattern?

Many times two classes are incompatible because of incompatible interfaces. Adapter helps us to wrap a class around the existing class and make the classes compatible with each other. Consider the below figure 'Incompatible interfaces' both of them are collections to hold string values. Both of them have a method which helps us to add string in to the collection. One of the methods is named as 'Add' and the other as 'Push'. One of them uses the collection object and the other the stack. We want to make the stack object compatible with the collection object.

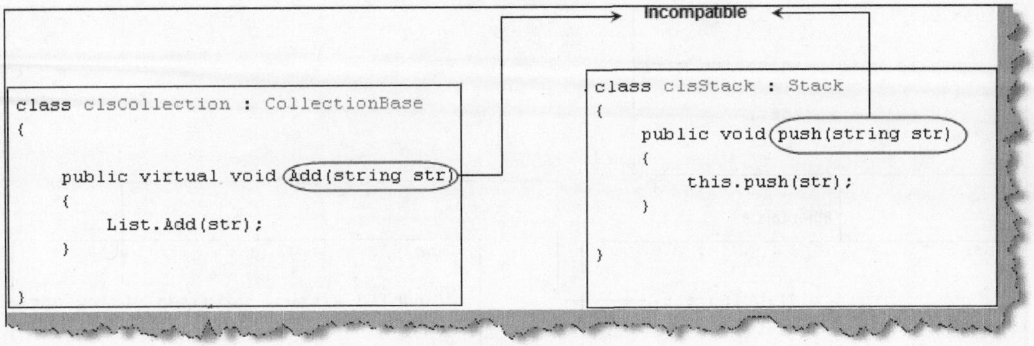

Figure: Incompatible interfaces

There are two way of implementing adapter pattern one is by using aggregation (this is termed as the object adapter pattern) and the other inheritance (this is termed as the class adapter pattern). First let's try to cover object adapter pattern.

Figure 'Object Adapter pattern' shows a broader view of how we can achieve the same. We have a introduced a new wrapper class 'clsCollectionAdapter' which wraps on the top of the 'clsStack' class and aggregates the 'push' method inside a new 'Add' method, thus making both the classes compatible.

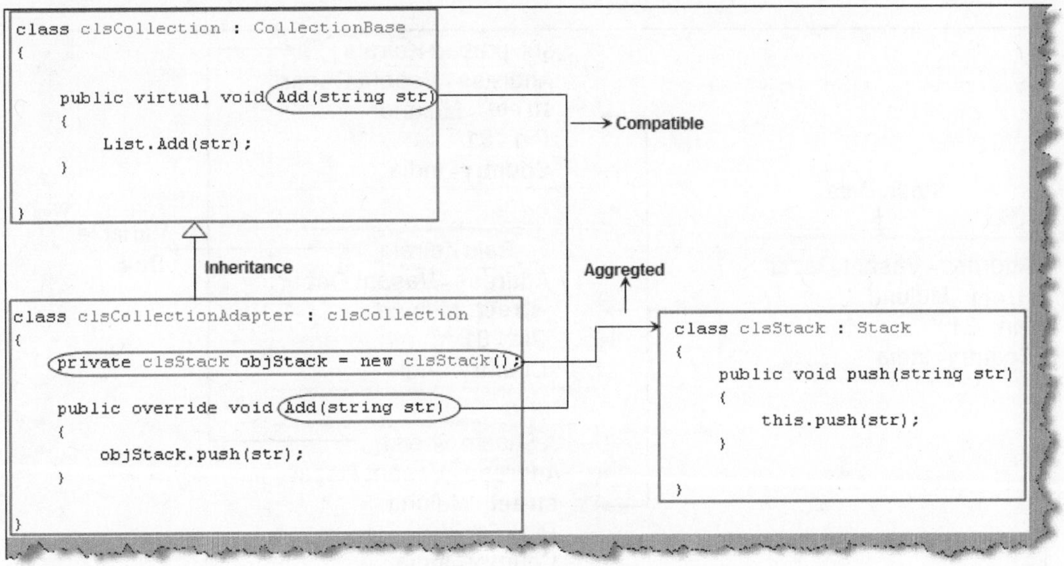

Figure: Object Adapter pattern

The other way to implement the adapter pattern is by using inheritance also termed as class adapter pattern. Figure 'Class adapter pattern' shows how we have inherited the 'clsStack' class in the 'clsCollectionAdapter' and made it compatible with the 'clsCollection' class.

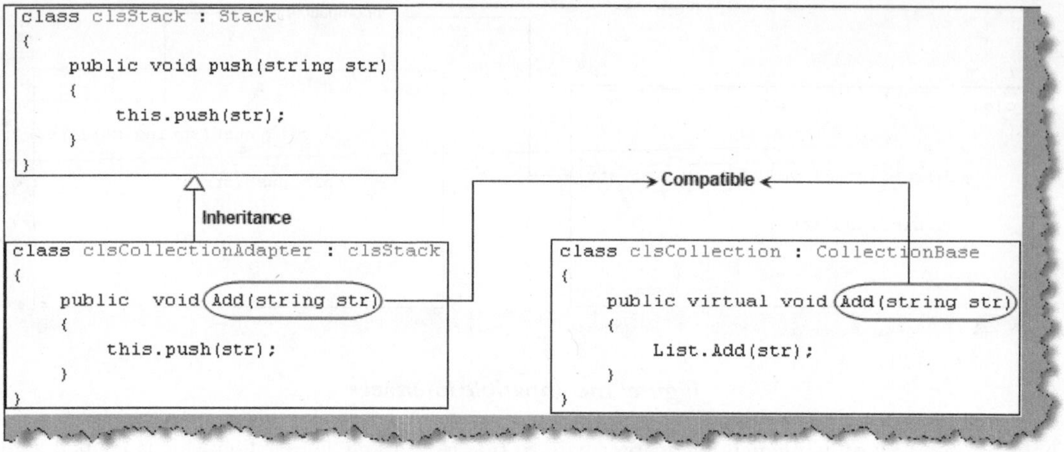

Figure: Class adapter pattern

Note: *You can the above C# example in the adapter folder of the CD.*

(I) What is fly weight pattern?

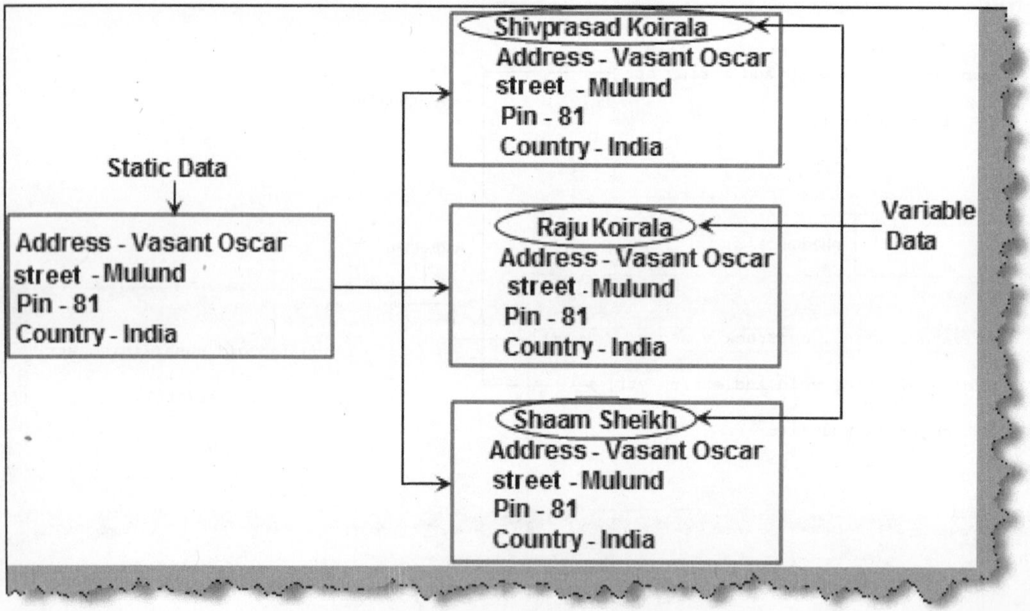

Figure: Objects and common data

Fly weight pattern is useful where we need to create many objects and all these objects share some kind of common data. Consider figure 'Objects and common data'. We need to print visiting card for all employees in the organization. So we have two parts of data one is the variable data i.e. the employee name and the other is static data i.e. address. We can minimize memory by just keeping one copy of the static data and referencing the same data in all objects of variable data. So we create different copies of variable data, but reference the same copy of static data. With this we can optimally use the memory.

Below is a sample C# code demonstration of how flyweight can be implemented practically. We have two classes, 'clsVariableAddress' which has the variable data and second 'clsAddress' which has the static data. To ensure that we have only one instance of 'clsAddress' we have made a wrapper class 'clsStatic' and created a static instance of the 'clsAddress' class. This object is aggregated in the 'clsVariableAddress' class.

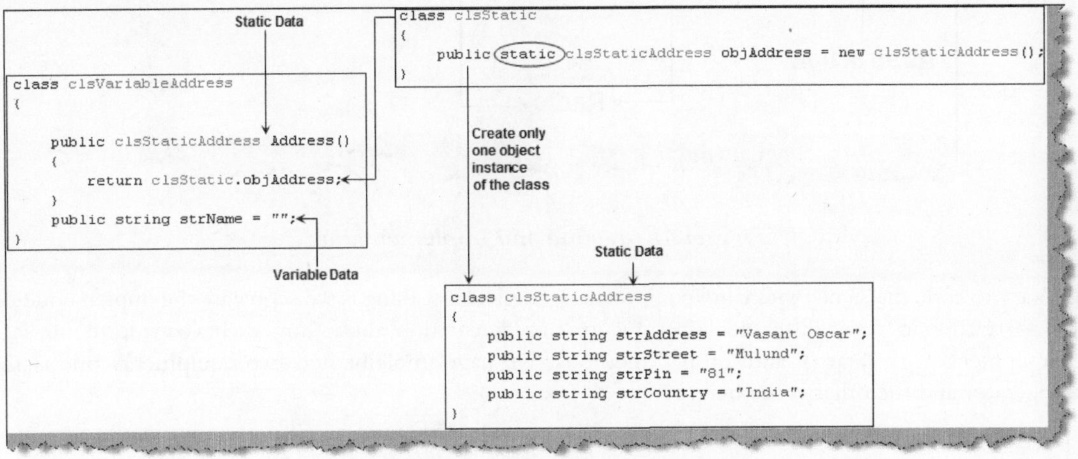

Figure: Class view of flyweight

Figure 'Fly weight client code' shows we have created two objects of 'clsVariableAddress' class, but internally the static data i.e. the address is referred to only one instance.

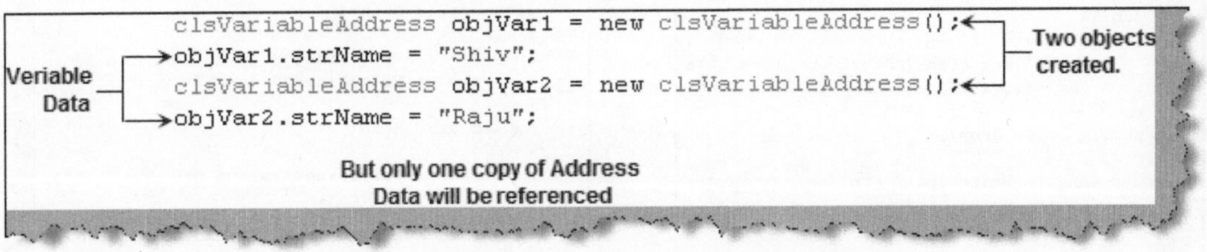

Figure: Fly weight client code

(A) Can you explain bridge pattern?

Bridge pattern helps to decouple abstraction from implementation. With this if the implementation changes it does not affect abstraction and vice versa. Consider the figure 'Abstraction and Implementation'. The switch is the abstraction and the electronic equipments are the implementations.

The switch can be applied to any electronic equipment, so the switch is an abstract thinking while the equipments are implementations.

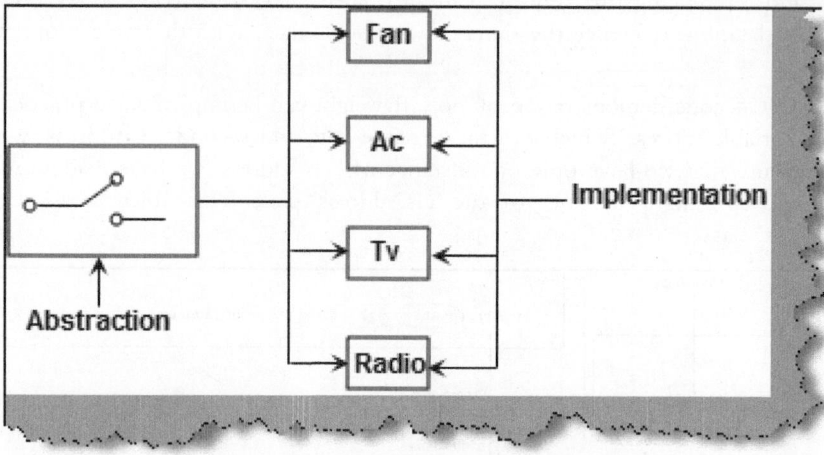

Figure: Abstraction and Implementation

Let's try to code the same switch and equipment example. First thing is we segregate the implementation and abstraction in to two different classes. Figure 'Implementation' shows how we have made an interface 'IEquipment' with 'Start()' and 'Stop()' methods. We have implemented two equipments one is the refrigerator and the other is the bulb.

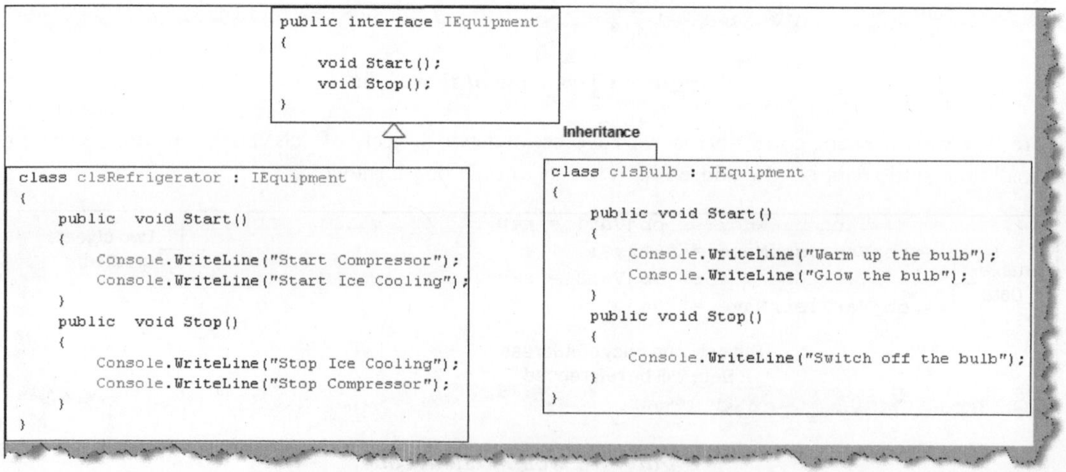

Figure: Implementation

The second part is the abstraction. Switch is the abstraction in our example. It has a 'SetEquipment' method which sets the object. The 'On' method calls the 'Start' method of the equipment and the 'off' calls the 'stop'.

```
interface ISwitch
{
    void On();
    void Off();
}
class Clsswitch : ISwitch
{
    private IEquipment objEquipment;
    public void setEquipMent(IEquipment Equipment)
    {
        objEquipment = Equipment;
    }
    public void On()
    {
        objEquipment.Start();

    }
    public void Off()
    {
        objEquipment.Stop();

    }
```

Abstraction interface

Aggregated Equipment object reference

Implement both the interface

Figure: Abstraction

```
clsBulb objBulb = new clsBulb();
clsRefrigerator objRefrig = new clsRefrigerator();
Clsswitch objSwitch = new Clsswitch();

objSwitch.setEquipMent(objBulb);
objSwitch.On();
objSwitch.Off();


objSwitch.setEquipMent(objRefrig);
objSwitch.On();
objSwitch.Off();
Console.ReadLine();
```

Create the implementation objects

Abstraction objects

Implementation is seperate from abstraction

Figure: Client code using bridge

Finally we see the client code. You can see we have created the implementation objects and the abstraction objects separately. We can use them in an isolated manner.

Figure: *You can find the C# code for bridge in the 'BridgePattern' folder.*

(A) Can you explain composite pattern?

Composite pattern allows treating different objects in a similar fashion. Figure 'Uniformity' shows how different objects are called in a uniform manner.

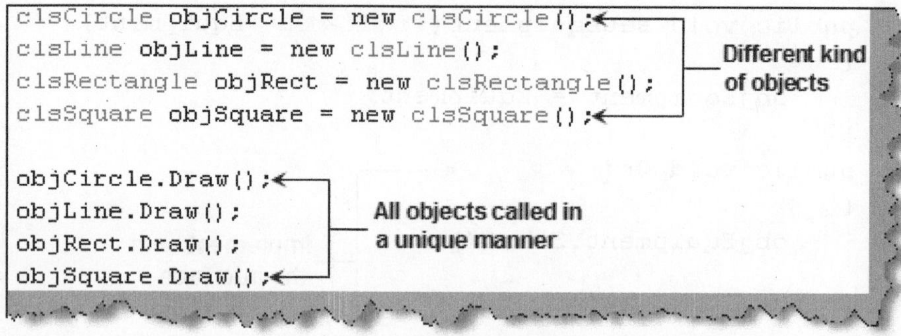

Figure: Uniformity

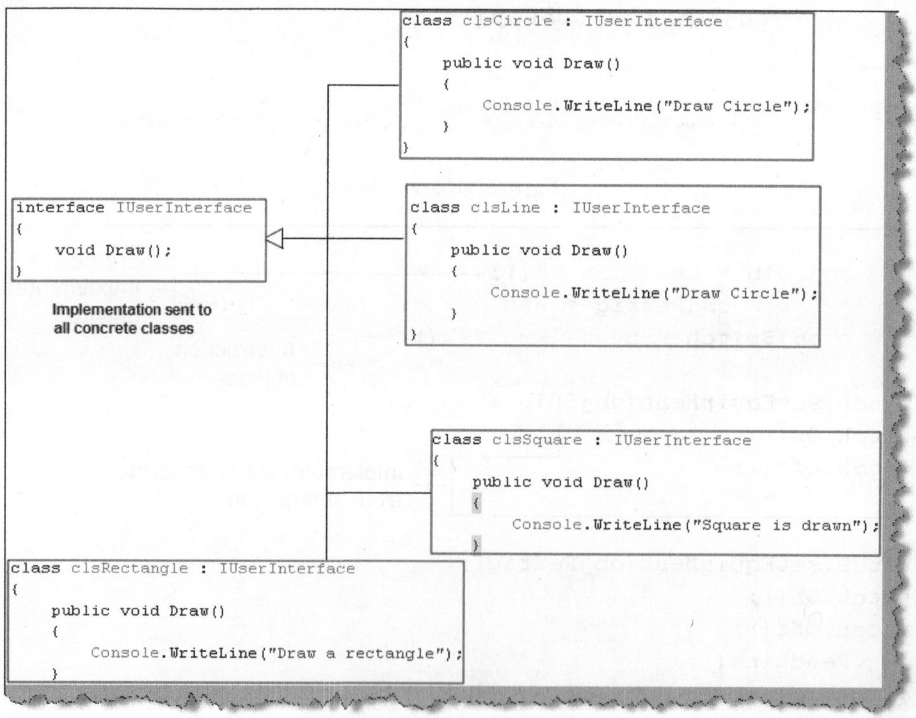

Figure: Common interface

In order to treat objects in a uniformed manner we need to inherit them from a common interface. Figure 'Common Interface' shows the objects inheriting from a common interface.

Figure 'Client code for composition' shows how we added all the different kind of objects in to one collection and then called them in a uniform fashion.

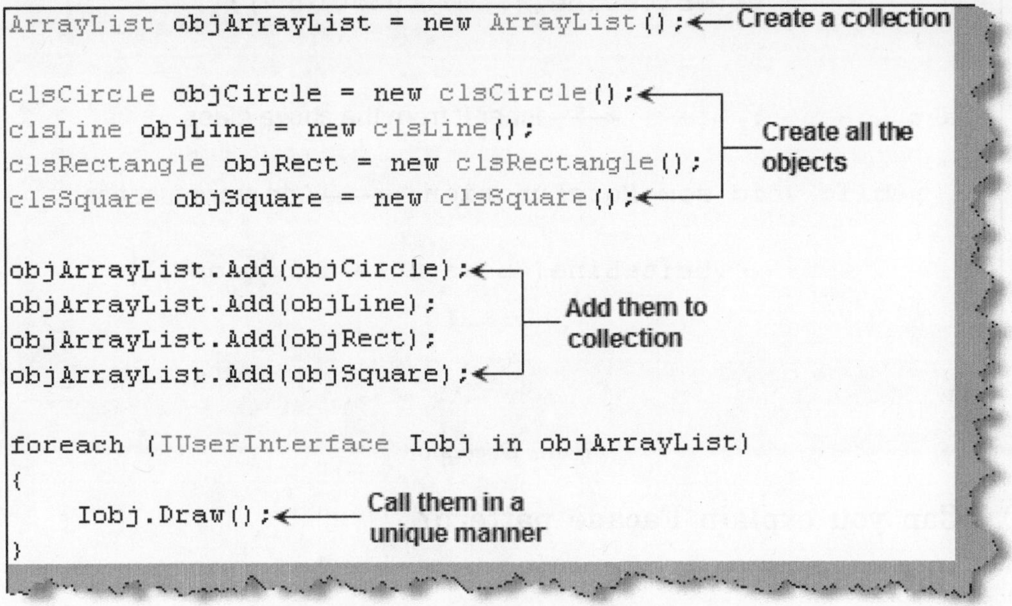

Figure: Client code for composition

> **Note:** *You can find C# code for composition in the 'Composite' folder.*

(I) Can you explain decorator pattern ?

Decorator pattern allows creating inherited classes which are sum of all part of the parent. For instance figure 'Decorator' has class1 which has method called as 'SomeFunction' now we inherit and add one more method called as 'SomeMoreFunction'. So Class2 is the addition of 'SomeFunction' plus 'SomeMoreFunction'.

```
class Class1
{
    public void someFunction()<——Some function
    {
        Console.WriteLine("Some function");
    }
}
class Class2 : Class1<——Inher it from the above class
{
    public void someMoreFunction()<——Add more function
    {
        Console.WriteLine("Some more function");
    }
}
```

Figure: Decorator

(A) Can you explain Façade pattern?

Façade pattern sits on the top of group of subsystems and allows them to communicate in a unified manner.

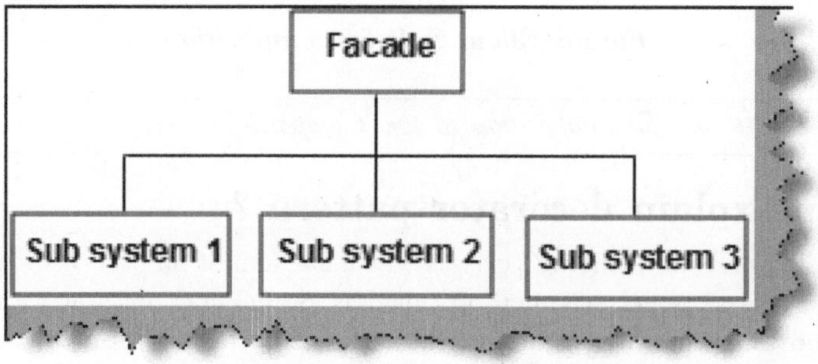

Figure: Façade and Subsystem

Figure 'Order Façade' shows a practical implementation of the same. In order to place an order we need to interact with product, payment and invoice classes. So order becomes a façade which unites product, payment and invoice classes.

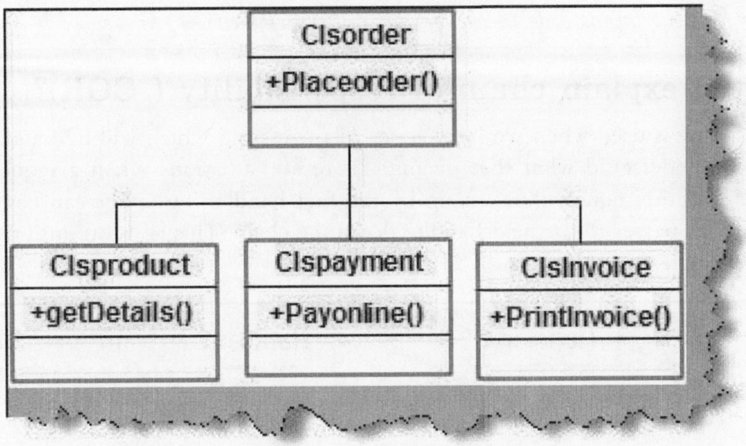

Figure: Order Facade

Figure 'façade in action' shows how class 'clsorder' unifies / uses 'clsproduct','clsproduct' and 'clsInvoice' to implement 'PlaceOrder' functionality.

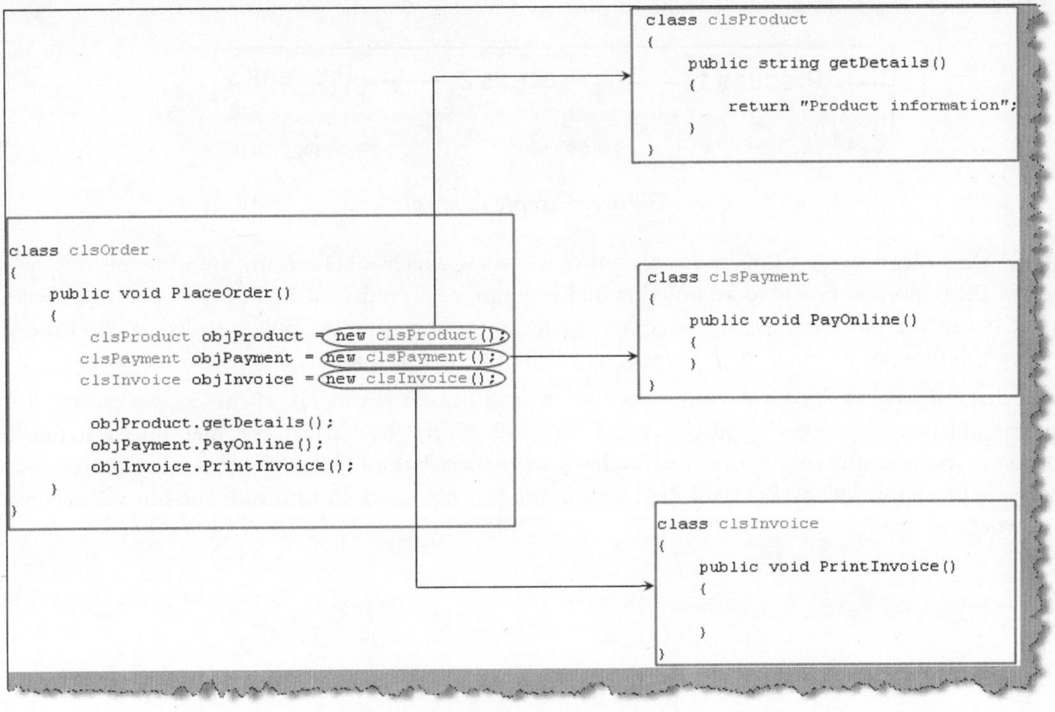

Figure: Façade in action

Note: *You can find the façade code in the 'façade pattern' folder.*

(A) Can you explain chain of responsibility (COR)?

Chain of responsibility is used when we have series of processing which will be handled by a series of handler logic. Let's understand what that means. There are situations when a request is handled by series of handlers. So the request is taken up by the first handler, he either can handle part of it or can not, once done he passes to the next handler down the chain. This goes on until the proper handler takes it up and completes the processing.

Figure: Concept of Chain of Responsibility

Let's try to understand this concept by a small sample example. Consider figure 'Sample example' where we have some logic to be processed. So there are three series of processes which it will go through. So process 1 does some processing and passes the same to process 2. Process 2 does some kind of processing and passed the same to process 3 to complete the processing activity.

Figure: Sample example

Figure 'class diagram for COR' the three process classes which inherit from the same abstract class. One of the important points to be noted is that every process points to the next process which will be called. So in the process class we have aggregated one more process object called as 'objProcess'. Object 'ObjProcess' points to next process which should be called after this process is complete.

Now that we have defined our classes its time to call the classes in the client. So we create all the process objects for process1 , process2 and process3. Using the 'setProcess' method we define the link list of process objects. You can see we have set process2 as a link list to process1 and process2 to process3. Once this link list is established we run the process which in turn runs the process according to the defined link list.

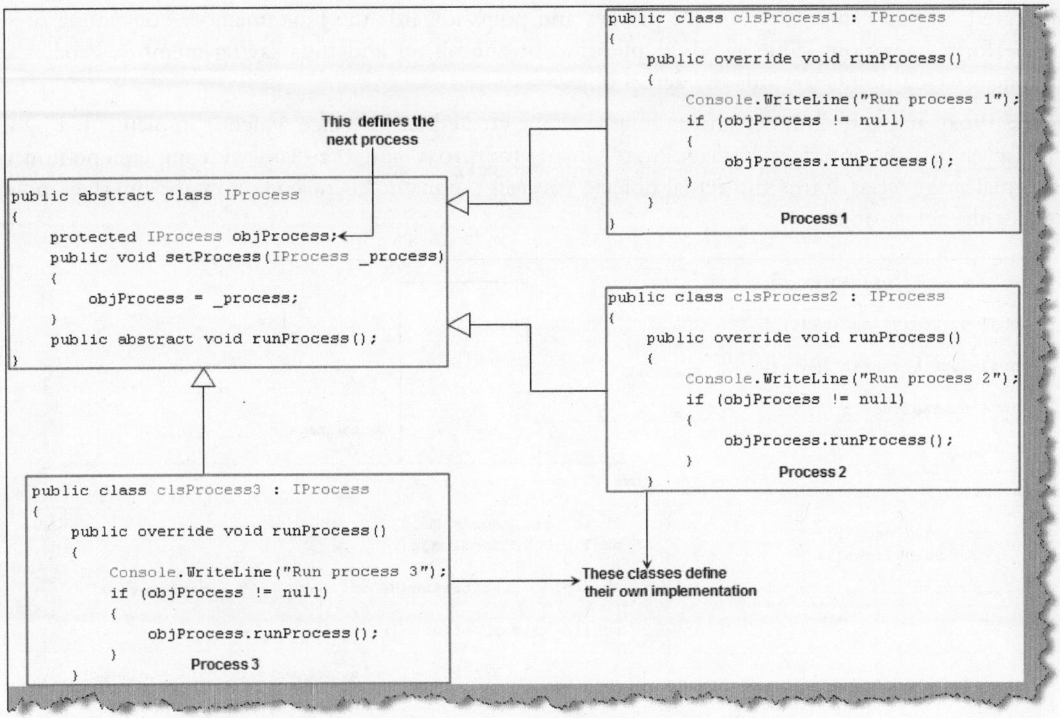

Figure: Class diagram for COR

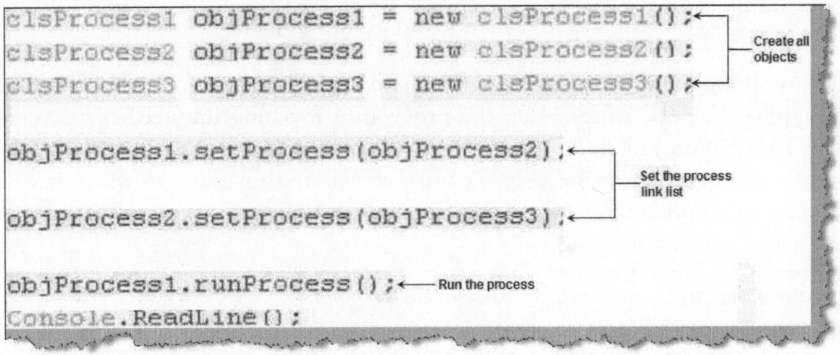

Figure: COR client code

Note: *You can get the code for the same in C# in 'ChainOfResponsibility' folder.*

(I) Can you explain proxy pattern?

Proxy fundamentally is a class functioning as in interface which points towards the actual class which has data. This actual data can be a huge image or an object data which very large and can not be duplicated. So you can create multiple proxies and point towards the huge memory consuming object and perform operations. This avoids duplication of the object and thus saving memory. Proxies are references which points towards the actual object.

Figure 'Proxy and actual object' shows how we have created an interface which is implemented by the actual class. So the interface 'IImageProxy' forms the proxy and the class with implementation i.e. 'clsActualImage' class forms the actual object. You can see in the client code how the interface points towards the actual object.

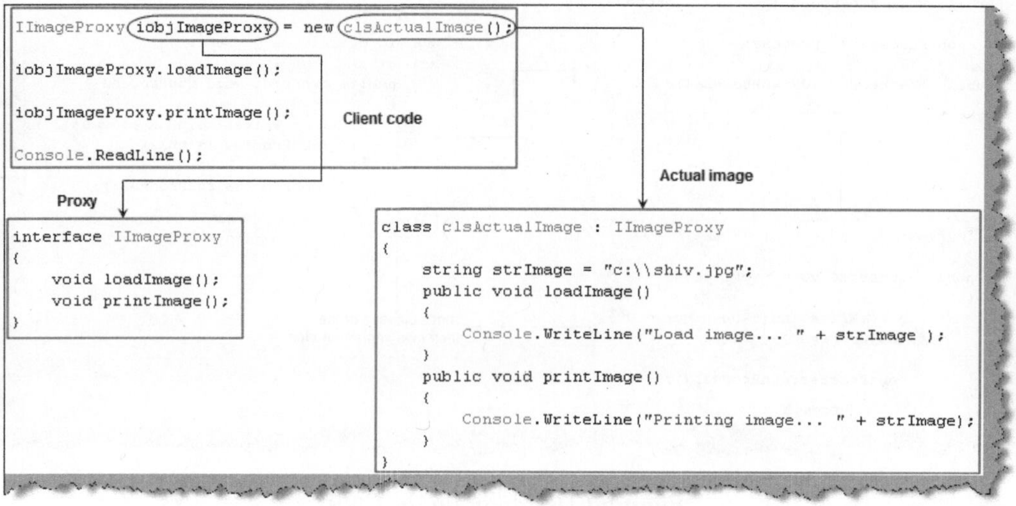

Figure: Proxy and actual object

The advantages of using proxy are security and avoiding duplicating objects which are of huge sizes. Rather than shipping the code we can ship the proxy, thus avoiding the need of installing the actual code at the client side. With only the proxy at the client end we ensure more security. Second point is when we have huge objects it can be very memory consuming to move to those large objects in a network or some other domain. So rather than moving those large objects we just move the proxy which leads to better performance.

Note: *You can get the proxy code in the 'Proxy Pattern' folder.*

(B) Can you explain template pattern?

In template pattern we have an abstract class which acts as a skeleton for its inherited classes. The inherited classes get the shared functionality. The inherited classes take the shared functionality and add enhancements to the existing functionality. In word or power point how we take templates and then prepare our own custom presentation using the base. Template classes works on the same fundamental.

Figure 'Template abstract class' shows we have created a customer class 'ClsCustomer' which has set/ get properties. Now we can inherit from this class and create add and update customer classes.

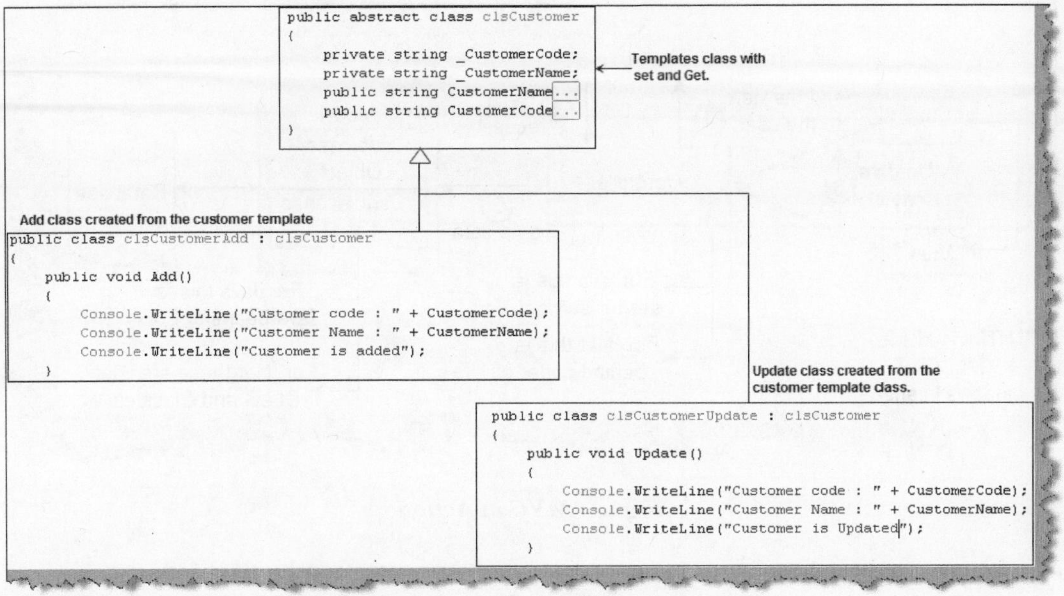

Figure: Template abstract class

Note: *You can find the above C# source code in 'Template Pattern' folder.*

(B) Can you explain MVC?

MVC is a design approach to separate the GUI from the application model. The main motive behind MVC to separate the view of data from the actual processing of data. MVC stands for model, view and controller. So let's define these three components and understand the MVC fundamental in a more precise format.

View: View represents the look and feel of an application; in one line they represent the GUI of a system. So view gets data and put in cosmetic formatting before displaying on the UI. It can be HTML, JAVA Applets, Windows form, XSL etc.

Model: They are responsible for processing the data, managing database connections, implementing business rules and querying database. It processes data and passes it on to the view with out worrying about the final cosmetic looks. Model gets requests from the controller and they notify the corresponding views regarding the data. In Microsoft technologies they are .NET DLL while in Java they are Java beans.

Controller: Controllers accept user events like mouse click, button enter etc and reacts accordingly. Controllers get these events from views and they trigger events to change the model to update their state. Once models have updated their states they communicate the same to the corresponding views to refresh the display. In .NET technologies they the behind code while in Java it's the Service method of the servlet.

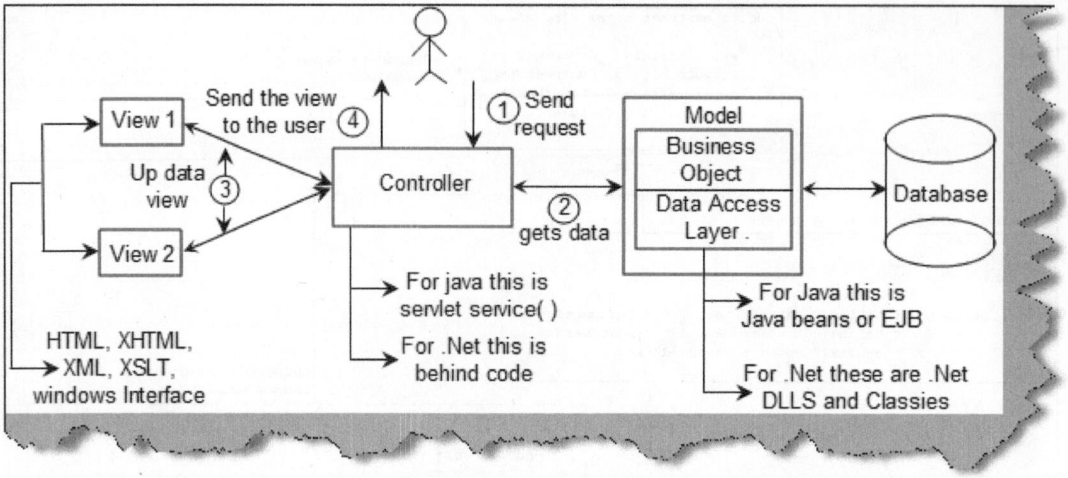

Figure: MVC in Action

So looking at the above figure we can say there are four main steps by which MVC works:

1. User sends an event like keyboard, button click or enter event to the controller.
2. Controller sends this event to the model who in turn updates himself and sends the data to the controller.
3. Controller updates the corresponding view depending on the event.
4. This view is then viewed by the end user.

> **Note:** *We have shown in the above figure how MVC will be implemented for .NET and JAVA. It's not necessary that an architecture follows the same approach. What we mean to say is these are the common ways of doing it. For instance architecture can use an ISAPI filter rather than a behind code to implement the controller.*

(A) What is aspect oriented programming?

> **Note:** *This is something which is catching up the market so interviewer can ask you to see how you are in touch with the market. So probably this explanation can be quiet long but bear with me it is worth of it*

We will try to make it as short as possible as this book is not a reference book. First, let us try to define it, which can probably save you during interview

> *Aspect-oriented software development is a new technology for separation of concerns (SOC) in software development. The techniques of AOSD make it possible to modularize crosscutting aspects of a system.*

Ok that statement can save you for the first stage let us get down actually what is it. Let us revisit back how software development cycle evolved.

When we look back at times of COBOL where we used to break the modules in small functionalities and use reusability to its maximum.

Then came the time when we talked in terms of Objects where things were clearer as software was modeled in terms of real life examples. It worked fine and until today is the most accepted way of implementing and organizing project. So why AOP?

Aspect oriented programming does not oppose OOP's but rather supports it and make's it more maintainable. So remove the logic from head the AOP is replacement of OOP. No its brother of OOP helping him to be better.

When we talk in terms of objects, it is an entity, which maps to real world domain. Object has attributes, which represent the state of object and define its behavior. By rule of object, oriented programming object should be stand alone and communicate with other objects using messages or defined interface.

One object should not communicate with other object directly rather communicate through defined interfaces. Every object satisfies some "Concern" in relation to the system.

Twist: What is Concern in AOP?

"A concern is a particular goal, concept, or area of interest"

There are mainly two types of concern from an object perspective:

- Core / Main concerns, which it should satisfy and is his work.
- System concerns which are not related to business functionalities but software related concerns example audit trail, Error handling, Security etc.

Ok let us try to understand this principle by some actual example.

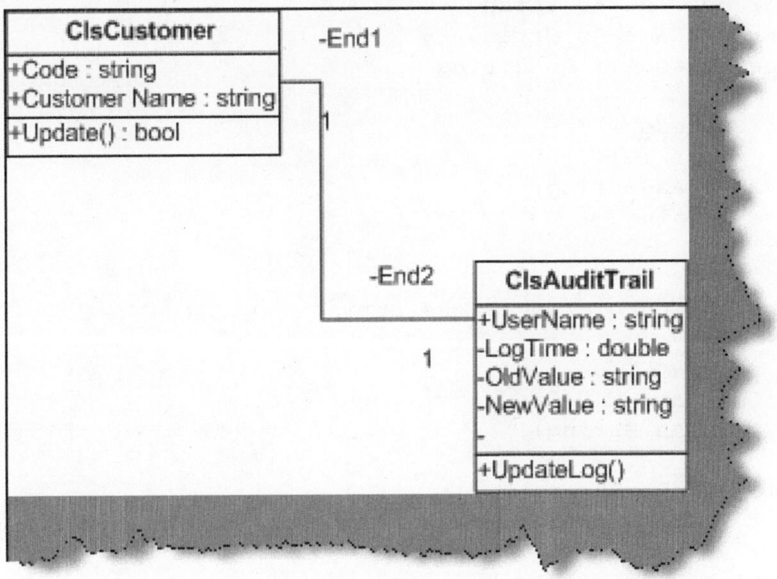

Figure: Customer and Audit trail relationships

Above is a class diagram, which shows relationshipbetween two classes "ClsCustomer" and "ClsAuditTrail". "ClsCustomer" class does inserting of new customers in to database and "ClsAuditTrail" does the auditing of what is changed in the customer class.

Now there are two concerns in this project:

- Customer code should not exceed than 10 lengths (Business level concern) greater
- All customer data, which is updated, should be audited. (System level concern)

Here goes the class code. If you see the ClsCustomer implementation in the update method, we have called the Audit trail implementation. If you really look from object-oriented point of view, we are doing something in customer class, which is supposed to be not his implementation: Audit Trail logging. Thus, we have also broken down the rule of encapsulation. In short, the class not only handles his work but also some other work which is not his concern.

Ok now let us define crosscutting which is one of important aspects of AOP.

Twist: What is cross cutting in AOP?

When one or many concerns span across module it is called as cross cutting. Example in our audit trail example we will probably need to audit trail for customer as well as supplier. So Audit trail can span across other objects also that is termed as cross cutting.

Below are both the classes actually implemented as per class diagram 'Customer and Audit trail relationship'. If you see the "Update" method of the customer class, its doing both of the concerns that is checking for customer code length, and also maintaining the audit trail using the audit trail class.

```
Public Class ClsCustomer
Private pstrCustcode As String
Private pstrCustName As String
Public Property Code() As String
Get
Return pstrCustcode
End Get
Set(ByVal Value As String)
pstrCustcode = Value
End Set
End Property
Public Property CustomerName() As String
Get

Return pstrCustName End Get
Set(ByVal Value As String)

pstrCustName = Value
End Set
End Property
Public Function Update() As Boolean
' first / core concern
```

```
If pstrCustcode.Length() > 10 Then
Throw New Exception("Value can not be greater than 10")
End If
' usingthe customer audit trail to do auditing
' second concern / system concern
Dim pobjClsAuditTrail As New ClsAuditTrail
With pobjClsAuditTrail
.NewValue = "1001"
.OldValue = "1003"
.UserName = "shiv"
.Update()
End With
' then inserting the customer in database
End Function
End Class
Public Class ClsAuditTrail
Private pstrUserName As String
Private pstrOldValue As String
Private pstrNewValue As String
Private pdblLogTime As Double
Public Property UserName() As String

Return pstrUserName
End Get
Set(ByVal Value As String)
pstrUserName = Value
End Set
End Property
Public Property OldValue() As String
Get
Return pstrOldValue
End Get
Set(ByVal Value As String)
pstrOldValue = Value
End Set
End Property
Public Property NewValue() As String
Get
Return pstrNewValue
End Get
Set(ByVal Value As String)
pstrNewValue = Value

End Set
      End Property
      Public Property LogTime() As Double
           Get
```

```
                Return pdblLogTime
            End Get
            Set(ByVal Value As Double)
                pdblLogTime = Value
            End Set
        End Property
        Public Sub Update()
            ' do the logging activity here
        End Sub
End Class
```

In short, the customer class is doing much activity. There is lot of tangling of code. So how do we overcome this problem...? Simple, separate the System level concern (Audit Trail) from the core level concern (Customer code check). This is achieved at this moment in .NET using attribute programming as shown in the below code snippet.

```
Here is the change to the customer class
Imports System.Reflection
Public Class ClsCustomer
        Private pstrCustcode As String
        Private pstrCustName As String
        Public Property Code() As String
            Get
                Return pstrCustcode
            End Get
            Set(ByVal Value As String)

                pstrCustcode = Value
            End Set
        End Property
        Public Property CustomerName() As String
            Get
                Return pstrCustName
            End Get
            Set(ByVal Value As String)

                pstrCustName = Value
            End Set
        End Property
        <ClsAuditTrail("Shiv", "1001", "1003", 12)> _
        Public Function Update() As Boolean
            If pstrCustcode.Length() > 10 Then
                Throw New Exception("Value can not be greater than
                10")
            End If
            ' usingthe customer audit trail to do auditing
```

```
'th End Function

End Class
```

And here is the change to the audit trail class

```
Imports System.Reflection
<AttributeUsage(AttributeTargets.All)> _
Public Class ClsAuditTrail
Inherits Attribute
Private pstrUserName As String
Private pstrOldValue As String
Private pstrNewValue As String
Private pdblLogTime As Double
Public Property UserName() As String
Get
Return pstrUserName
End Get
Set(ByVal Value As String)
pstrUserName = Value
End Set
End Property
Public Property OldValue() As String
Get
Return pstrOldValue
End Get
Set(ByVal Value As String)
pstrOldValue = Value
End Set
End Property
Public Property NewValue() As String
Get
            Return pstrNewValue
      End Get
      Set(ByVal Value As String)
            pstrNewValue = Value
      End Set
End Property
      Public Property LogTime() As Double
            Get
                  Return pdblLogTime
            End Get
            Set(ByVal Value As Double)
                  pdblLogTime = Value
            End Set
      End Property
      Public Sub New(ByVal pstrUserName As String, _
            ByVal pstrOldValue As String, _
```

```
            ByVal pstrnewValue As String, _
            ByVal plng As Long)
      Update()
End Sub
```

In .NET AOP is currently support by using attribute programming. In JAVA you can use Annotation/JBOSS for implementing AOP.

(A) What is Inversion of control?

Inversion of control in acronym it's also termed as Dependency Inversion Principle. Let's say we have class A. Class A uses Class B. In short Class A depends on Class B. In short Class A can not be used with out Class B. Second Class B can not use Class A. In order to remove the dependency that Class A can not be used with out Class B we need to introduce an Interface in between them. This is termed as IOC or DIP. So now both of the classes will communicate through this interface thus leading to loosely coupled and independent architecture.

(I) What is OR mapping?

OR mapping is process in which we map classes to relation tables. Mapping places object attributes in one or more database fields. Ok let's try understanding this with a simple example.

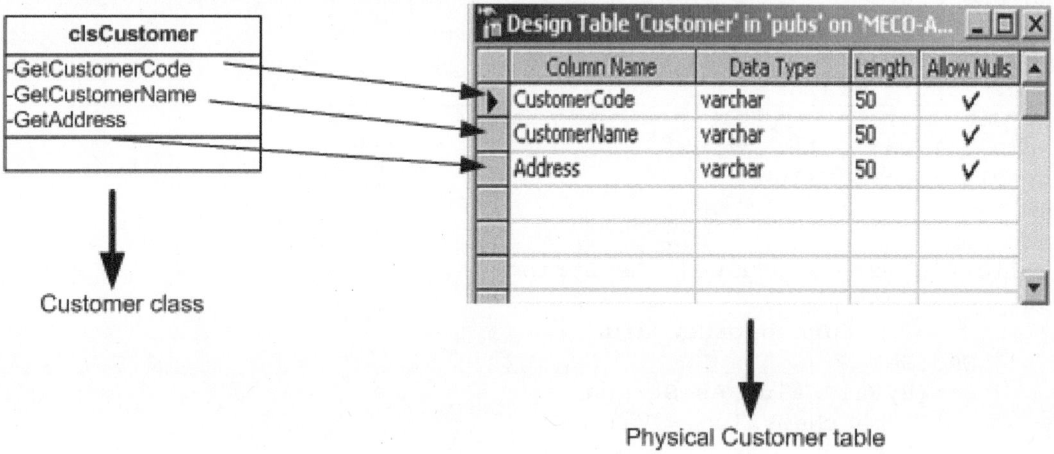

Figure: OR mapper in action

In the above figure you can see on the right hand side we have physical customer table with three attributes Customer Code , CustomerName and Address. All these three attributes map the customer class defined in the right hand side. If the table has one to many relation ship similar mapping will be done on the class side also. Due the above mapping you can now handle save and retrieve more effectively. There are many OR mapping tools available in market which read your schema and create classes accordingly. It generates full persistence objects due to which you can minimize your code to a lot greater extent.

5

SOA (Service Oriented Architecture)

(B) What is SOA?

SOA stands for service oriented architecture. Before we define SOA lets first define a service. In real world service is what we pay for and we get the intended service. For instance you go to a hotel and order food. Your order first goes to the counter and then it goes to the kitchen where the food is prepared and finally the waiter serves the food.

Figure: Hotel and services

So in order to order a item from a hotel you need the three logical departments / services to work together (counter, kitchen and waiter).

In the same manner in software world these services are termed as business services. They are self contained and logical. So let's first define a business service, SOA definition will be just an extension of the same.

Definition of business service: It's a logical encapsulation of self contained business functionality.

For instance figure 'order system' shows a simple ordering system which is achieved by different services like payment gateway, stock system and delivery system coming together. All the services are self contained and logical. They are like black boxes. In short we do not need to understand the internal details of how the business service works. For the external world it's just a black box which takes messages and serves accordingly. For instance the 'payment gateway' business service takes message 'check credit' and gives out output does the customer have credit or not. For the 'order system' business service 'payment gateway' service is a black box.

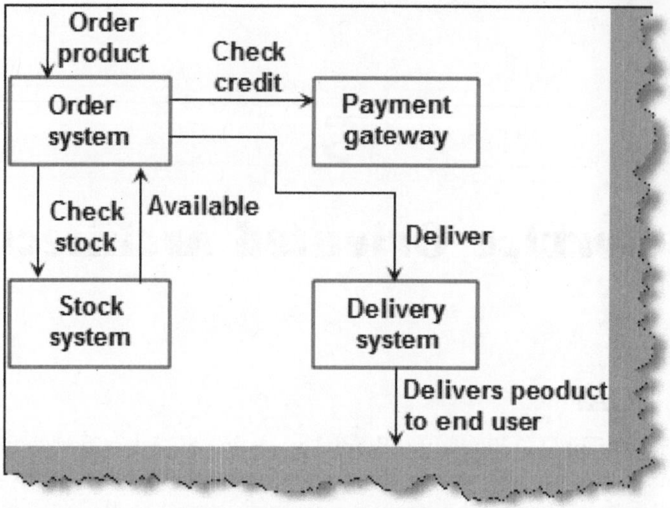

Figure: Order system

Now let's revise some bullet points of SOA before we arrive to a definition of SOA.

- **SOA components are loosely coupled**. When we say loosely coupled means every service is self contained and exist in alone logically. For instance we take the 'payment gateway' service and attach it to a different system.
- **SOA services are black boxes**. In SOA services hide there inner complexities. They only interact using messages and send services depending on those messages. By visualizing services as black boxes services become more loosely coupled.

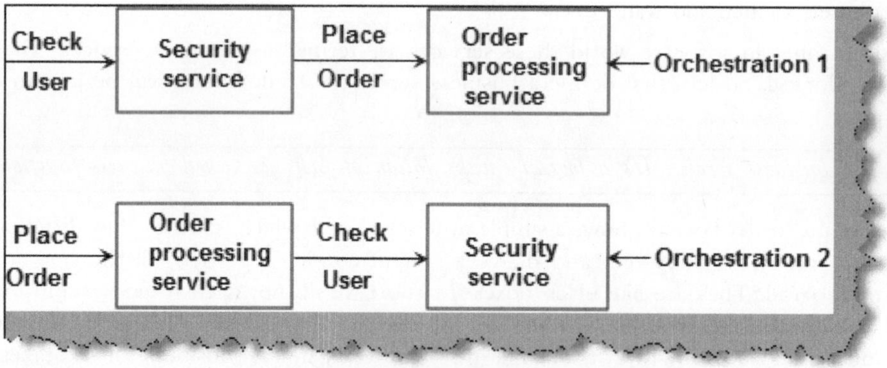

Figure: Orchestration

- **SOA service should be self defined:** SOA services should be able to define themselves.
- **SOA Services are maintained in a listing**: SOA services are maintained in a central repository. Applications can search the services in the central repository and use them accordingly.

- **SOA components can be orchestrated and linked to achieve a particular functionality.** SOA services can be used/orchestrated in a plug and play manner. For instance figure 'Orchestration' shows two services 'Security service' and 'Order processing service'. You can achieve two types of orchestrations from it one you can check the user first and then process order or vice-versa. Yes you guessed right using SOA we can manage work flow between services in a loosely coupled fashion.

So lets define SOA.

SOA is a architecture for building business applications using **loosely coupled services** which act like **black boxes** and can be **orchestrated** to achieve a specific functionality by linking together.

(I) In SOA do we need to build systems from scratch?

No. If you need to integrate or make an existing system as a business service, you just need to create loosely coupled wrappers which will wrap your custom systems and expose the systems functionality in generic fashion to the external world.

(I) Can you explain business layers and plumbing layers in SOA?

In SOA we can divide any architecture in two layers. The first which has direct relevance to business as it carries out business functions. The second layer is a technical layer which talks about managing computer resources like database, web server etc. This division is needed to identify a service. Consider the figure 'Simple order system'. It has various components which interact with each other to complete the order system functionality.

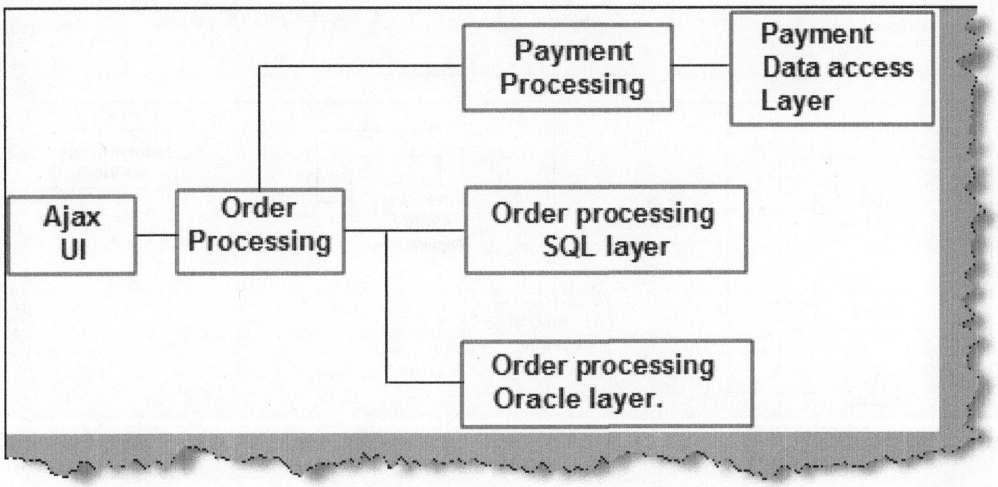

Figure: Simple order System

The simple order system can be divided in to two layers (see figure 'business and plumbing layer' one which is business related and second which is more technical related. You can see the plumbing layer consisting of data access layer , AJAX , yes more of technical stuff.

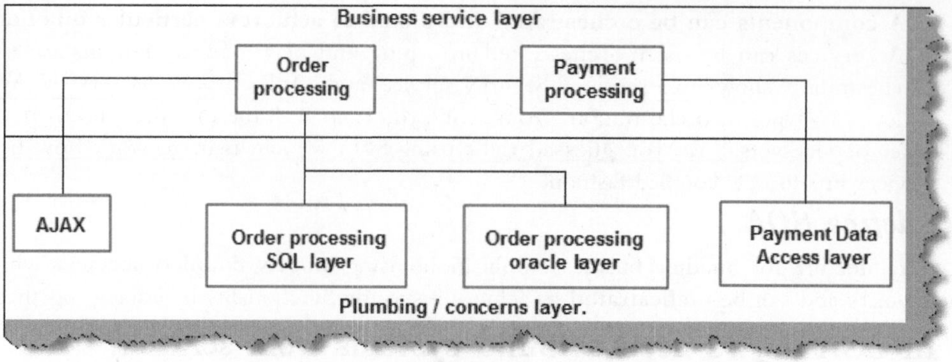

Figure: Business layer and plumbing layer

(I) What's the difference between services and components?

Services are logical grouping of components to achieve business functionality. Components are implementation approaches to make a service. The components can be in JAVA, C#, C++ but the services will be exposed in a general format like Web Services.

(A) Can you describe the complete architecture of SOA?

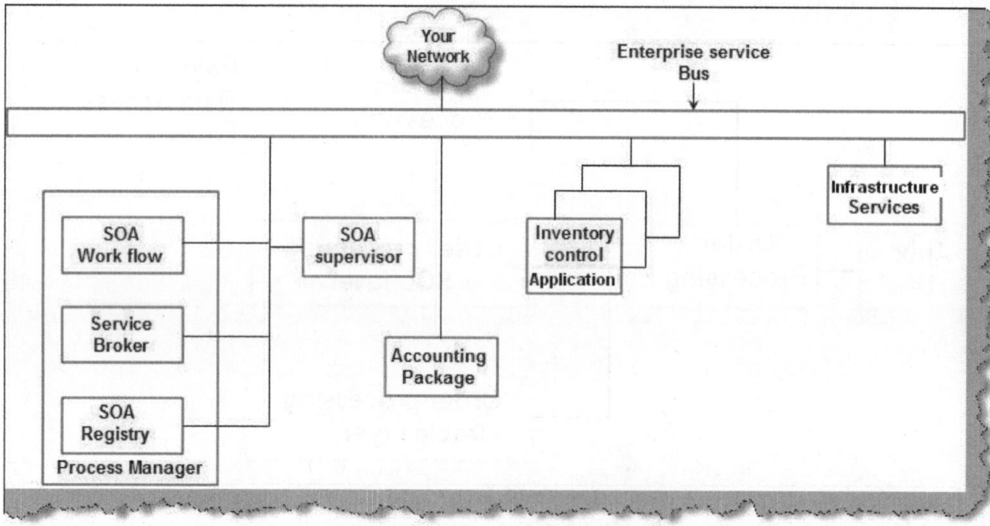

Figure: Architecture of SOA

Figure 'Architecture of SOA' shows a complete view of a SOA. Please note this architecture diagram is not tied up with implementation of Microsoft, IBM etc. It's a general architecture. Any vendor who implements SOA needs to fulfill the below SOA components. How they do it is completely their own technological implementation.

The main goal of SOA is to connect disparate systems. In order that these disparate system work they should messages to each other. **ESB (Enterprise service bus)** acts like a reliable post office which guarantees delivery of messages between systems in a loosely coupled manner. ESB is a special layer which delivers messages between applications. In the figure we have shown a huge plump pipe. It's not hardware or some wire etc. It's a group of components/software which helps you to send and receive messages between the disparate applications. Do not try to code your own ESB, you can think of buying one from Microsoft, IBM, Oracle, progress etc.

SOA registry is like a reference database of services. It describes what each services do, where are they located and how can they communicate. It's a central reference of meta-data for services.

SOA workflow allows us to define work flow using the services in SOA registry. We will read more about BPM in the further questions.

Service broker reads the work flow and takes services from the SOA registry and ties them together. Service brokers are normally middleware like EAI (Enterprise application Integration) products. You can get a list of decent EAI from Sun, Microsoft, and IBM etc.

Process manager is nothing but the collection of SOA registry, SOA workflow and service broker.

SOA supervisor is traffic cop ensuring that services do not have issues. It deals mainly with performance issues of the system so that appropriate service levels are met. If any of the services have performance problems it sends messages to the proper infrastructure to fix the issue.

> **Note:** *The above explanation is of general architecture for SOA. Any vendor (Microsoft, IBM, SUN etc) who gives solution for SOA should have the above components in some or other manner. As this is a Software architecture book, we will not be covering specific vendor implementation. We would advise the reader to map the same to their vendor products for better understanding.*

(I) Can you explain a practical example in SOA?

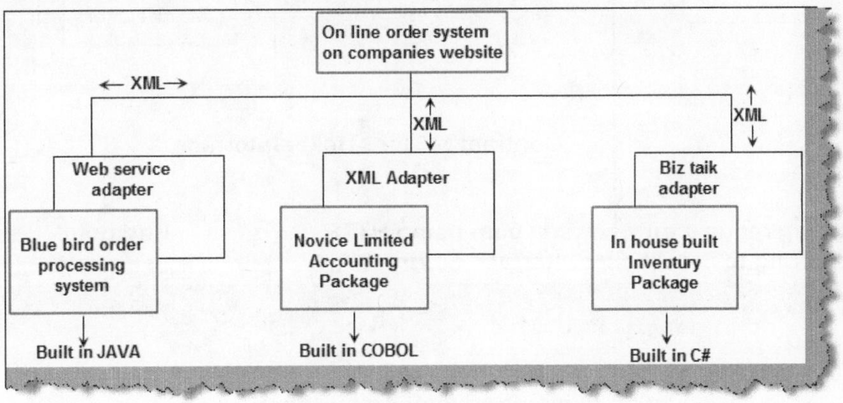

Figure: Practical example

Figure 'practical example' shows how different systems are integrated to define online order system service. The main important point is that data communication is in xml.

(I) What are ends, contract, address, and bindings?

These three terminologies on which SOA service stands. Every service must expose one or more ends by which the service can be available to the client. End consists of three important things where, what and how:

- ***Contract (What)***

Contract is an agreement between two or more parties. It defines the protocol how client should communicate with your service. Technically, it describes parameters and return values for a method.

- ***Address (Where)***

An Address indicates where we can find this service. Address is a URL, which points to the location of the service.

- ***Binding (How)***

Bindings determine how this end can be accessed. It determines how communications is done. For instance, you expose your service, which can be accessed using SOAP over HTTP or BINARY over TCP. So for each of these communications medium two bindings will be created.

Below figure, show the three main components of end. You can see the stock ticker is the service class, which has an end hosted on www.soa.com with HTTP and TCP binding support and using Stock Ticker interface type.

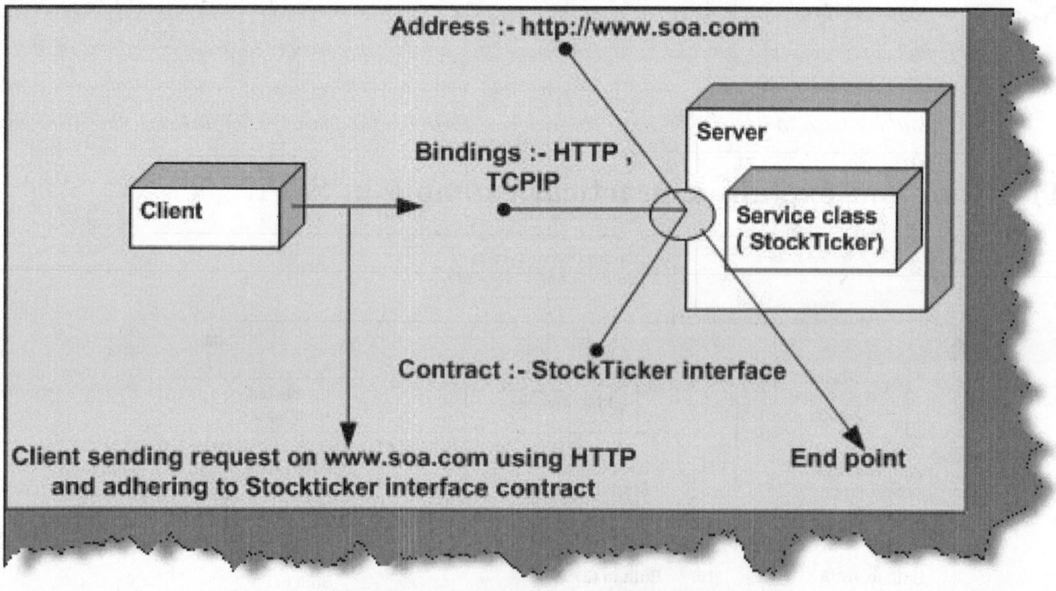

Figure: Endpoint Architecture

Note: *You can also remember the end point by ABC where A stands for Address, B for bindings and C for Contract.*

(I) Are web-services SOA ?

SOA is a thinking, it's an architectural concept and web service is one of the technical approach to complete it. Web services are the preferred standards to achieve SOA.

- In SOA we need the services to be loosely coupled. A web service communicates using SOAP protocol which is XML based which is very loosely coupled. It answers the what part of the service.
- SOA services should be able to describe themselves.WSDL describes how we can access the service.
- SOA services are located in a directory.UDDI describes where we can get the web service. This nothing but implementation of SOA registry.

(B) What is SOAP?

SOAP is an XML-based protocol that enables software components and applications to communicate with one another. It defines rules to translate application and platform-specific data into the XML format. SOAP allows you to communicate with the Web Service using protocols such as HTTP and Simple Mail Transfer Protocol.

SOAP has three main sections:

- **Envelope:** Contains elements such as the header and body of the SOAP messaging structure. It also includes an encodingStyle attribute that specifies the representation of data in messages.
- **Header:** Encapsulates extended messages without adding or modifying the standard message flow.
- **Body:** Contains Web application-specific data. It defines the purpose of sending the message. The body element should be the first element under the envelope element if there is no header element.

Below is a snippet of a sample SOAP header.

```
POST/Inventory HTTP/1.1
Host: localhost
Content-Type: text/xml; charset="utf-8"
Content-Length: <content_length>
SOAPAction: "<URI specified>"
<SOAP-ENV:Envelope  xmlns:SOAP-ENV="http://schemas.xmlsoap.org/soap/
envelope/">
<SOAP-ENV:encodingStyle="http://schemas.xmlsoap.org/soap/encoding/">
<SOAP-ENV:Body>
<m:GetLastName xmlns:m="Test_URI">
<symbol></symbol>
</m:GetLastName>
</SOAP-ENV:Body>
</SOAP-ENV:Envelope>
```

(B) What is WSDL ?

WSDL is an XML-based file that describes a Web service. A WSDL document describes the methods provided by a Web service and the input, output, and connection parameters.

```
<?xml version="1.0"?>
<definitions name="virtual-library"
targetNamespace="http://soapservice.com/ virtual-library.wsdl"
xmlns:tns="http://soapservice.com/ virtual-library.wsdl"
xmlns:xsd="http://www.w3.org/2000/10/XMLSchema"
xmlns:xsd1="http://soapservice.com/ virtual-library.xsd"
xmlns:soap="http://schemas.xmlsoap.org/wsdl/soap/"
xmlns="http://schemas.xmlsoap.org/wsdl/">
<message name="GetFlowerList">
      <part name="symbol" element="xsd:string"/>
</message>
<message name="GetFlowerList">
      <part name="result" type="xsd:float"/>
</message>
<portType name=" virtual-libraryPortType">
      <operation name="GetLastRecord"-*">
            <input message="tns:GetPriceInput"/>
            <output message="tns:GetStockPriceOutput"/>
      </operation>
</portType>
<binding name="virtual_librarySoapBinding"
type="tns:virtual_libraryPortType">
      <soap:binding style="rpc"
      transport="http://schemas.xmlsoap.org/soap/http"/>
      <operation name="GetLastRecord">
            <soap:operation soapAction="http://soapservice.com/
            GetLastRecord"/>
            <input>
                  <soap:body use="encoded" namespace="http://
                  soapservice.com/virtual_library"
                  encodingStyle="http://schemas.xmlsoap.org/soap/
                  encoding/"/>
            </input>
            <output>
                  <soap:body use="encoded" namespace="http://
                  soapservice.com/virtual_library"
                  encodingStyle="http://schemas.xmlsoap.org/soap/
                  encoding/"/>
            </output>
      </operation>>
</binding>
<service name="virtual_libraryService">
```

```
      <documentation>Virtual Library Service</documentation>
      <port name="virtual_libraryPort" binding="tns:
      virtual_librarySoapBinding">
      <soap:address location="http://soapservice.com/virtual_
      library"/>
      </port>
</service>
</definitions>
```

(B) Can you explain UDDI ?

Universal Description, Discovery, and Integration (UDDI) is an industry standard that is used to locate Web services on the Internet. It is an XML-based registry that enables enterprises to list their Web services on the Internet. UDDI enables organizations to perform secure online transactions.

The UDDI company registry contains a comprehensive list of available Web services and provides links to discovery documents of Web services. These discovery documents, called DISCO files, contain links to WSDL documents.

(A) What is BPEL?

Business Process Execution Language (BPEL) is an XML-based language for creating a process, which is a set of logical steps to define a workflow. One of the important points we stressed while defining SOA is orchestration. BPEL is the answer to do orchestration in SOA.

BPEL uses WSDL to describe the web services that come in a process and how the services interact. For example, the following WSDL entry describes one of the services in the purchase order process:

```
<portType name="purchaseOrderPT">
      <operation name="sendPurchaseOrder">
            <input message="pos:POMessage"/>
            <output message="pos:InvMessage"/>
            <fault name="cannotCompleteOrder"
                  message="pos:orderFaultType"/>
      </operation>
</portType>
```

The following entry describes the flow of the purchase order process:

```
<sequence>
      <receive partnerLink="purchasing"
            portType="lns:purchaseOrderPT"
            operation="sendPurchaseOrder"
            variable="PO">
      </receive>
      <flow>
            <links>
                  <link name="ship-to-invoice"/>
                  <link name="ship-to-scheduling"/>
            </links>
```

(A) What are WS-* specifications?

WS-* specifications are standard specification defined by Microsoft, IBM, SUN and many other big companies so that they can expose there service through a common protocol. Let's go through some of WS-* specifications:

- **Messaging (WS-Addressing)**: SOAP is the fundamental protocol for web services. WS Addressing defines some extra additions to SOAP headers, which makes SOAP free from underlying transport protocol. One of the good things about Message transmission is MTOM, also termed as Message Transmission Optimization Mechanism. They optimize transmission format for SOAP messages in XML-Binary formant using XML optimized packaging (XOP). Because the data will sent in binary and optimized format, it will give us huge performance gain.
- **Security (WS-Security, WS-Trust, and WS-Secure Conversation)**: All the three WS- define authentication, security, data integrity and privacy features for a service.
- **Reliability (WS-Reliable Messaging)**: This specification ensures end-to-end communication when we want SOAP messages to be traversed back and forth many times.
- **Transactions (WS-Coordination and WS-Atomic Transaction)**: These two specifications enable transaction with SOAP messages.
- **Metadata (WS-Policy and WS-Metadata exchange)**: WSDL is a implementation of WS-Metadata Exchange protocol. WS-Policy defines more dynamic features of a service, which cannot be expressed by WSDL.

We have stressed on the WS-* specification as it is a specification which a service has to follow to be compatible with other languages. WS-* specification allows us to achieve the above functionalities between cross language like JAVA, C#, C++ etc. That means we can use features like transactions, security, messaging etc in a seamless manner between services of different programming languages.

(A) Can you explain SOA governance?

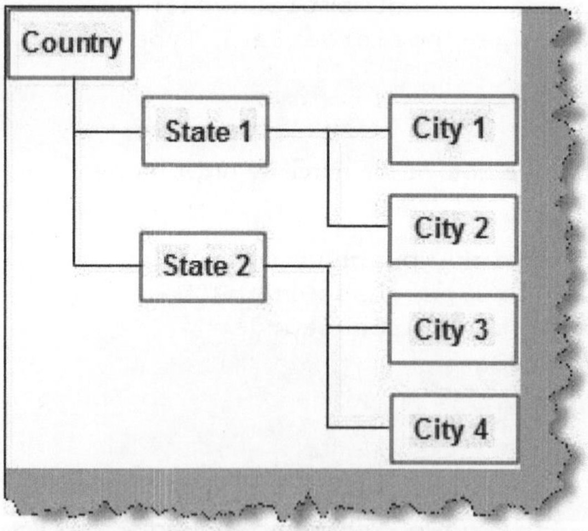

Figure: Real world governance

Governance defines policies which in turn will define how organizations will behave. Think about how normal governance works. Every city has his own legal norms, but they have some legal norms which are forced from the state. In the same way every state has some legal policies but they need to also inherit from of the policies from the country legal norms.

If you look at the model it's more like global policies and overriding those global policies by local policies according to the local needs. Organizations resemble the same pattern as we have seen for country, state and city. It's like we have head office which defines global policies and then we have local / branch offices which will inherits those global policies but tailor some according to their local branches.

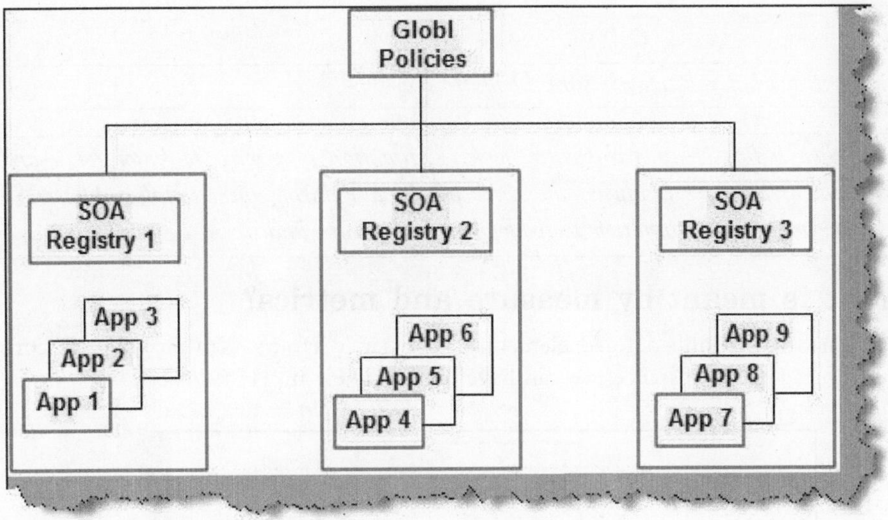

Figure: SOA governance in action

With proper SOA policies in place this will be a breeze. For instance figure 'SOA governance in action' shows how this achieved by SOA. We can define global policies for all applications in an organization, but we would like to have specific policies defined for specific group of application. This can be achieved by defining different SOA registry and implementing policies according to those groups of applications.

Note: *As this is an architecture interview question book. We have not covered vendor specific products for SOA given by Microsoft, IBM etc. It's left to the readers to compare those products with the SOA fundamentals.*

6

Estimation, Metrics and Measure

You can not control what you can measure: Demarco 87

Note: *Even though this is an architecture book. Estimation is a must to know for a architecture. Technical architecture is always an active participant during the estimation phase. So we will cover the most used estimation methodologies in software industry.*

(B) What is meant by measure and metrics?

Measures are quantitative unit defined elements for instance Hours, Km etc. Metrics comprises of more than one measure for instance, we can have metrics like Km/Hr, M/S etc.

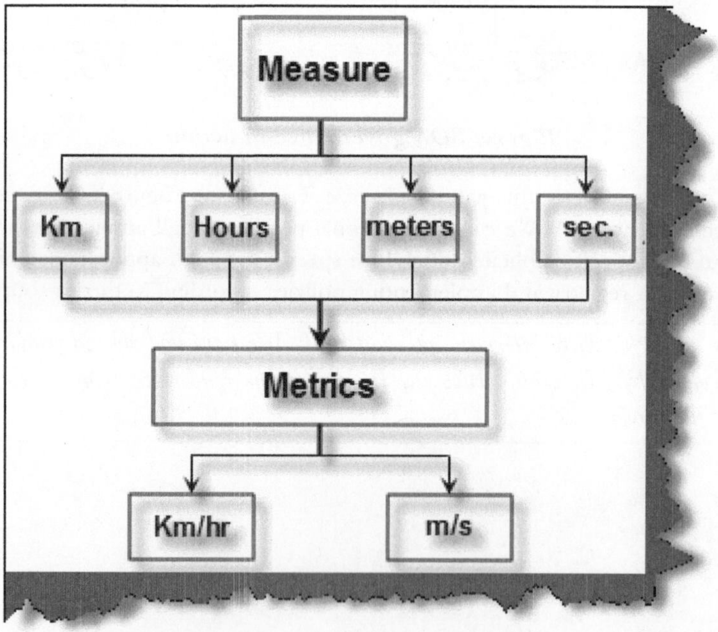

Figure: Measure and Metrics

(B) What are the various common ways of estimation?

There are many ways of estimation in software industry. Frankly we can not really say which estimation methodology can be asked during interview. But let's concentrate on those estimation methodologies which are widely accepted. Below are some of the most used methodologies:

- LOC (Lines of Code).
- COCOMO.
- Function Points.
- Use case points.
- SMC (Simple, Medium and Complex).

(B) Can you explain LOC method of estimation?

LOC (Lines of Code) is a metric to measure size of software program by counting the number of lines in the program's source code. There are two types of LOC units:

- **Physical Lines of Code**: In physical lines of code means counting even comments, spaces, automated generated code etc.
- **Logical Lines of Code**: In logical lines of code we only count the code which actually contributes towards running the program. For instance comments and spaces are not counted.

For instance the below code snippet has 5 physical lines of code while 2 logical lines of code (we excluded comments and curly brackets when we count logical lines of code).

```
// Loop and display the value
for (int i = 0; i < 10; i++)
{
     System.Console.WriteLine(Convert.ToString(i));
}
```

SEI (Software Engineering Institute) has come out with a check list called as 'Logical Source Statement of code'. So if we want to get the logical lines of code we should follow the below simplified SEI table.

Litmus Test	Include in Counting or Not
Depending on Statement Type	
Executable	Yes
Non-executable	
Declarations	Yes
Compiler directives	Yes
Comments	
On their Own lines	No
On lines with Source Code	No

Banners and nonblank spacers	No
Blank (Empty) Comments	No
Blank Lines	No
How Produced	
Programmed = =	Yes
Generated with Source Code Generators	Yes
Converted with automated Translators	Yes
Copied or reused without Change	Yes
Modified	Yes
Removed	No
Origin	
New Work: no Prior Existence	Yes
Prior Work: Taken or adapted from	
A previous version, build or release	Yes
COTS Commercial, off- the- shelf Software, other then reuse libraries	Yes
Another Product	Yes
A vendor- supplied language support library (unmodified)	No
A vendor- supplied Operating system or utility (unmodified)	No
A local or modified language support Library or operating System	Yes
Other Commercial library	Yes
A reuse library (software designed for reuse)	Yes
Other software component or library	Yes
Usage	
In or as part of primary product	Yes
External to or in support of the primary product	Yes
Delivery	
Delivered	
Delivered as Source	Yes
Delivered in Compiled or executable form, but not as source	Yes
Not delivered	
Under Configuration control	No
Not under configuration control	No
Functionality	
Operative	Yes
Inoperative (Dead, bypassed, unused, unreferenced or unaccessed)	
Functional (Intentional Dead Code, reactivated for special purpose)	Yes
Nonfunctional (unintentionally present)No	No
Replications	

Master Source Statements (originals)	Yes
Physical replicates of master statements, stored in master code	Yes
Copies inserted, instantiated, or expanded when compiling or linking	No
Postproduction replicates- as in distributed, redundant or reparameterized systems	No
Development status	
Estimated or planned	No
Designed	No
Coded	No
Unit tests Completed	No
Integrated into components	No
Test readiness review completed	No
Software (CI) test completed	No
System test completed	Yes

Table: SEI check list (Courtesy SEI)

If you count line of code with out using SEI check list that means it is physical lines of code.

Advantages of LOC

- Counting LOC is Simple.
- As they are final deliverables they can be used as Base Line to define companies' productivity.

Disadvantages of LOC

- Earlier estimation is difficult.
- Difficult to convince the end customer saying that project is 1000 lines of code so the cost is "XYZ" dollars.

(B) How do we convert LOC in to effort?

LOC finally needs to be converted to man days/man hours or man months. There are two ways either by using baseline technique or using COCOMO. In base line technique we have a company history which says that a developer for this language can delivery x amount of LOC so for this much LOC how much.

COCOMO is covered in depth in the coming questions.

(B) Can you explain COCOMO?

COCMO (Constructive Cost Model) is a parametric estimation model. It is not a size measurement methodology. On the contrary its takes in size and then applies non-functional characteristics of a project. When we say non-function characteristic we mean by:

- Is the team interaction good or bad?
- Are we using prototype model?
- Which software life cycle process are we following?

The above things can not be measured. So what COCOMO does is it take size as a parameter and applies these non-functional aspects of the project. In short it is a formula. The size input is LOC and the effort output is in man months. Below figure shows how COCOMO works. It takes LOC and gives the effort in man months.

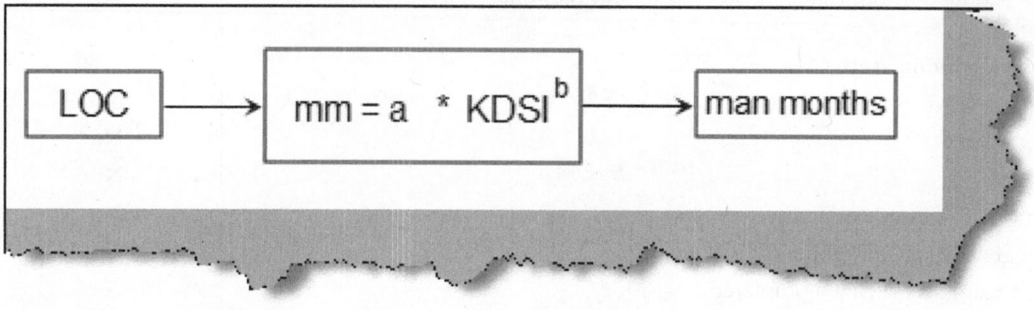

Figure: Basic COCOMO

Before we go in depth of the above formula, let's understand the principle on which COCOMO works. COCOMO says that any software has two aspects to be considered for estimation. One aspect is the complexity of the software and the other project development mode.

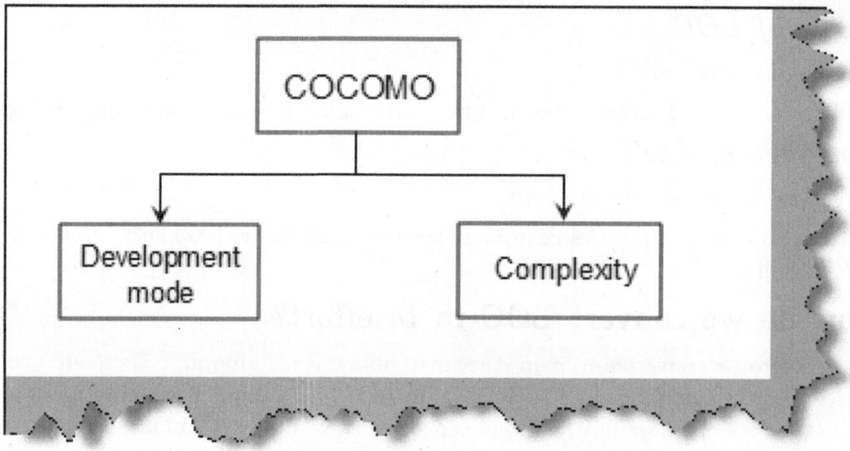

Figure: COCOMO Estimation view

Complexity Aspect

COCOMO views two types of complexity in a software project, one is the multiplicative complexity and the other is the exponential complexity. Exponential complexities of a project are those aspects, if they change slightly the estimation changes in a very huge manner. Multiplicative complexities are those aspects if they change only a proportional changes happen to estimation. For instance a changing customer issue is an exponential factor while a new technology is a multiplicative factor.

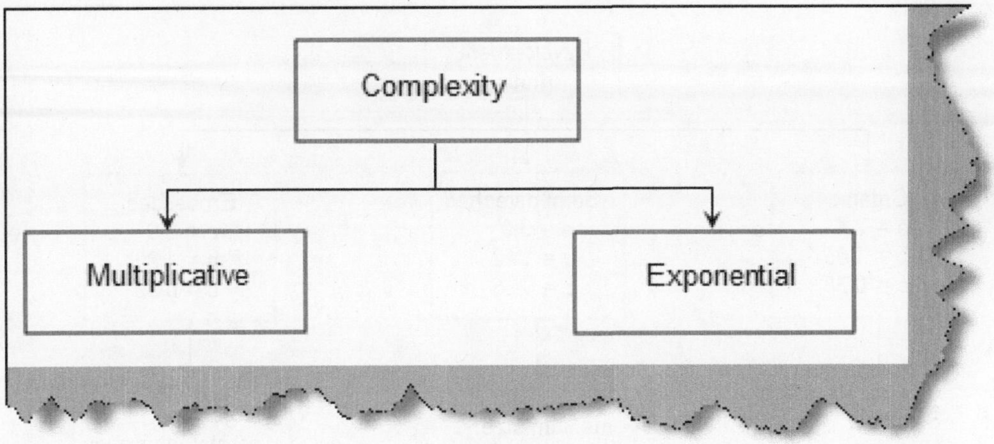

Figure: COCOMO Complexity

Below is the formula for COCOMO.

a: This coefficient represents multiplicative complexity.

b: This coefficient represents exponential complexity.

KDSI: KDSI is the delivered source instruction. In short they are physical lines of code.

MM: Man month i.e. one month of effort by one person or one staff.

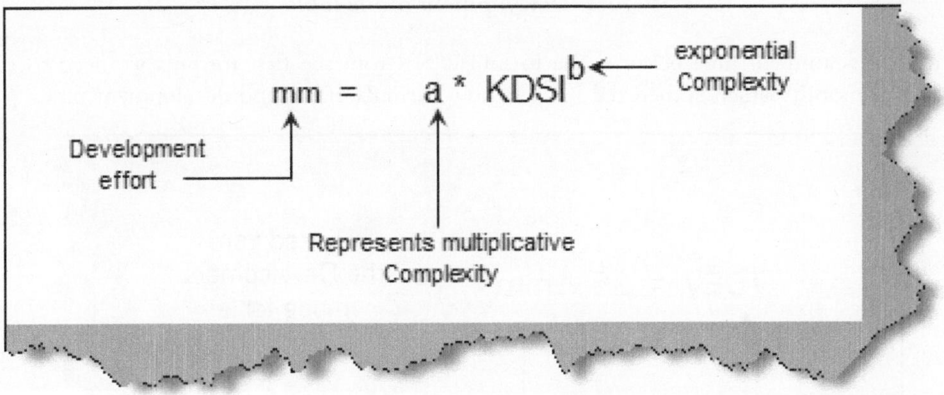

Figure: COCOMO Formulae

Project development mode

The above two coefficients 'a' and 'b' depends on project development mode. Below figure 'Development mode table' shows the different development mode. There are basically three development modes which are decided on basis of size, innovation, how is the deadline and the development environment. Depending on the same we have given values for 'a' and 'b'. There is one more coefficient introduced 'c' which will be used to calculate development time.

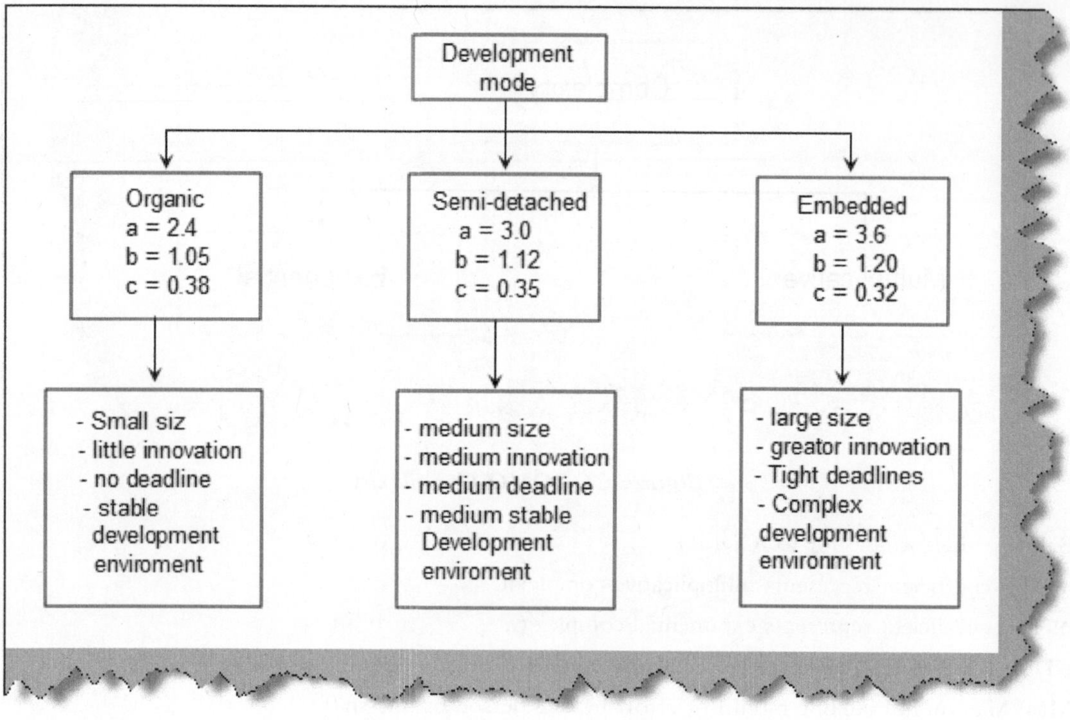

Figure: Development mode table

To calculate development time below is the formulae. So from the first formula we need to calculate the MM (man month) which is then fed in the below formula effort and development time.

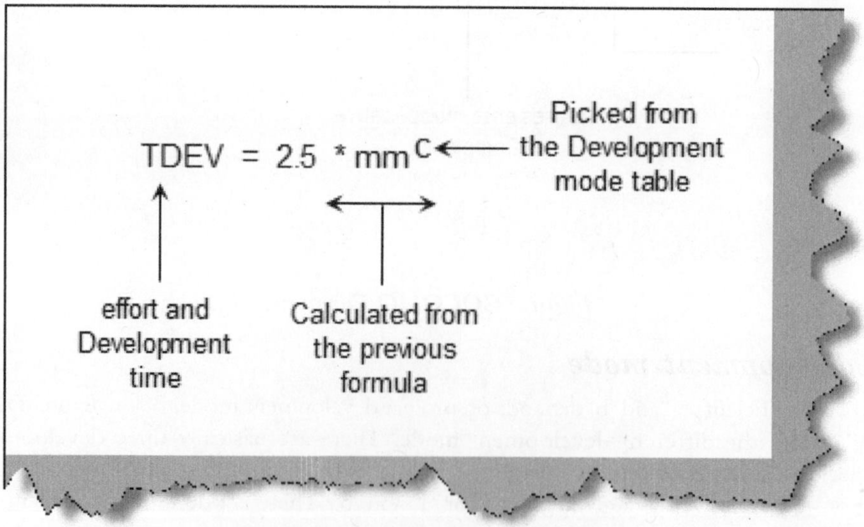

Figure: Effort and Development time

Let's try to understand COCOMO with small sample. Below figure 'Sample Calculation' explains the same in a more detailed manner. We have considered development mode as organic and 1000 lines of code. There are two steps first we get the "MM" and then we use the same to calculate 'TDEV'. For coefficient value 'a','b' and 'c' we have referred the figure 'Development mode table'. As we have considered organic so a=2.4, b=1.05 and c=0.38. So MM is 3390 and using the same we calculate TDEV which comes around 54 man months.

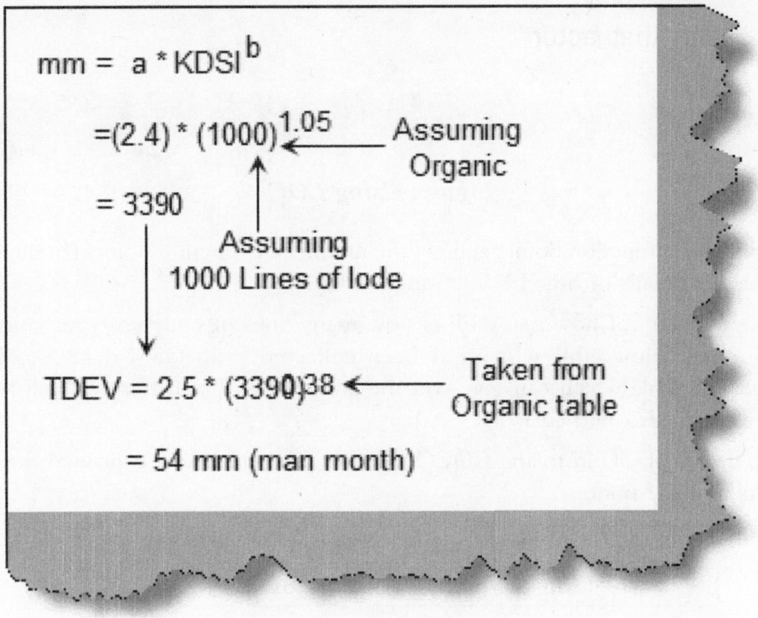

Figure: Sample Calculation

(I) Can you explain Intermediate COCOMO and COCOMO II?

COCOMO is now not a much used technique. From interview perspective knowing the basic COCOMO is more than enough. But in case you are looking for more details like intermediate COCOMO and COCOMO II, please do go through my book 'How to prepare Software Quotations?'. It is shipped free in the CD with name 'HowtoPrepareSoftwareQuotations.pdf'.

(B) How do you estimate using LOC?

In LOC we can not determine the LOC just by pure requirements. There are two ways of estimating. First is either you have a history of data or either FP. We will try to understand how to estimate using FP, because history of LOC can be very inconsistent. To estimate effort using LOC in man/days or man/hours we need to also use COCOMO and FP. Alone LOC can not help us as such. Below figure 'Using LOC' shows how we can get the effort.

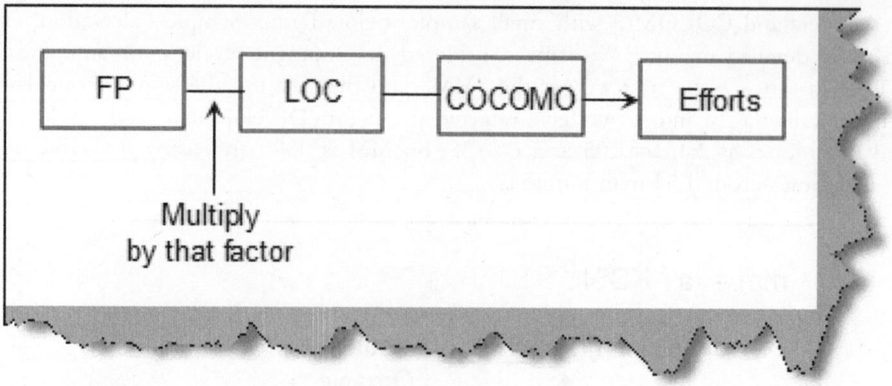

Figure: Using LOC

Step 1: We estimate using function points and get the number of function points (In the further chapters we have given the full details of how FP counting works).

Step 2: If you have history of how many FP is how many lines of code use your company history or else you can refer the below table which has been collected from QSM database. There are many standard databases available which can give you the conversion. From this you will know how many LOC will be derived for that particular FP.

Step 3: Feed the derived LOC in to the COCOMO formula which was explained previously and you will get the results in man/months.

Below table is taken from Source http://www.qsm.com/FPGearing.html

Language	SLOC / FP
Access	38
ADA	-
Advantage	38
APS	83
ASP	62
Assembler**	157
C **	104
C++ **	53
C#	59
Clipper	39
COBOL **	77
Cool:Gen/IEF	31
Culprit	-
DBase III	-
DBase IV	-
Easytrieve+	34

Excel	46
Focus	42
FORTRAN	-
FoxPro	35
HTML**	42
Ideal	52
IEF/Cool:Gen	31
Informix	31
J2EE	50
Java**	59
JavaScript**	54
JCL**	48
JSP	-
Lotus Notes	22
Mantis	27
Mapper	81
Natural	52
Oracle**	29
Oracle Dev 2K/FORMS	30
Pacbase	48
PeopleSoft	32
Perl	-
PL/1**	58
PL/SQL	31
Powerbuilder**	24
REXX	-
RPG II/III	49
Sabretalk	89
SAS	41
Siebel Tools	13
Slogan	82
Smalltalk**	32
SQL**	35
VBScript**	34
Visual Basic**	42
VPF	95
Web Scripts	15

Table: QSM database

Let's do a simple sample estimation using LOC. Below are the assumptions for the project.

Assumptions	
Function points	400
Language	C#
Development mode	Organic

Table: Assumptions for COCOMO

Below figure 'LOC calculation' shows the effort calculation using LOC. Basically there are three steps:

- We convert function points in to LOC using the QSM database. You can see how to do function point counting in the further questions. So according to the assumption function point value is 400 and from the QSM database the C# LOC for one FP is 59. So LOC is 23600 lines of code.

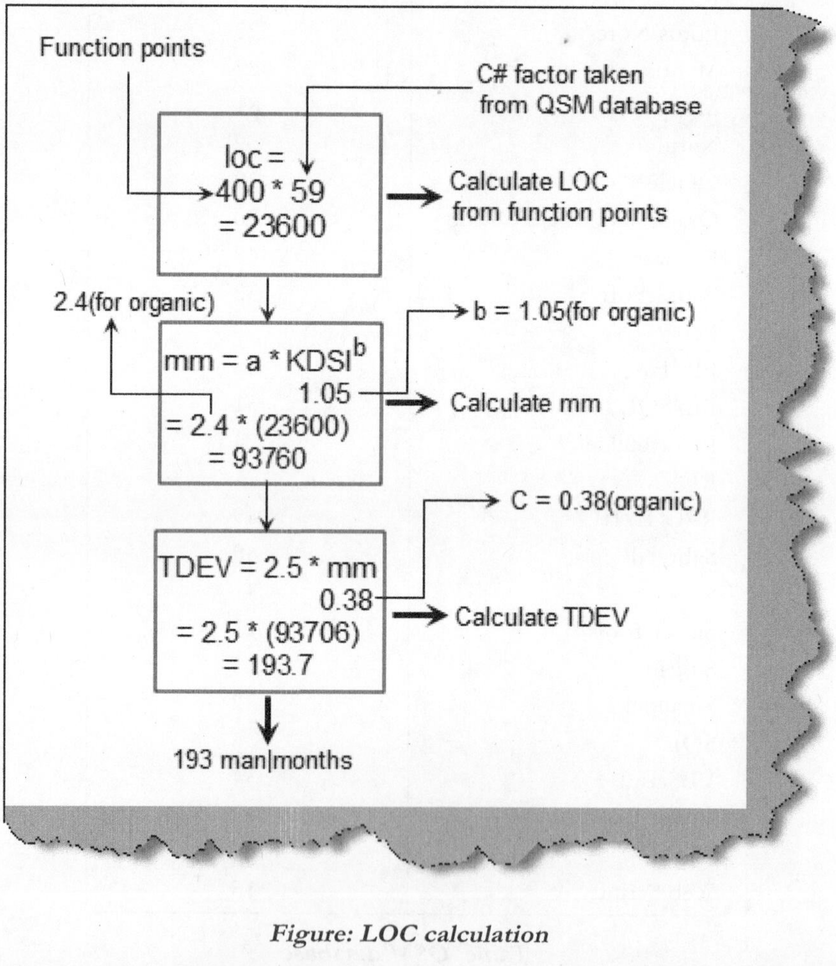

Figure: LOC calculation

- Assuming that the development mode is organic so a = 2.4 and b=1.05. Man month effort comes to 93706.
- Using the man month effort we calculate TDEV. As its organic the value of c = 0.38. The final calculation comes to 193 man month.

Above diagram shows the above calculation in a phase wise manner.

(A) Can you explain in brief Function points?

Note: *It's rare that some one will ask you to say full details of function points in one shot. They will rather ask specific sections like GSC, ILF etc. The main interest of the interviewer will do you have a broader idea of estimating using function points.*

Introduction to Function Points

"This document contains material which has been extracted from the IFPUG Counting Practices Manual. It is reproduced in this document with the permission of IFPUG."

Function Point Analysis was developed first by Allan J. Albrecht in the mid 1970s. It was an attempt to overcome difficulties associated with lines of code as a measure of software size, and to assist in developing a mechanism to predict effort associated with software development. The method was first published in 1979, then later in 1983. In 1984 Albrecht refined the method and since 1986, when the International Function Point User Group (IFPUG) was set up, several versions of the Function Point Counting Practices Manual have been coming out.

"The best way to understand any complicated system is breaking the system in to smaller subsystem and try to understand those smaller sub-systems . In Function Point you break complicated huge system into smaller systems and estimate those smaller pieces, then total up all the subsystem estimate to come up with final estimate."

Basics of Function Points

Following are some terms used in FPA [Function Point analysis].

(B) Can you explain the concept Application boundary?

Application Boundary

The first step in FPA is defining boundary. There are two types of major boundaries:

- Internal Application Boundary
- External Application Boundary

We will state features of external application boundary, so that internal application boundary would be self explained.

External Application Boundary can be identified using following litmus test:

- Does it have or will have any other interface to maintain its data, which is not Developed by you. Example: Your Company is developing an "Accounts Application" and at the end of accounting year, you have to report to tax Department. Tax department has his own website where companies can connect and report there Tax transaction. Tax department application has other Maintenance and reporting screens been developed by tax software department. These maintenance screens are used internally by the Tax department. So Tax Online interface has other interface to maintain its data which is not your scope, thus we can identify Tax website reporting as External Application.

- Does your program have to go through a third party API or layer? In order your application interacts with Tax Department Application probably your code have to interact through Tax Department API.
- The best litmus test is to ask yourself do you have full access over the system. If you have full rights or command to change then its internal application boundary or else external application boundary.

(B) Can you explain the concept of elementary process?

(B) Can you explain the concept of static and dynamic elementary process?

Elementary Process

As said in introduction FPA is breaking huge systems in to smaller pieces and analyzing them. Software application is combination of set of elementary processes.

> *EP is smallest unit of activity that is meaningful to the user. EP must be self contained and leave the application in a consistent state.*

When elementary processes come together they form a software application.

> **Note:** *Elementary process is not necessarily completely independent or can exist by itself.So, we can define elementary process as small units of self contained functionality from user perspective.*

Dynamic and static elementary process

There are two types of elementary process:

- Dynamic Elementary process.
- Static Elementary process.

Dynamic elementary process moves data from internal application boundary to external Application boundary or vice-versa.

Examples of dynamic elementary process:

- Input data screen where user inputs data in to application. Data moves from the input screen inside application.
- Transaction exported in export files in XML or any other standard.
- Display reports which can come from external application boundary and internal application boundary.

Examples of static elementary process:

- Static elementary process maintains data of application either inside application boundary or in external application boundary.

For instance in a customer maintenance screen maintaining customer data is static elementary process.

(I) Can you explain concept of FTR, ILF, EIF, EI, EO , EQ and GSC ?

Elements of Function Points

Following are the elements of FPA.

Internal Logical Files (ILF)

Following are points to be noted for ILF:

- ILF are logically related data from user point of view.
- They reside in Internal Application boundary and are maintained through Elementary process of application.
- ILF can have maintenance screen or probably not.

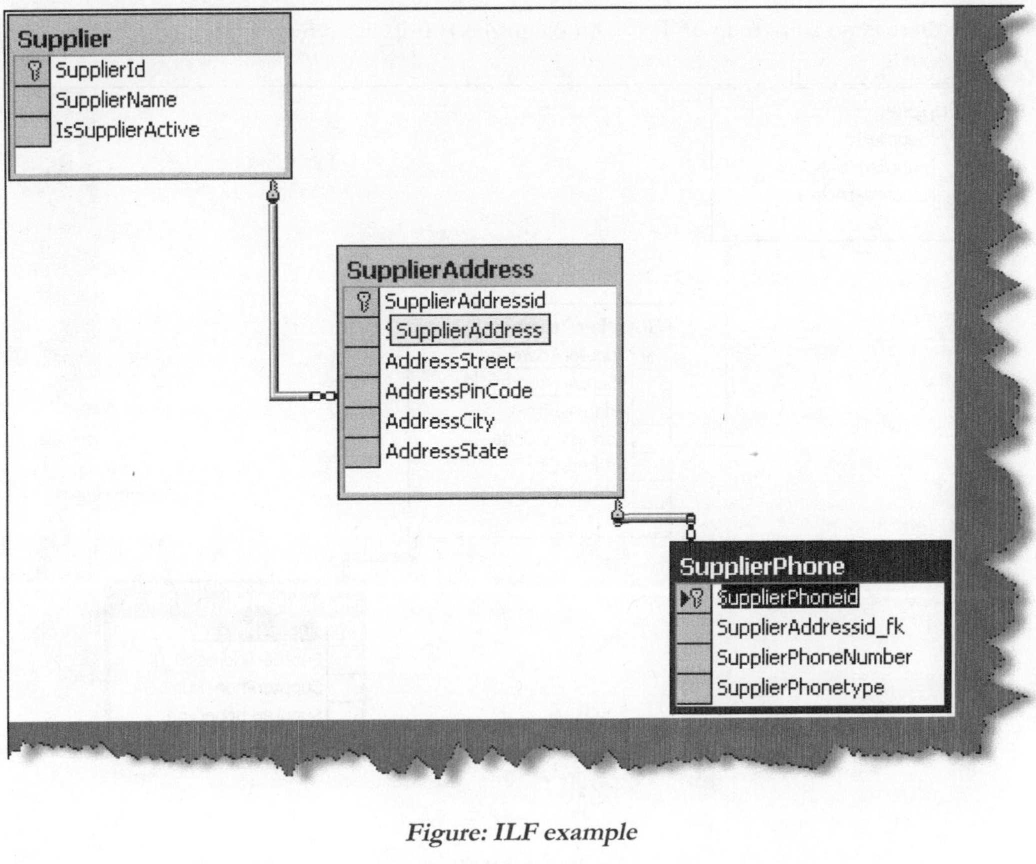

Figure: ILF example

Caution: *Do not make a mistake of mapping one to one relationship between ILF and technical database design, then FPA can go very misleading. The main difference between ILF and technical database is ILF is logical view and database is physical structure (Technical Design). Example Supplier database design will have tables like Supplier, Supplier Address, SupplierPhonenumbers, but from ILF point of view its only Supplier. As logically they are all Supplier details.*

External Interface File (EIF)

- They are logically related data from user point of view.
- EIF reside in external application boundary.
- EIF is used only for reference purpose and are not maintained by internal application.
- EIF is maintained by external application.

Record Element Type (RET)

Following are points to be noted for RET

- RET are sub-group element data of ILF or EIF.
- If there is no sub-group of ILF then count the ILF itself as one RET.

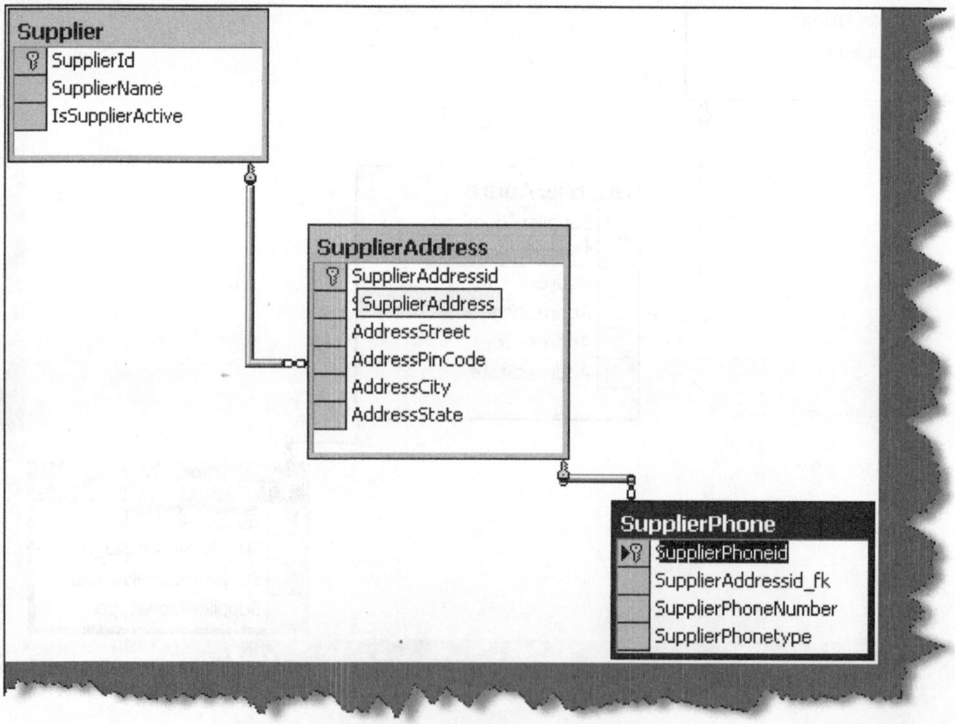

Figure: RET

- A group of RET's within ILF are logically related. Most probably with a parent child relationship. Example: Supplier had multiple addresses and every address can have multiple phone numbers (See detail image below which shows database diagrams).So Supplier, Supplier Address and Supplier phone numbers are RET's.

Please note the whole database is one supplier ILF as all belong to one logical section. RET quantifies the relationship complexity of ILF and EIF.

DET (Data element types)

Following are the points to be noted for DET counting:

- Each DET should be User recognizable. Example in the above given figure we have kept auto increment field (Supplierid) for primary key. Supplierid field from user point of view never exists at all , its only from software designing aspect, so does not qualifies for DET.
- DET should be non-recursive field in ILF. DET should not repeat in the same ILF again, it should be counted only once.
- Count foreign keys as one DET. "Supplierid" does not qualifies as DET but its relationship in "supplieraddress" table is counted as DET. So "Supplierid_fk" in supplieraddress table is counted as DET. Same folds true for "Supplieraddressid_fk".

File Type Reference (FTR)

Following are points to be noted for FTR:

- FTR is files or data referenced by a transaction.
- FTR should be ILF or EIF. So count each ILF or EIF read during process.
- If the EP is maintaining an ILF then count that as FTR. So by default you will always have one FTR in any EP.

External Input (EI)

Following are points to be noted for EI:

- It's a dynamic elementary process [For definition see "Dynamic and Static Elementary Process" Section] in which data is received from external application boundary.

  Example: User Interaction Screens, when data comes from User Interface to Internal Application.

  EI may maintain ILF of the application, but it's not compulsory rule.

  Example: A calculator application does not maintain any data, but still the screen of calculator will be counted as EI.
- Most of time User Screens will be EI, again no hard and fast rule. Example: An import batch process running from command line does not have screen, but still should be counted as EI as it helps passing data from External Application Boundary to Internal Application Boundary.

External Inquiry (EQ)

Following are points to be noted for EQ:

- It's a dynamic elementary process in which result data is retrieved from one or more ILF or EIF.

- In this EP some input request has to enter the application boundary.
- Output results exits the application boundary.
- EQ does not contain any derived data. Derived data means any complex calculated data. Derived data is not just mere retrieval but are combined with additional formulae to generate results. Derived data is not part of ILF or EIF, they are generated on fly.
- EQ does not update any ILF or EIF.
- EQ activity should be meaningful from user perspective.
- EP is self contained and leaves the business in consistent state.
- DET and processing logic is different from other EQ's.
- Simple reports form good base as EQ.

Note: *No hard and fast rules that only simple reports are EQ's.Simple view functionality can also be counted as EQ.*

External Output (EO)

Following are points to be noted for EO:

- It's a dynamic elementary process in which derived data crosses from Internal Application Boundary to External Application Boundary.
- EO can update an ILF or EIF.
- Process should be the smallest unit of activity that is meaningful to end user in business.
- EP is self contained and leaves the business in a consistent state.
- DET is different from other EO's.So this ensures to us that we do not count EO's twice.
- They have derived data or formulae calculated data.

Major difference between EO and EQ is that data passes across application boundary. Example: Exporting Accounts transaction to some external file format like XML or some other format. Which later the external accounting software can import. Second important difference is in EQ its non-derived data and EO has derived data.

General System Characteristic Section (GSC)

This section is the most important section. All the above discussed sections are counting sections. They relate only to application. But there are other things also to be considered while making software, like are you going to make it an N-Tier application, what's the performance level the user is expecting etc these other factors are called GSC. These are external factors which affect the software a lot and also the cost of it. When you submit a function point to a client, he normally will skip everything and come to GSC first. GSC gives us something called as VAF (Value Added Factor).

There are 14 points considered to come out with VAF (Value Added factor) and its associated rating table.

Data Communications

How many communication facilities are there to aid in the transfer or exchange of information with the application or system?

Rating	Description
0	Application is pure batch processing or a standalone PC.
1	Application is batch but has remote data entry or remote Printing.
2	Application is batch but has remote data entry and remote Printing.
3	Application includes online data collection or TP (Teleprocessing) front end to a batch process or query system.
4	Application is more than a front-end, but supports only one Type of TP communications protocol.
5	Application is more than a front-end, and supports more than One type of TP communications protocol.

Table: Data Communication

Distributed data processing

How are distributed data and processing functions handled?

Rating	Description
0	Application does not aid the transfer of data or processing Function between components of the system.
1	Application prepares data for end user processing on another component of the system such as PC spreadsheets and PC DBMS
2	Data is prepared for transfer, then is transferred and processed on another component of the system (not for end-user Processing).
3	Distributed processing and data transfer are online and in One direction only.
4	Distributed processing and data transfer are online and in Both directions.
5	Processing functions are dynamically performed on the most Appropriate component of the system

Table: Distributed data processing

Performance

Did the user require response time or throughput?

Rating	Description
0	No special performance requirements were stated by the User.
1	Performance and design requirements were stated and Reviewed but no special actions were required.
2	ResponsetimeorthroughputiscriticalduringpeakhoursNospecialdesignforCPU utilization was required. Processing deadline is for the next business day.
3	Response time or through put is critical during all business hours. No special design

	for CPU utilizationwasrequired.Processingdeadlinerequirementswithinterfacing systems Are constraining.
4	In addition, stated user performance requirements are stringent enough to require performance analysis tasks in the Design phase.
5	In addition, performance analysis tools were used in the design, development, and/ or implementation phases to meet The stated user performance requirements.

Table: Performance

Heavily used configuration

How heavily used is the current hardware platform where the application will be executed?

Rating	Description
0	No explicit or implicit operational restrictions are included.
1	Operational restrictions do exist, but are less restrictive than a typical application. No special effort is needed to meet the Restrictions.
2	Some security or timing considerations are included.
3	Specific processor requirement for a specific piece of the Application is included.
4	Stated operation restrictions require special constraints on the application in the central processor or a dedicated Processor.
5	In addition, there are special constraints on the application in The distributed components of the system.

Table: Heavily used configuration

Transaction rate

How frequently are transactions executed; daily, weekly, monthly, etc.?

Rating	Description
0	No peak transaction period is anticipated.
1	Peak transaction period (e.g., monthly, quarterly, seasonally, Annually) is anticipated.
2	Weekly peak transaction period is anticipated.
3	Daily peak transaction period is anticipated.
4	High transaction rate(s) stated by the user in the application requirements or service level agreements are high enough to Require perform ance analysis tasks in the design phase.
5	High transaction rate(s) stated by the user in the application requirem ents or service level agreements are high enough to require performance analysis tasks and, in addition, require the use of performance analysis tools in the design, Development, and/or installation phases.

Table: Transaction rate

On-Line data entry

What percentage of the information is entered On-Line?

Rating	Description
0	All transactions are processed in batch mode.
1	1% to7% of transactions is interactive data entry.
2	8% to15% of transactions is interactive data entry.
3	16% to23% of transactions is interactive data entry.
4	24% to30% of transactions is interactive data entry.
5	M orethan30% of transactions is interactive data entry.

Table: Online data entry

End-user efficiency

Was the application designed for end-user efficiency? There are seven end-user efficiency factors which govern how this point is rated.

Sr no	End-user Efficiency Factor
1	Navigational aids(for example, function keys, jumps, dynamically generated menus)
2	Menus
3	Online help and documents
4	Automated curs or movement
5	Scrolling
6	Remote printing(via online transactions)
7	Preassigned function keys
8	Batch jobs submitted from online transactions
9	Cursor selection of screen data
10	Heavy use of reverse video, highlighting, colors underlining, and other indicators
11	Hard copy user documentation of online transactions
1 2	Mouse interface
1 3	Pop-up windows
14	.As few screens as possible to accomplish a business function
15	Bilingual support(supports two languages; count as four items)
16	Multilingual support (supports more than two languages; count as six items).

Table: End user efficiency factor

Rating	Description
0	None of the above.
1	One to three of the above.
2	Four to five of the above.
3	Six or more of the above, but there are no specific user Requirements related to efficiency.
4	Six or more of the above, and stated requirements for end-user efficiency are strong enough to require design tasks for human factors to be included (for example, minimize keystrokes, maximize defaults, use of templates).
5	Six or more of the above, and stated requirements for end-user efficiency are strong enough to require use of special tools and processes to demonstrate that the objectives have been achieved.

Table: End user efficiency

On-Line update

How many ILF's are updated by On-Line transaction?

Rating	Description
0	None of the above.
1	Online update of one to three control files is included. Volume of updating I slow and recovery is easy.
2	Online update off our or more control files is included. Volume of updating is low and recovery easy.
3	Online update of major internal logical files is included.
4	In addition, protection against data lost is essential and has been specially designed and programmed in the system.
5	In addition, high volumes bring cost considerations into the Recovery process. Highly automated recovery procedures With minimum operator intervention are included.

Table: Online update

Complex processing

Does the application have extensive logical or mathematical processing?

Sr no	Complex Processing Factor
1	Sensitive control(for example, special audit processing)and/or application specific security Processing
2	Extensive logical processing
3	Extensive mathematical processing

4	Much exception processing resulting in incomplete transactions that must be processed again, for example, incomplete ATM transactions caused by TP interruption, missing data values, or failed edits
5	Complex processing to handle multiple input/output possibilities, for example, multimedia, or device independence

Table: Complex processing factor

Rating	Description
0	None of the above.
1	Any one of the above.
2	Any two of the above.
3	Any three of the above.
4	Any four of the above.
5	All five of the above

Table: Complex processing

Reusability

Was the application developed to meet one or many user's needs?

Rating	Description
0	No reusable code.
1	Reusable code is used within the application.
2	Less than 10% of the application considered more than one user's needs.
3	Ten percent (10%) or more of the application considered more than one user's needs.
4	The application was specifically packaged and/or documented to ease re-use, and the application is customized by the user at source code level.
5	The application was specifically packaged and/or documented to ease re-use, and the application is customized for use by means of user parameter maintenance.

Table: reusability

Installation ease

How difficult is conversion and installation

Rating	Description
0	No special considerations were stated by the user, and no special setup is required for installation.
1	No special considerations were stated by the user but special setup is required for installation.

2	Conversion and installation requirements were stated by the user and conversion and installation guides were provided and tested. The impact of conversion on the project is not considered to be important.
3	Conversion and installation requirements were stated by the user, and conversion and installation guides were provided And tested. The impact of conversion on the project is Considered to be important.
4	In addition to 2 above, automated conversion and installation Tools were provided and tested.
5	In addition to 3 above, automated conversion and installation Tools were provided and tested.

Table: Installation ease

Operational ease

How effective and/or automated are start-up, back up, and recovery procedures?

Rating	Description
0	No special operational considerations so other than the normal Back- up procedures were stated by the user.
1-4	One, some, or all of the following items apply to the Application. Select all that apply. Each item has a point Value of one, except as noted otherwise. Effective start-up, back-up, and recovery processes were Provided, but operator intervention is required. Effective start-up, back-up, and recovery processes were provided, but no operator intervention is required(count as Two items). The application minimizes the need for tape mounts. The application minimizes the need for paper handling.
5	The application is designed for unattended operation. Unattended operation means no operator intervention is required to operate the system other than to startup or shutdown the application.Automatic error recovery is a feature Of the application.

Table: operational ease

Multiple sites

Was the application specifically designed, developed, and supported to be installed at multiple sites for multiple organizations?

Rating	Description
0	User requirements do not require considering the needs of More than one user/ installation site.
1	Needs of multiple sites were considered in the design, and the application is designed to operate only under identical Hardware and software environments.

2	Needs of multiple sites were considered in the design, and the application is designed to operate only under similar Hardware and or software environments.
3	Needs of multiple sites were considered in the design, and the application is designed to operate under different Hardware and or software environments.
4	Documentation and support plan are provided and tested to support the application at multiple sites and the application is as described by 1 or 2.
5	Documentation and support plan are provided and tested to support the application at multiple sites and the application is as described by 3.

Table: Multiple sites

Facilitate change

Was the application specifically designed, developed, and supported to facilitate change?.

The following characteristics can apply for the application

Sr no	Facilitate factors
0	None of above
1	Flexible query and report facility is provided that can handle simple requests; for example, and/or logic applied to only one internal logical file (count as one item).
2	Flexible query and report facility is provided that can handle requests of average complexity for example, and/or logic applied to more than one internal logical file (count as two items).
3	Flexible query and report facility is provided that can handle complex requests, for example, and/or logic combinations on one or more internal logical files (count as three items).
4	Business control data is kept in tables that are maintained by the user with online interactive Processes, but changes take effect only on the next business day.
5	Business control data is kept in tables that are maintained by the user with online interactive Processes and the changes take effect immediately (count as two items)

Table: Facilitate change factors

Rating	Description
0	None of the above.
1	Any one of the above.
2	Any two of the above.
3	Any three of the above.
4	Any four of the above.
5	All five of the above

Table: Facilitate change

All the above GSC are rated from 0-5.Then VAF is calculated from the equation below:

VAF = 0.65 + ((sum of all GSC factor)/100).

> **Note:** *GSC has not been accepted in software industry widely. Many software companies use Unadjusted Function point rather than adjusted. ISO has also removed GSC from its books and only kept unadjusted function points as the base for measurement. Read GSC acceptance in software industry Rating Tables for All elements of Function Points.*

Below shown are look up tables which will be referred during counting.

EI Rating Table			
	Data Elements		
FTR	**1to 4**	**5 to 15**	**Greater than 15**
Less than 2	3	3	4
Equal to 2	3	4	6
Greater than 2	4	4	6

Table: EI rating table

This table says that in any EI (External Input), if your DET count (Data Element) and FTR (File Type Reference) exceed these limits, then this should be the FP (Function Point). Example, if your DET (data element) exceeds >15 and FTR (File Type Reference) is greater than 2, then the Function Point count is 6. The rest down tables also show the same things. These tables will be there before us when we are doing function point count. The best is put these values in Excel with formulae so that you have to only put quantity in the appropriate section and you get the final value.

EO Rating Table			
	Data Elements		
FTR	**1 to 5**	**6 to 19**	**Greater than 19**
Less than 2	4	4	5
2 or 3	4	5	7
Greater than 2	5	7	7

Table: EO rating table

EQ Rating Table			
	Data Elements		
FTR	**1 to 5**	**6 to 19**	**Greater than 19**
Less than 2	3	3	4
2 or 3	3	4	6
Greater than 2	4	6	6

Table: EQ rating table

ILF Rating Table			
Data Elements			
RET	**1 to 19**	**20 to 50**	**51 or more**
1 RET	7	7	10
2 to 5	7	10	15
Greater than 6	10	15	15
EIF Rating Table			
RET	**1 to 19**	**20 to 50**	**51 or more**
1 RET	5	5	7
2 to 5	5	7	10
Greater than 6	7	10	10

Table: ILF rating table.

Steps to Count Function Points

This section will discuss the practical way of counting the FP and coming out with a Man/Days on a project.

- Counting the ILF, EIF, EI, EQ, RET, DET, FTR (this is basically all sections discussed above): This whole FP count will be called as "unadjusted function point".
- Then put rating values 0 to 5 to all 14 GSC. Adding total of all 14 GSC to come out with total VAF. Formula for VAF = 0.65 + (sum of all GSC factor/ 100).
- Finally, make the calculation of adjusted function point. Formula: Total function point = VAF * Unadjusted function point.
- Make estimation how many function points you will do per day. This is also called as "Performance factor".
- On basis of performance factor, you can calculate Man/Days]

Let's try to implement these details in a sample customer project.

Sample Customer Project

We will be evaluating the customer GUI. So we will just scope what the customer GUI is all about.

Following is the scope of the customer screen:

- Customer screen will be as shown below.
- After putting the customer code and Customer name. They will be verified credit card check.
- Credit Card check is a external system.
- Every Customer can have multiple addresses.
- Customer will have add, update functionality.

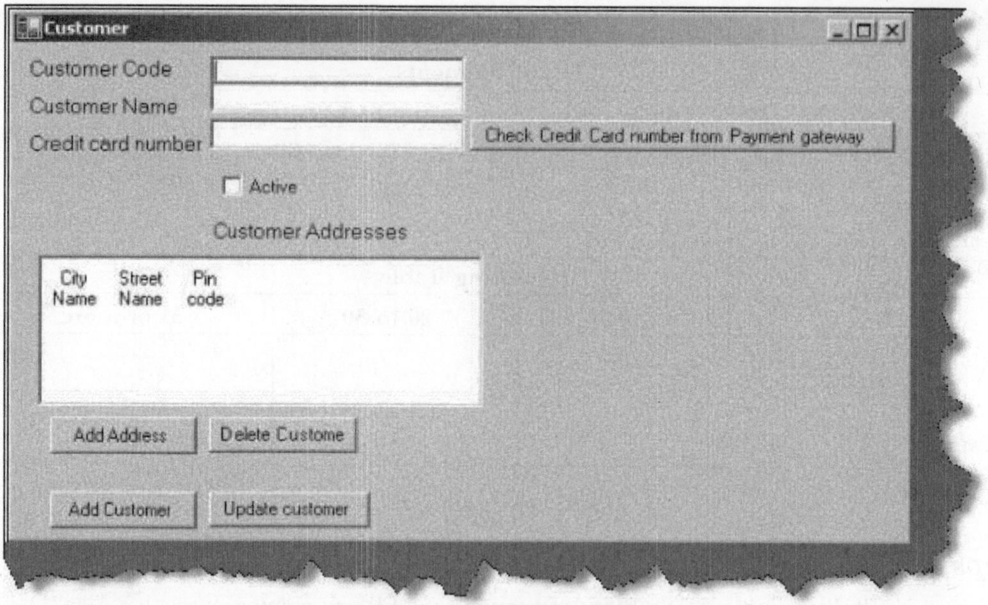

Figure: Custom screen

There is one ILF in the above screen:

- The customer ILF.

There is one EIF in the above form.

- Credit Card System

Following the ILF counting rules

- ILF are logically related data from user point of view. Customer and Customer addresses belong logically to customer category.
- ILF reside in Internal Application boundary and are maintained through Elementary process of application. Customer resides in inside application boundary as we have full access over it.

So hence goes the counting below for ILF

ILF Customer		
Description	**Number of DET**	**Number of RET**
There are total 9 DETs, alladd and update buttons, even the credit check button, the address list box, check box active, all text boxes. There is only one RET, the customer addresses.	9	1
So according to the above ILF ranking table	**Total function**	**7**

Table: ILF for the customer

EIF lie outside the application boundary.

EI Credit Card Information		
Description	**Number of DET**	**Number of RET**
The credit card information referenced is EIF. Note this file is only referenced for credit card check.There's only one textbox credit card number and hence one DET is put in the side column. And RET 0.Looking at the above rating table the total FP is 5.	1	1
So according to the above ranking table	**Total function**	5

Table: EI for the customer

Following EIF rules define in the previous sections:

- It's a dynamic elementary process [For definition see "Dynamic and Static Elementary Process" Section] in which data is received from external application boundary. Customer detail is received from external boundary that is customer input screen.
- EI may maintain ILF of the application, but it's not compulsory rule. In this sample project Customer ILF is maintained.
- So there are two EI one for Add and one from update.

It is two because processing logic for add and update is different.

EI Add Customer		
Description	**Number of DET**	**Number of FTR**
There are total 9 DETs, all add and update buttons, even the credit check button, the address list box, check box active, all text boxes.There are 3 FTRs, one is the address and the second is the credit card information and third is customer himself.	9	3
So according to the above ranking table	**Total function**	6

Table: EI for the add customer

EI Update Customer		
Description	**Number of DET**	**Number of RET**
There are total 9 DETs, all add and update buttons, even the credit check button, the address list box, check box active, all text boxes.There are 3 FTRs, one is the address	9	3

and the second is the credit card information and third is customer himself.		
So according to the above ranking table	**Total function**	6

Table: EI for the update customer

While counting EI I have seen many people multiplying it by 3.That means we are going to do all CRUD functionality (ADD, UPDATE, and DELETE).This is not fair as it just shows laziness of the Cost estimation team. Here the customer screen has add and update. I can say the 2 * 6 that's = 12 FP for this EI customer. But later when some refers to your FP sheet he will be completely lost.

Following are rules to recognize EO:

- Data should cross application boundary and it should involve complex logic.

Credit card check process can be complex as the credit card API complexity is still not known. Data that is credit card information crosses from credit card system to Customer system.

EO check credit card		
Description	**Number of DET**	**Number of RET**
One DET Credit Card number and one RET credit card itself. Note if there are no RET we count default as one. Look for RET counting rules defined in previous section.	1	1
So according to the above ranking table	**Total function**	4

Table: EO to check the credit card

Following are rules to recognize EQ:

- It's a dynamic elementary process in which result data is retrieved from one or more ILF or EIF. For editing the customer we will need to retrieve the customer details.
- In this EP some input request has to enter the application boundary. The customer code is inputted from the same screen.
- Output results exits the application boundary. The customer details is displayed while the customer is editing the customer data.
- EQ does not contain any derived data. The above customer data which is displayed does not contain any complex calculations.

EQ Display Customer Edit Information		
Description	**Number of DET**	**Number of FTR**
There are 5 DETs to be retrieved Customer Code, Customer Name, Credit Card number, Active, Customer Address. Only customer details and customer address will be referenced.	5	2
So according to the above ranking table	**Total function**	3

Table: EQ to display customer edit

So now, let's add the total function point got from above tables:

Function Point	Section Name Counted
ILF Customer	
EO Credit Card check system	4
EIF credit card information	5
EI Customer (Add and update)	12
EQ display customer edit information	3
Total UnadjustedFunction Points	31

Table: Total of all function point

So unadjusted function point comes to 31.Please note I have said this as Unadjusted function as we have not accounted other variance factor of project (Programmers leaving job, Language we will use, what architecture etc etc).

In order to make it adjusted function point, we have to calculate and tabulate the GSC and come out with the VAF.

GSC	Value(0-5)
Data communications	1
Distributed data processing	1
Performance	4
Heavily used configuration	0
Transaction rate	1
On-Line data entry	0
End-user efficiency	4
On-Line update	0
Complex processing	0
Reusability 3	
Installation ease	4
Operational ease	4
Multiple sites	0
Facilitate change	0
Total	**22**

Table: GSC

VAF = 0.65 + ((sum of all GSC factor)/100). = 0.65 + (22/100) = 0.87.

This factor affects the whole FP like anything, be very particular with this factor. So now, calculating the Adjusted FP = VAF * Total unadjusted

*FP = 0.87 * 31 = 26.97 = rounded to 27 FP.*

Now we know that the complete FP for the customer GUI is 27 FP. Now calculating the efficiency factor, we say that we will complete 3 FP per day that is 9 working days. So, the whole customer GUI is of 9 working days (Note do not consider Saturday and Sundays in this). I know upper manager people will say make it 7 FP per day and over load the programmer. That's why programmer works at night.

Considering SDLC (System Development Life Cycle)

Before reading this section please refer to different SDLC cycles questions in the previous chapters.

The main intention of introducing this section is because quotations are heavily affected by which software life cycle you follow. Because deliverables change according to SLDC model the project manager chooses for the project. Example for waterfall model we will have Requirement documents, Design documents, Source code and testing plans. But for prototyping models in addition to the documents above we will also need to deliver the rough prototype. For build and fix model we will not deliver any of the documents and the only document delivered will be source code. So according to SDLC model deliverables change and hence the quotation. We will divide the estimation across requirement, design, implementation (coding) and testing .In what way the estimation has to divide across all deliverables is all up to the project manager and his plans.

Phase	Percentage distribution effort
Requirements	10% of total effort
Design Phase	20% of total effort
Coding	100 % of total effort
Testing	10% of total effort

Table: Phase wise distribution of effort

The above sample is total 100 % distribution of effort across various phases. But note function point or any other estimation methodology only gives you total execution estimation. So you can see in the above distribution we have given coding as 100 %. But as said it up to the project manager to change according to scenarios .Ok now from the above function point estimation is 9 days let's try to divide it across all phases.

Phase	Percentage distribution effort	Distribution of man/ days across phases
Requirements	10 % of total effort	0.9 days
Design Phase	20 % of total effort	1.8 days
Coding	100 % of total effort	9 days
Testing	10 % of total effort	0.9 days
Total		**12.6 day**

Table: Phase wise effort distribution of man days

The above table shows the division of project man/days across project. Now let's put down the final quotation. Just a small comment about test cases.

Total number of Test Cases = (Function Point) raised to power of 1.2.This is as suggested from caper Jones.

(A) How can you estimate number of acceptance test cases in a project?

*Number of Acceptance Test Cases = 1.2 * Function Points*

20-25 % of total effort can be allocated to testing phase. Test cases are non-deterministic. That means if test passes it takes "X" amount of time and if it does not then to amend it take "Y" amount of time.

Final Quotation

One programmer will sit on the project with around 1000 $ salary / Month. So his 12.6 days salary comes to 386.4 dollars approx. The upper quotation format is in its simplest format. Every company has his quotation format accordingly. So no hard and fast rule of quotation template. But still if interested http://www.microsoft.com/mac/resources/templates.aspx?pid=templates has good collection of decent templates.

<table>
<tr><th colspan="5">XYZ SOFTWARE COMPANY</th></tr>
<tr><td colspan="5">To:
TNC Limited, Western road 17, California.
Quotation number: 90
Date: 1/1/2004
Customer ID: Z- 20090DATAENTRY</td></tr>
<tr><th>Quantity</th><th>Description</th><th>Discount</th><th>Taxable</th><th>Total</th></tr>
<tr><td>1</td><td>Customer Project</td><td>0%</td><td>0%</td><td>386.4 dollars</td></tr>
<tr><td colspan="5">Quotation Valid for 100 days
Goods delivery date with in 25 days of half payment
Quotation Prepared by: XYZ estimation department
Approved by: SPEG department XYZ.</td></tr>
</table>

Table – Final bill

CustomerSampleFP.xls is provided with the CD which has all estimation details which you can refer for practical approach.

GSC Acceptance in Software industry

GSC factors have been always a controversial topic. Most of the software companies do not use GSC, rather than they base line UAFP or construct there own table depending on company project history. ISO has also adopted function point as unit of measurement, but they also use UAFP rather than AFP. Let's do a small experiment to view relationship between FP, AFP, GSC and VAF. In this experiment we will assume UAFP = 120 and then lot graph with GSC increment of five. So the formulae is VAF = 0.65 + (GS/100).

Here's the table with every five incremental values in formulae and plot.

FP	GSC
78	0
84	5
90	10
96	15
102	20
108	25
114	30
120	35
126	40
132	45
138	50
144	55
150	60
156	65
162	70

Table: GSC acceptance

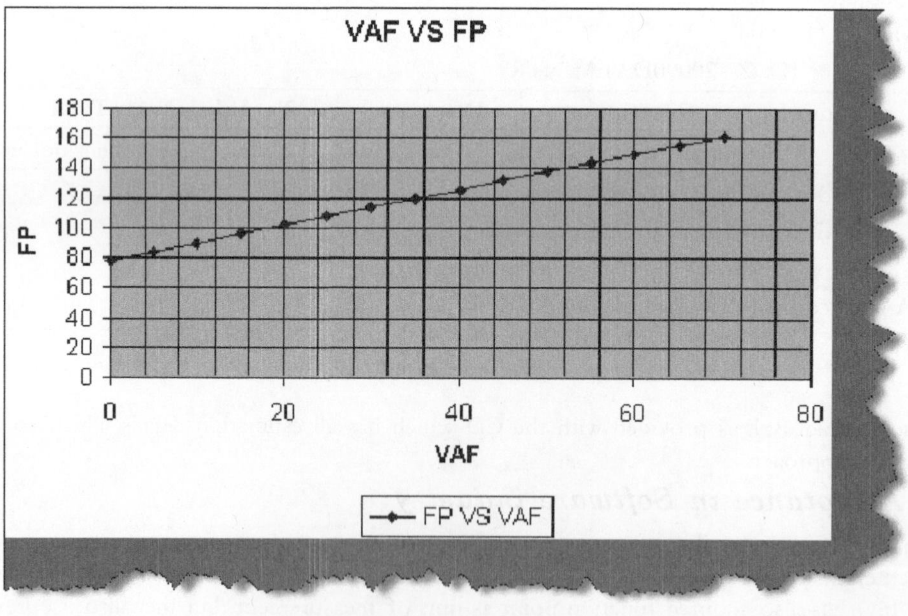

Figure: FP versus VAF

The following are the observation from the table and plot:

- Graph is linear. It also captures that nature of complexity is linear.
- If the GSC value is zero then VAF is 0.65. So the graph starts from UAFP*0.65.GSC = 35 AFP = UAFP. So the VAF = 1.
- When GSC < 35 then AFP < UAFP. That means complexity decreases.
- When GSC > 35 then AFP > UAFP. That means complexity increases.

Readers must be wondering why 0.65? There are fourteen GSC factor from zero to five. So the maximum value of VAF = 0.65 + (70/100) = 1.35. In order that VAF does not have any affect i.e. UAFP = FP VAF should be one. VAF will be one when GSC is 35 i.e. half of 70. So in order to complete value "1" value "0.65" is taken. Note value is 0.35 when GSC is 35 to complete the one factor "0.65" is required.

But following is the main problem related to GSC. GSC is applied throughout FP even when some GSC does not apply to whole function points. Here's the example to demonstrate GSC problem.

Let's take 11th GSC factor "installation ease". The project is of 100 UAFP and there is no consideration of installation previously by client so the 11th factor is zero.

GSC with installation ease with ZERO	
GSC	**Value(0-5)**
Data communications	1
Distributed data processing	1
Performance	4
Heavily used configuration	0
Transaction rate	1
On-Line data entry	0
End-user efficiency	4
On-Line update	0
Complex processing	0
Reusability	3
Installation ease	0
Operational ease	4
Multiple sites	0
Facilitate change	0
Total	**18**

Table: GSC with installation ease zero

VAF = 0.65 + (18/100) = 0.83. So the FP = 100 * 0.83 = 83 Function Points. But later the client demanded for full blown installation for the project with auto updating when new version is released. So we change out GSC table with installation ease to 5.

GSC with installation ease with FIVE	
GSC	**Value(0-5)**
Data communications	1
Distributed data processing	1
Performance	4
Heavily used configuration	0
Transaction rate	1
On-Line data entry	0
End-user efficiency	4
On-Line update	0
Complex processing	0
Reusability	3
Installation ease	5
Operational ease	4
Multiple sites	0
Facilitate change	0
Total	**23**

Table: GSC with Installation ease 5

So VAF = 0.65 + (23/100) = 0.88 so the FP = 100 * 0.88 = 88. The difference is of only 5 FP which from no way a proper effort estimate. To make an auto updation for a software versioning can no way be done in 5 function points , just think downloading new version, deleting the old version , updating any database structure changes etc etc. So that's the reason GSC is not accepted in software industry. Best ways is baseline you're UAFP and make your estimation on base of UAFP.

Enhancement Function Points

Major software project fail not because of programmer's or project managers but due to moody and changing customers. In one of our huge projects we had good programmers, very enthusiastic. The project started of well but customer called ten times in a day to change something or other. Believe me programmers get pissed if the customer is changing his plans every fortnight. Well from this book point of view we have to evaluate this changes which can be addition or deletion of requirements. Function point group has come out with a methodology called as "Enhancement Function Points".

Down is the formulae

*Formulae of EFP (Enhanced Function Points) = (ADD + CHGA) * VAFA + (DELFP) * VAFB*

ADD: This is new function points added. This value is achieved by counting all new EP (Elementary process) given in change request.

CHGA: Function points which are affected due to CR. This value is achieved by counting all DET, FTR, ILF, EI, EO and EQ which are affected. Do not count elements which are not affected.

VAFA: This is VAF factor which is because of CR. Example previously the application was desktop and now is changed to web so the GSC factor is affected.

DELFP: When CR is for removing some functionality this value is counted. It's rare that customer removes functionalities (at least in India), but if they ever estimator has to take note of it by counting the deleted elementary process.

VAFB: Again removal affects Value added factor.

Once we are through with calculating enhanced function points, it time to count total function points of the application.

Total Function points = [UFPB + ADD + CHGA] – [CHGB – DELFP]

UFPB: Function points previously counted before enhancement.

ADD: Newly added functionality which leads to new function points after enhancements.

CHGA: Changed function points counted after enhancements.

CHGB: Changed function points before enhancements.

DELFP: Deleted function points.

(I) Can you explain the concept of Use Case's?

Use case is used to capture the functional requirement of a project. Use case describes the functional requirement of a project in terms of actor, roles and sequence of steps.

(I) Can you explain the concept of Use case points?

Use Case Point is software sizing and measurement based on Use Case Document. "Use Case Point" is based on work by Gustav Karner in 1993. It was written as a diploma thesis at the University of Linkoping. This work is a modification of work by Allen Albrecht on function points.

(B) What is a use case transaction?

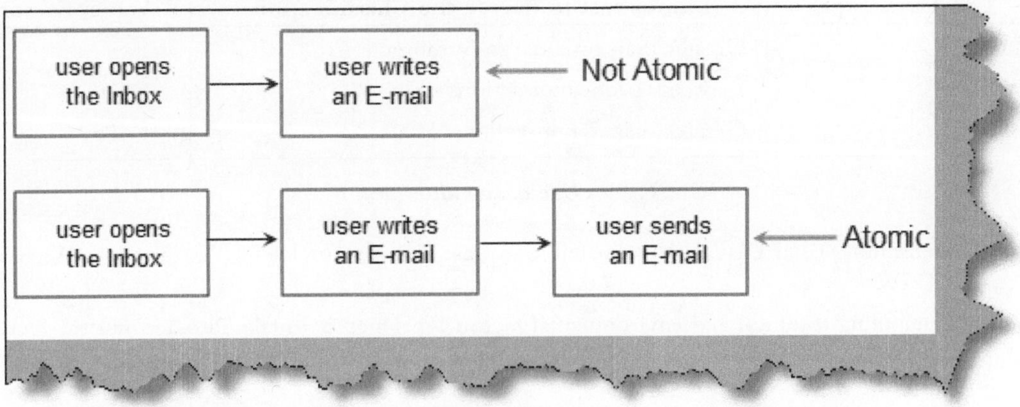

Figure: Atomic

Use case transactions are atomic set of activities which are either performed or not performed at all. For instance below figure 'Atomic' shows the meaning of atomic in context of use case transaction. The first transaction cycle does not show a complete atomic activity; rather the transaction is in between and is not in persistent state. If you see the second transaction cycle it's atomic because after the user sends the email it's in persistent state and is sitting on the mail server.

(B) How do we estimate using Use Case Points?

Steps for UCP (Use Case Points) Estimation

- Determine the UAW (Unadjusted Actor weight): The first step is to classify all the actors in to the following classification. Table 'Actor Classification' will give you a clear idea of how to classify the actors. Second column is the litmus test for making a decision of which type of actor falls in which category. The last column provides the factor of complexity.

Classification	Litmus test to recognize classifications	Value/Factor
Simple actors	Simple actors are those which communicate to system through API.	1
Average actors	Average actors are recognized if they have the following properties: ● Actors who are interacting with the system through some protocol (HTTP, FTP, or probably some user defined protocol). ● Actors which are data stores (Files, RDBMS).	2
Complex	Complex actor is interacting normally through GUI.	3

Table: Actor classification

- Determine number of UUCW (Unadjusted Use case Weight): The second step is to count Use Cases and assign weights depending on number of scenarios and number of transactions.

Use Case Type	Litmus test to decide the Classification	Value/Factor
Simple	Greater than or equal to 3 transactions	5
Average	Between 4 to 7 transactions	10
Complex	Greater than 7 transactions	15

Table: Use case value factor

- Determine Total UUCP (Unadjusted Use Case Point): Total UUCP = Total UAW + Total UUCW.
- Computing technical and environmental factor: Final step is to take into account the technical complexity. All technical factors will be assigned a value from 0 to 5 depending on complexity.

	Technical factor	Weight	Description
t1	Distributed System	2	Is the system having distributed architecture or centralized architecture?
t2	Response time	1	Does the client need the system to fast? Is time response one of the important criteria?
t3	End user efficiency	1	How's the end user's efficiency?
t4	Complex internal processing	1	Is the business process very complex? Like complicated accounts closing, inventory tracking, heavy tax calculation etc.
t5	Reusable code	1	Do we intend to keep the reusability high? So will increase the design complexity.
t6	Installation ease	0.5	Is client looking for installation ease? By default, we get many installers which create packages. But the client might be looking for some custom installation, probably depending on modules. One of our client has a requirement that when the client wants to install, he can choose which modules he çan install. Is the requirement such that when there is a new version there should be auto installation? These factors will count when assigning value to this factor.
t7	Easy use	0.5	Is user friendliness a top priority?
t8	Portable	2	Is the customer also looking for cross platform implementation?
t9	Easy to change	1	Is the customer looking for high customization in the future? That also increases the architecture design complexity and hence this factor.
t10	Concurrent	1	Is the customer looking at large number of users working with locking support? This will increase the architecture complexity and hence this value.
t11	Security objectives	1	Is the customer looking at having heavy security like SSL? Or do we have to write custom code logic for encryption?
t12	Direct access to third parties	1	Does the project depend in using third party controls? For understanding the third-party controls and studying its pros and cons, considerable effort will be required. So, this factor should be rated accordingly.
t13	User training facilities	1	Will the software from user perspective be so complex that separate training has to be provided? So this factor will vary accordingly.

Table: Technical Factor

- Equation for Tfactor = sum(T1....T13)
- TCF (Technical Complexity Factor): TCF = 0.6 + (0.01 * Tfactor).
- EF (Environmental Factor): There are other factors like trained staff, motivation of programmers etc. which have quiet a decent impact on the cost estimate.

	Environmental Factor	**Weight**	**Description**
e1	Familiarity with project	1.5	1.5 Are all the people working in the project familiar with domain and technical details of the project? Probably you will spend most of your time in explaining them all know-how's.
e2	Application experience	0.5	How much is the application experience?
e3	Object-oriented programming experience	1	As use-case documents are inputs to object oriented design, it's important that people on the project should have basic knowledge of OOP concepts.
e4	Lead analyst capability	0.5	How is the analyst who is leading the project? Does he have enough knowledge of the domain?.
e5	Motivation	1	Are the programmers motivated for working on the project? Instability in the project will always lead to people leaving half way through their source code. And the hand over becomes really tough. This factor you can put according to how software industry is going on? Example, if the software market is very good, put this at maximum value. More good the market, more the jobs and more the programmers will jump.
e6	Stable requirements	2	Is the client clear of what he wants? I have seen clients' expectations are the most important factor in the stability of requirements. If the client is of highly changing nature, put this value to maximum.
e7	Part-time Staff	-1	Are there part-time staff in projects, like consultants etc.?
e8	Difficult programming language	-1	How much is the language complexity, Assembly, VB 6.0, C++, C etc.

Table: Environmental factor

- Efactor = SUM(e1...e8).
- Calculating Environmental Factor = EF = 1.4 + (-0.03 * Efactor).
- AUCP (Adjusted Use Case Points). Finally, calculating the Adjusted Use case points: AUCP = UUCP * TCF * EF
- Multiplying by Man/Hours Factor: AUCP * Person/Hours/AUCP.

Karner[13] proposed a factor of 20 staff hours per Use Case point for a project estimate. While Sharks states that field experience has shown that effort can range from 15 to 30 hours per Use Case point.Schneider and Winters proposed number of staff hours per Use Case point depends on the environmental factors. The number of factors in E1 through E6 that are below 3 are counted and added to the number of factors in E7 through E8 that are above 3. If the total is 2 or less, the general idea is to use twenty staff hours per UCP; if the total is 3 or 4, use twenty-eight staff hours per UCP. If the number exceeds 5, it is usually recommended that changes should be made to the project so the number can be adjusted, because in this case, the risk is unacceptably high. Another possibility is to increase the number of staff hours to thirty-six per

Sample project scope (Sample Data Entry Project)

Let's start with a sample fiction project. Here's the scope of the project. TNC company till now was using manual way of maintaining its customer database and there credit card information. Data entry operator manually validates credit card information from external payment gateway. They maintain customer code, customer name, customer address, customer phone and validated customer credit card information in Customer registry. Customer code is unique for a customer. So, TNC manually checks for the validations and enters in the customer registry. TNC wants the data entry project to be automated. TNC is looking for the following automation:

- Customer code assigned should be checked for uniqueness automatically.
- Customer code should not exceed 8 length.
- Credit card validation should be automatic for the current system. TNC has already given the API documentation of how to interact with the third party payment system.
- Credit card length should not exceed more than 10 length.
- Data entry operator should be able to add/update/delete customer information.
- The database will be in the TNC head office and only data entry operators will be allowed to use the data entry software.
- Software should work on Windows platform. At this moment, TNC has Windows 2000 client installed in all computers.

Writing Use Case for Sample Data Entry Project:

I have used Alistair Cockburn's template for the "Use Case point" example. Use Case template varies from person to person, project to project, and organization to organization. I found Alistair's template to be complete, so just took it. But there's no hard and fast rule that you have to follow this template. What will matter is what steps you write in the Use Case.

Use Case Transactions: It's an atomic set of activities that are either performed entirely or not all. What is a Use Case transaction and what's not: just see if the transaction is adding any business value or else do not include it as a transaction. Example: the user switches on the computer, user clicks on add button or any GUI, are not valid business transaction steps. But the customer code validated for credit card information is a valid business transaction. Use Case points are heavily affected by the way the Actors and their transactions are identified. So a Use Case Document should be written by predefined guidelines, uniformly in a project. Just take a meeting with the whole project team before starting writing Use Cases. The depth of the Use Case Document will affect estimation by 40%.

Use Case #	DATAENTRYPROJECTCUST-1009
Use Case name	Maintain Customer
Description	This Use Case depicts full maintenance of customer from project "Data Entry".
Scope and level	Data Entry System (Internal) Credit Card System (External)
Level	User Goal Level (If this property is not understood, look at the reference for the book Writing Effective Use Cases (**PRE-PUB. DRAFT#3**): Alistair Cockburn Humans and technology)
Primary and secondary actors	Data Entry operator.
Stakeholders and interests	
Trigger	Data entry operator clicks on menu: "Add New Customer"
Preconditions	Data entry operator should be logged in. Data entry operator should have access to Internet.
Assumptions	Customer information received is entered manually. No automated import routine is in the scope.
Failed End condition	Customer is not added to database and appropriate error message is displayed. Customer code already existing in the customer database. Customer code length limit is exceeded. Customer credit card limit is exceeded. Customer credit card validation failed with the payment gateway.
Action	Add new customer
Main success scenario (or basic Flow):	Data entry operator receives customer information. Data entry operator enters following information: Customer code Customer name Customer address Customer phone Customer code is checked if it exists in Customer table. If the customer code is existing then "Duplicate Customer Code" error is raised. If the customer code is more than 8 length, then "Customer code length limit crossed" error is raised. After step 3 is passed OK. Data entry operator enters credit card information. If the credit card length is more than 10 length, then "Credit card length limit crossed" error is raised. Credit card information is send to the external payment gateway. Appropriate APIs of the external payment gateway will be used for validity. External payment gateway returns "OK" if credit card is validated or else will return "NOT VALID" flag. Data entry operator then adds the customer in database.
Alternate scenario (Extensions):	Update Existing Customer Data entry operator enters customer code to retrieve the customer who has to be updated. Data entry operator makes appropriate changes to the customer information. All steps and business validation from 1 to 6 of Add new Customer is repeated. Data Entry operator updates the customer information.

Alternate scenario (Extensions):	Delete Existing Customer Data entry operator enters customer code to retrieve the customer who has to be deleted. Data entry operator deletes the customer. Data entry operator is alerted "Are you sure you want to delete the Customer?" If the data entry operator clicks "Yes", then the customer is deleted from the database. If the data entry operator clicks "NO", no action is taken.
Success Guarantee (Post conditions):	Customer is added to Customer database. Customer is updated to Customer database. Customer is deleted from Customer database.
Special Requirements (including business rules):	
Technology and Data Variations List:	If credit card payment gateway API changes, the interaction of the data entry customer module will have to be changed accordingly.
Frequency of occurrence:	
Notes and Open Issues:	

Table 6.0

Applying Use Case Points

Let's start applying Use Case Points to the above given document.

- Determining Unadjusted Use Actor Weights (UAW): In this project, we have identified only one actor "Data Entry Operator". The upper Actor (data entry operator) is complex as data entry operator will be interacting through GUI. So UAW=3 as per Table:2.0.
- Determine number of UUCW (Unadjusted Use case Weight): There are 12 transactions [Adding also the alternative flows] in Table 6.0 Use Case. So the above Use Case is complex according to Table 'Use case value factor'. So referring Table 'Use case value factor', UUCW=15.
- Now calculating the total UUCP = 15 + 3 = 18.
- Determining the technical factor

	Technical Factor	Weight	Value	Weighted Value	Explanation
t1	Distributed System	2	1	2	Simple two tier architecture is decided.
t2	Response time	1	4	4	Speed is of importance as the data entry operator has to enter data quiet fast.
t3	End user efficiency	1	3	3	Data entry operator has high user efficiency.
t4	Complex Internal Processing	1	2	2	Its simple entry screen and no business process has been scoped by the client. Only credit card check and

					duplicate customer code is the business check.
t5	Reusable Code	1	1	1	No reusability as project is small and customer is not looking for any further changes for at least two years.
t6	Installation Ease	0.5	0	0	TNC has good in house development team, and installation problems will be handled by them. Technology thought is C#, and .NET setup wizard will be enough to make the installation process easy.
t7	Easy use	0.5	4	2	Yes, data entry operator has to have user friendly menus and shortcut keys for fast entry of data.
t8	Portable	2	1	2	TNC has Windows 2000 client as specified in the scope document.
t9	Easy to change	1	0	0	None specified by client.
t10	Concurrent	1	0	0	Client has not clarified about this issue as such in the scope document. So assumed least concurrent.
t11	Security objectives	1	0	0	None specified by client. Even credit card information will be passed with out encryption.
t12	Direct access to third parties	1	3	3	Using the credit card check API.
t13	User training facilities	1	0	0	The screen is simple, and data entry operator can operate without any training.
	Total			19	

Table 7.0

- Depending on the table, calculating the Technical Factor: TCF = 0.6 + (0.01 * Tfactor) = 0.6 + (0.01 * 19) = 0.79
- Calculating environmental factor

	Environmental	Value Factor	Weight	Weighted Columns	Explanation for the value assigned
e1	Familiarity with project	5	1.5	7.5	It's a simple project, so familiarity with project is not so much needed.
e2	Application experience	5	0.5	2.5	It's a simple application.
e3	Object-oriented programming experience	5	1	5	Every one has good OOP knowledge.
e4	Lead analyst capability	5	0.5	2.5	It's a simple project; no lead analyst needed till now.
e5	Motivation	1	1	1	Motivation is little down as programmers are reluctant to work on the project because of its simplicity.
e6	Stable requirements	4	2	8	Client is very clear with what he wants?
e7	Part-time Staff	0	-1	0	No part time staff.
e8	Difficult programming language.	3	-1	-3	C# will be used. And most of the programming guys are new to C# and .NET technology.

Table 8.0

According to [Kirsten Ribu Master of Science Thesis], Environmental factor plays a very important role in the estimation. A slight variation will increase the Use Case point by a very, very drastic amount. Even small adjustments of an environmental factor, for instance by half a point, can make a great difference to the estimate. Difference of 3 to 2.5 increased the estimate by 4580 hours, from 10831 to 15411 hours, or 42.3 percent. This means that if the values for the environmental factors are not set correctly, there may be disastrous .

- Using formulae for calculating EF = 1.4 + (-0.03 * Efactor) = 1.4 + (-0.03 * 23.5) = 0.695.
- Calculating AUCP = UUCP * TCF * EF = 18 X 0.79 X 0.695 = 9.88 approx = 10 Use Case Points. I have done the approximation as its only creates 3 to 4 hours of difference.
- Calculating according to Karner, i.e., 20 staff hours per Use Case points = 10 X 20 = 200 hours for the total project. If programmer works for 8 hours for a day, then 340/8 = 25 days.
- Calculating according to Schneider and Winters, from e1 to e6 there are only 3 properties that are below 3. And from e7 to e8, there are none whose value is above 3. So the total is 3. We use 28 staff hours. 10 X 28 = 280 hours.

If programmer works for 8 hours, then 35 days. If this step is not understood, look at the steps defined in theory of Use Case points. If we apply sixth sense, we will find Karner approach is coming to round about figure. It really depends what you want to follow: Karner or Schneider approach. Best is that after two or three projects, whatever is coming accurate from history, take that approach. Best approach is to use Excel and incorporate formulas properly.

Note: *Check for the use case points estimation sheet in the CD.*

7

Project Management Interview Questions

Architectures are senior persons and mainly responsible to looks after the technical aspects of the project. Many organization expect architects to have a know how of project management basics. In this book we have mainly focused on the technical aspect. We have a complete dedicated book on project management. You can buy the same from Bpb. For details please email bpb@bol.net.in or to bpb@vsnl.com .

Below are the questions from the book.

Basics of project management

Define project?

Who is a stakeholder?

Can you explain Scope triangle?

Can you explain what's a vision and a goal?

What is ROI?

Can you explain project life cycle?

You have people in your team who do not meet there deadlines or do not perform what are the actions you will take?

Are risk constant through out the project?

Explain SDLC (Software development Life Cycle) in detail?

Can you explain waterfall model?

Can you explain big-bang waterfall model?

Can you explain phased waterfall model?

Explain Iterative model, Incremental model, Spiral model, Evolutionary model and VModel?

Explain Unit testing, Integration tests, System testing and Acceptance testing?

What's the difference between system and acceptance testing?

Which is the best model?

What is CAR (Causal Analysis and Resolution)?

What is DAR (Decision Analysis and Resolution)?

Can you explain the concept of baseline in software development?

What is the software you have used for project management?

What does a project plan consist?

When do you say the project has finished?

Can you explain what a PMO office is?

How many members in your team you have handled?

Is GANTT chart a project plan?

Two resources are having issues how do you handle the same?

What is a change request?

How did you manage change request in your project?

Can you explain traceability matrix?

What is configuration management?

What is CI?

Define stakeholders?

Can you explain versioning?

Can you explain the concept of sign off?

How will you start a project?

What is an MOU?

What where the deliverables in your project?

Can you explain your project?

Do you also participate in technical activities?

How did you manage code reviews?

You have team member who does not meets his deadlines how do you handle it?

Did you have project audits if yes how was it handled?

What is a non-conformance report (NCR)?

How did you estimate your project?

How did you motivate your team members?

Did you create leaders in your team if yes how?

How did you confirm that your modules are resource independent?

Was your project show cased for CMMI or any other project process standardization?

What are the functions of the Quality Assurance Group (QAG)?

Can you explain milestone?

How did you do assessme nt of team members?

What does entry and exit criteria mean in a project?

How much are you as leader and how much are you as PM ?

How can he handle the conflicts between peers and subordinates?

In your team you have highly talented people how did you ha ndle their motivation ?

How can you balance between underperforming and outperforming people ?

You need to make choice between delivery and quality what's your take ?

Risk Management

Define risk?

What is risk break down structure?

How did you plan your risk?

What is DR, BCP and contingency planning?

Schedule Management

Can you explain WBS?

Can you explain WBS numbering?

How did you do resource allocation?

Can you explain the use of WBS?

Can you explain network diagram?

What are the different types of network diagram?

What is the advantage of using network diagrams?

Can you explain Arrow diagram and Precendence diagram?

What are the different types of Network diagrams?

Can you explain Critical path?

Can you define EST, LST, EFT, LFT?

Can you explain Float and Slack?

Can you explain PERT?

Can you explain GANTT chart?

What is the disadvantage of GANTT chart?

What is Monte-Carlo simulation?

Costing

Can you explain PV, AC and EV?

Can you explain BCWS, ACWS and BCWP?

What are the derived metrics from Earned Value?

Can you explain earned value with a sample?

Estimation, Metrics and Measure

What is meant by measure and metrics?

Which metrics have you used for tracking purpose?

What are the various common ways of estimation?

Can you explain LOC method of estimation?

How do we convert LOC in to effort?

Can you explain COCOMO?

Can you explain Intermediate COCOMO and COCOMO II?

How do you estimate using LOC?

Can you explain in brief Function points?

Can you explain the concept Application boundary?

Can you explain the concept of elementary process?

Can you explain the concept of static and dynamic elementary process?

Can you explain concept of FTR, ILF, EIF, EI, EO , EQ and GSC ?

How can you estimate number of acceptance test cases in a project?

Can you explain the concept of Use Case's?

Can you explain the concept of Use case points?

What is a use case transaction?

How do we estimate using Use Case Points?

Can you explain on what basis does TPA actually work?

How did you do estimation for black box testing?

How did you estimate white box testing?

Is there a way to estimate acceptance test cases in a system?

Can you explain Number of defects measure?

Can you explain number of production defects measure?

Can you explain defect seeding?

Can you explain DRE?

Can you explain Unit and system test DRE?

How do you measure test effectiveness?

Can you explain Defect age and Defect spoilage?

Software process

What is a Software process?

What are the different cost eleme nt involved in implementing process in an organization?

What is a model?

What is maturity level?

Can you explain the concept of process area in CMMI?

Can you explain the concept of tailoring?

CMMI

What is CMMI?

What's the difference between implementation and Institutionalization?

What are different models in CMMI?

Can you explain staged and continuous models in CMMI?

Can you explain the different maturity levels in staged representation?

Can you explain capability levels in continuous representation?

Which model should we use and under what scenarios?

How many process areas are present in CMMI and in what classification do they fall in?

What the difference between every level in CMMI?

What different sources are needed to verify authenticity for CMMI implementation?

Can you explain SCAMPI process?

How is appraisal done in CMMI?

Which appraisal method class is the best?

Can you explain the importance of PII in SCAMPI?

Can you explain implementation of CMMI in one of the Key process areas?

Explanation of all process areas with goals and practices?

Can you explain the process areas?

Six Sigma

What is six sigma?

Can you explain the different methodology for execution and design process in SIX sigma?

What does executive leaders, champions, Master Black belt, green belts and black belts mean?

What are the different kinds of variations used in six sigma?

Can you explain the concept of standard deviation?

Can you explain the concept of fish bone/ Ishikawa diagram?

What is Pareto principle?

Can you explain QFD?

Can you explain FMEA?

Can you explain X bar charts?

Can you explain Flow charting and brain storming?

Agile Development

What does Agile mean?

Can you explain Agile modelling?

What are core and supplementary principles in Agile modeling?

What is the main principle behind Agile documentation?

What are the different methodologies to implement Agile?

What is XP?

What are User Stories in XP and how different are they from requirement?

Who writes User stories?

When do we say a story is valid?

When are test plans written in XP?

Can you explain the XP development life cycle?

Can you explain how planning game works in Extreme Programming?

How do we estimate in Agile?

On What basis can stories be prioritized?

Can you point out simple differences between Agile and traditional SDLC?

Can you explain the concept of refactoring?

What is a feature in Feature Driven Development?

Can you explain the overall structure of FDD project?

Can you explain the concept of time boxing?

When to choose FDD and when to choose XP?

What is SCRUM?

What does product owner, product back log and sprint mean in SCRUM?

Can you explain how SCRUM flows?

Can you explain different roles in SCRUM?

Can you explain DSDM?

Can you explain different phases in DSDM?

Can you explain in detail project life cycle phase in DSDM?

Can you explain LSD?

Can you explain ASD?

8

.NET Interview Questions

What is an IL?

What is a CLR?

What is CTS?

What is a CLS (Common Language Specification)?

What is a Managed Code?

What is a Assembly?

What are the different types of Assembly?

What is NameSpace?

What is Difference between NameSpace and Assembly?

If you want to view an Assembly how do you go about it?

What is Manifest?

Where is version information stored of an assembly?

Is versioning applicable to private assemblies?

What is GAC?

What is the concept of strong names?

How to add and remove an assembly from GAC?

What is Delay signing?

What is garbage collection?

Can we force garbage collector to run?

What is reflection?

What are different types of JIT?

What are Value types and Reference types?

What is concept of Boxing and Unboxing ?

What is the difference between VB.NET and C#?

What is the difference between System exceptions and Application exceptions?

What is CODE Access security?

What is a satellite assembly?

How to prevent my .NET DLL to be decompiled?

What is the difference between Convert.toString and .toString () method?

What is Native Image Generator (Ngen.exe)?

If we have two version of same assembly in GAC how do we make a choice?

What is CodeDom?

How can we use COM Components in .NET?

We have developed the COM wrapper do we have to still register the COM?

How can we use .NET components in COM?

How can we make Windows API calls in .NET?

When we use windows API in .NET is it managed or unmanaged code?

What is COM?

What is Reference counting in COM?

Can you describe IUKNOWN interface in short?

Can you explain what DCOM is?

How do we create DCOM object in VB6?

How to implement DTC in .NET?

How many types of Transactions are there in COM + .NET?

How do you do object pooling in .NET?

What are types of compatibility in VB6?

What is equivalent for regsvr32 exe in .NET?

What is Multi-tasking?

What is Multi-threading?

What is a Thread?

Did VB6 support multi-threading?

Can we have multiple threads in one App domain?

Which namespace has threading?

What does Address Of operator do in background?

How can you reference current thread of the method?

What is Thread.Sleep () in threading?

How can we make a thread sleep for infinite period?

What is Suspend and Resume in Threading?

What the way to stop a long running thread?

How do I debug thread?

What is Thread.Join () in threading?

What are Daemon threads and how can a thread be created as Daemon?

How is shared data managed in threading?

Can we use events with threading?

How can we know a state of a thread?

What is use of Interlocked class ?

What is a monitor object?

What are wait handles?

What is ManualResetEvent and AutoResetEvent?

What is Reader Writer Locks?

How can you avoid deadlock in threading?

What is the difference between thread and process?

What is an application domain?

What is .NET Remoting?

Which class does the remote object has to inherit?

What are two different types of remote object creation mode in .NET ?

Describe in detail Basic of SAO architecture of Remoting?

What are the situations you will use singleton architecture in remoting?

What is fundamental of published or precreated objects in Remoting?

What are the ways in which client can create object on server in CAO model?

Are CAO stateful in nature?

To create objects in CAO with 'new' keyword what should be done?

Is it a good design practice to distribute the implementation to Remoting Client?

What are LeaseTime, SponsorshipTime, RenewonCallTime and LeaseManagerPollTime?

Which config file has all the supported channels/protocol?

How can you specify remoting parameters using Config files?

Can Non-Default constructors be used with Single Call SAO?

How can we call methods in remoting asynchronously?

What is Asynchronous One-Way Calls?

What is marshalling and what are different kinds of marshalling?

What is ObjRef object in remoting?

What is a Web Service?

What is UDDI?

What is DISCO?

What is WSDL?

What the different phase/steps of acquiring a proxy object in Web service?

What the different phase/steps of acquiring a proxy object in Web service?

What is file extension of Web services?

Which attribute is used in order that the method can be used as WebService?

What are the steps to create a web service and consume it?

Do webservice have state?

What is an application object?

What is the difference between Cache object and application object?

How can get access to cache object?

What are dependencies in cache and types of dependencies?

Can you show a simple code showing file dependency in cache?

What is Cache Callback in Cache?

What is scavenging?

What are different types of caching using cache object of ASP.NET?

How can you cache different version of same page using ASP.NET cache object?

How will implement Page Fragment Caching?

Can you compare ASP.NET sessions with classic ASP?

Which are the various modes of storing ASP.NET session?

Is Session_End event supported in all session modes?

What are the steps to configure StateServer Mode?

What are the steps to configure SQLServer mode?

Where do you specify session state mode in ASP.NET?

What are the other ways you can maintain state?

What are benefits and Limitation of using Hidden fields?

What is ViewState?

Does the performance for viewstate vary according to User controls?

What are benefits and Limitation of using Viewstate for state management?

How can you use Hidden frames to cache client data ?

What are benefits and limitations of using Hidden frames?

What are benefits and limitations of using Cookies?

What is Query String and What are benefits and limitations of using Query Strings?

What is Absolute and Sliding expiration?

What is cross page posting?

How do we access viewstate value of this page in the next page ?

Can we post and access view state in another application?

What is SQL Cache Dependency in ASP.NET 2.0?

How do we enable SQL Cache Dependency in ASP.NET 2.0?

What is Post Cache substitution?

Why do we need methods to be static for Post Cache substitution?

What is Object Oriented Programming?

What is a Class?

What is an Object?

What is the relation between Classes and Objects?

What are different properties provided by Object-oriented systems?

How can we achieve inheritance in VB.NET?

What are abstract classes?

What is a Interface?

What is difference between abstract classes and interfaces?

What is a delegate?

What are Events?

Do events have return type.

Can events have access modifiers?

Can we have shared events?

What is shadowing?

What is the difference between Shadowing and Overriding?

What is the difference between delegate and events?

If we inherit a class do the private variables also get inherited?

What is the different accessibility levels defined in .NET?

Can you prevent a class from overriding?

What is the use of "Must inherit" keyword in VB.NET?

Do interface have accessibility modifier.

What are similarities between Class and structure?

What is the difference between Class and structure's?

What does virtual keyword mean?

What are shared (VB.NET)/Static(C#) variables?

What is Dispose method in .NET?

What is the use of "Overrides" and "Overridable" keywords?

Where are all .NET Collection classes located?

What is ArrayList?

What is a HashTable?

What are queues and stacks?

What is ENUM? 6

What is nested Classes?

What is Operator overloading in .NET?

For the below code which constructor will fire first?

What is the significance of Finalize method in .NET?

How can we suppress a finalize method?

What is the use of DISPOSE method?

How do I force the Dispose method to be called automatically, as clients can forget to call Dispose method?

In what instances you will declare a constructor to be private?

Can we have different access modifiers on get/set methods of a property ?

If we write a goto or a return statement in try and catch block will the finally block execute?

What is Indexer?

Can we have static indexer in C#?

Can two catch blocks be executed?

What is the difference between System.String and System.StringBuilder classes?

What' is the sequence in which ASP.NET events are processed?

In which event are the controls fully loaded?

How can we identify that the Page is Post Back?

How does ASP.NET maintain state in between subsequent request?

How do we assign page specific attributes?

How do we ensure viewstate is not tampered?

What is the use of @ Register directives?

What is the use of Smart Navigation property?

What is AppSetting Section in "Web.Config" file?

Where is View State information stored?

What is the use of @ Output Cache directive in ASP.NET.

How can we create custom controls in ASP.NET?

How many types of validation controls are provided by ASP.NET?

Can you explain "AutoPostBack"?

How can you enable automatic paging in Data Grid?

What is the use of "GLOBAL.ASAX" file?

What is the difference between "Web.config" and "Machine.Config"?

What is a SESSION and APPLICATION object?

What is the difference between 'Server.Transfer' and 'response. Redirect' ?

What is the difference between Authentication and authorization?

What is impersonation in ASP.NET?

Can you explain in brief how the ASP.NET authentication process works?

What are the various ways of authentication techniques in ASP.NET?

How does authorization work in ASP.NET?

What is difference between Data grid, Datalist, and repeater?

From performance point of view, how do they rate?

What is the method to customize columns in Data Grid?

How can we format data inside Data Grid?

How to decide on the design consideration to take a Data grid, data list, or repeater?

Difference between ASP and ASP.NET?

What are major events in GLOBAL.ASAX file?

What order they are triggered?

Do session use cookies?

How can we force all the validation control to run?

How can we check if all the validation control are valid and proper?

If client side validation is enabled in your Web page, does that mean server side code is not run.
Which JavaScript file is referenced for validating the validators at the client side?

How to disable client side script in validators?

How can I show the entire validation error message in a message box on the client side?

You find that one of your validations is very complicated and does not fit in any of the validators, what will you do?

What exactly happens when ASPX page is requested from a browser?

How can we kill a user session?

How do you upload a file in ASP.NET?

How do I send email message from ASP.NET?

What are different IIS isolation levels?

ASP used STA threading model, what is the threading model used for ASP.NET.

What is the use of <%@ page aspcompat=true %> attribute?

(B) Explain the differences between Server-side and Client-side code?

Can you explain Forms authentication in detail?

How do I sign out in forms authentication?

If cookies are not enabled at browser end does form Authentication work?

How to use a checkbox in a data grid?

What are the steps to create a windows service in VB.NET?

What is the difference between "Web farms" and "Web garden"?

How do we configure "Web Garden"?

What is the main difference between Grid layout and Flow Layout?

What's the difference between trace and debug in ASP.NET?

How do you enable tracing in on an ASP.NET page?

Which namespace is needed to implement debug and trace ?

Can you explain the concept of trace listener?

What are trace switches?

What are design patterns?

What is the difference between Factory and Abstract Factory Patterns?

What is MVC pattern?

How can we implement singleton pattern in .NET?

How do you implement prototype pattern in .NET?

What are the situations you will use a Web Service and Remoting in projects?

Can you give a practical implementation of FAÇADE patterns?

How can we implement observer pattern in .NET?

What is three-tier architecture?

Have you ever worked with Microsoft Application Blocks, if yes then which?

What is Service Oriented architecture?

What are different ways you can pass data between tiers?

What is Windows DNA architecture?

What is aspect oriented programming?

What is the namespace in which .NET has the data functionality class?

Can you give an overview of ADO.NET architecture?

What are the two fundamental objects in ADO.NET?

What is difference between dataset and data reader?

What are major difference between classic ADO and ADO.NET?

What is the use of connection object?

What is the use of command objects?

What is the use of data adapter?

What are basic methods of Data adapter?

What is Dataset object?

What are the various objects in Dataset?

How can we connect to Microsoft Access, FoxPro, and Oracle etc?

How do we connect to SQL SERVER, which namespace do we use?

How do we use stored procedure in ADO.NET and how do we provide parameters to the stored procedures?

How can we force the connection object to close after my data reader is closed?

I want to force the data reader to return only schema of the data store rather than data.

How can we fine-tune the command object when we are expecting a single row?

Which is the best place to store connection string in .NET projects?

What are the steps involved to fill a dataset?

What are the various methods provided by the dataset object to generate XML?

How can we save all data from dataset?

How can we check that some changes have been made to dataset since it was loaded?

How can we add/remove row is in "Data Table" object of "Dataset"?

What is basic use of "Data View"?

What is the difference between "Dataset" and "Data Reader" ?

How can we load multiple tables in a Dataset?

How can we add relation between tables in a Dataset?

What is the use of Command Builder?

What's difference between "Optimistic" and "Pessimistic" locking ?

How many ways are there to implement locking in ADO.NET?

How can we perform transactions in .NET?

What is difference between Dataset? Clone and Dataset. Copy?

Can you explain the difference between an ADO.NET Dataset and an ADO Record set?

Explain in detail the fundamental of connection pooling?

What is Maximum Pool Size in ADO.NET Connection String?

How to enable and disable connection pooling?

What extra features does ADO.Net 2.0 have ?

What is normalization? What are different types of normalization?

What is denormalization?

What is a candidate key?

What are the different types of joins? What is the difference between them?

What are indexes? What is the difference between clustered and nonclustered indexes?

How can you increase SQL performance?

What is the use of OLAP?

What is a measure in OLAP?

What are dimensions in OLAP?

What are levels in dimensions?

What are fact tables and dimension tables in OLAP?

What is DTS?

What is fill factor ?

What is RAID and how does it work?

What is the difference between DELETE TABLE and TRUNCATE TABLE commands?

If locking is not implemented, what issues can occur?

What are different transaction levels in SQL SERVER?

What are the different locks in SQL SERVER?

Can we suggest locking hints to SQL SERVER?

What is LOCK escalation?

What are the different ways of moving data between databases in SQL Server?

What are advantages of SQL 2000 over SQl 7.0?

What is the difference between a HAVING CLAUSE and a WHERE CLAUSE?

What is the difference between UNION and UNION ALL SQL syntax?

How can you raise custom errors from stored procedure?

What is ACID fundamental? What are transactions in SQL SERVER?

What is DBCC?

What is the purpose of Replication?

What are the different types of replication supported by SQL SERVER?

What is BCP utility in SQL SERVER?

What are the different types of triggers in SQl SERVER?

If we have multiple AFTER Triggers on table how can we define the sequence of the triggers?

What is SQL injection?

What is the difference between Stored Procedure (SP) and User Defined Function (UDF)?

What is UML?

How many types of diagrams are there in UML?

What are advantages of using UML?

What is the sequence of UML diagrams in project?

Give a small brief explanation of all Elements in activity diagrams?

Explain Different elements of a collaboration diagram?

Explain all parts of a deployment diagram?

Describe the various components in sequence diagrams?

What are the elements in State Chart diagrams?

Describe different elements in Static Chart diagrams?

Explain the different elements of a Use Case?

What is project management?

Is spending in IT projects constant through out the project?

Who is a stakeholder?

Can you explain project life cycle?

Are risk constant through out the project?

Can you explain different software development life cycles?

What is triple constraint triangle in project management?

What is a project baseline?

What is effort variance?

How is normally a project management plan document organized?

How do you estimate a project?

What is CAR (Causal Analysis and Resolution)?

What is DAR (Decision Analysis and Resolution)?

What is a fish bone diagram?

What is Pareto principle?

How do you handle change request?

What is internal change request?

What is difference between SITP and UTP in testing?

Which software have you used for project management?

What are the metrics followed in project management?

People in your project do not peform , what will you do?

What is black box testing and White box testing?

What is the difference between Unit testing, Assembly testing and Regression testing?

What is V model in testing?

How do you start a project?

How did you do resource allocations?

How will you do code reviews?

What is CMMI?

What are the five levels in CMMI?

What is continuous and staged representation?

What is SIX sigma?

What are DMAIC and DMADV?

What are the various roles in Six Sigma implementation?

What are function points?

What are the different types of elementary process in FPA?

What are the different elements in Functions points?

Can you explain in GSC and VAF in function points?

What are unadjusted function points and how is it calculated?

Can you explain steps in function points?

What is the FP per day in your current company?

Do you know Use Case points?

What is COCOMO I, COCOMOII and COCOMOIII?

What is SMC approach of estimation?

How do you estimate maintenance project and change requests?

What is XML?

What is the version information in XML?

What is ROOT element in XML?

If XML does not have closing tag will it work?

Is XML case sensitive? 256

What is the difference between XML and HTML?

Is XML meant to replace HTML?

Can you explain why your project needed XML?

What is DTD (Document Type Definition)?

What is well formed XML?

What is a valid XML?

What is CDATA section in XML?

What is CSS?

What is XSL?

What is element and attributes in XML?

Which are the namespaces in .NET used for XML?

What are the standard ways of parsing XML document?

In What scenarios will you use a DOM parser and SAX parser?

How was XML handled during COM times?

What is the main difference between MSML and .NET Framework XML classes?

What are the core functionalitiès in XML .NET framework? Can you explain in detail those functionalities?

What is XSLT?

Define XPATH?

What is the concept of XPOINTER?

What is an XMLReader Class?

What is XMLTextReader?

How do we access attributes using "XmlReader"?

Explain simple Walk through of XmlReader.

What does XmlValidatingReader class do?

What is Unicode & Why was it introduced?

Does .NET support UNICODE and how do you know it supports?

What is the difference between localization and globalization?

What architecture decisions you should consider while planning for international software's?

How do we get the current culture of the environment in windows and ASP.NET?

Which are the important namespaces during localization and globalization?

What are resource files and how do we generate resource files?

Can resource file be in any other format other than resx extensions?

How is resource files actually used in project?

How can we use Culture Auto in project?

What are satellite assemblies?

How do we generate Satellite assemblies?

What is AL.EXE and RESGEN.EXE?

What is the use of resource manager class?

What precautions do we need to take while deploying satellite assemblies?

Can we get a strongly typed resource class rather than using resource manager?

Can you explain the fundamentals of "GetGlobalResourceObject" and "GetLocalResourceObject" functions?

Can we sign a satellite assembly?

Can you explain collation sequence in sql server?

How do we define collation sequence for database and tables?

Can we change the order in a select query with a specified collation sequence?

Can you list best practices for globalization and localization?

Why is the culture set to the current thread?

What are the important principles of SOA (Service oriented Architecture)?

What are ends, contract, address, and bindings?

Which specifications does WCF follow?

What are the main components of WCF?

Explain how Ends, Contract, Address, and Bindings are done in WCF?

What is a service class?

What is a service contract, operation contract and Data Contract?

What are the various ways of hosting a WCF service?

How do we host a WCF service in IIS?

What are the advantages of hosting WCF Services in IIS as compared to self-hosting?

What are the major differences between services and Web services?

What is the difference WCF and Web services?

What are different bindings supported by WCF?

Which are the various programming approaches for WCF? 2

What is one-way operation?

Can you explain duplex contracts in WCF?

How can we host a service on two different protocols on a single server?

How can we use MSMQ bindings in WCF?

Can you explain transactions in WCF?

What different transaction isolation levels provided in WCF?

Can we do transactions using MSMQ?

Can we have two-way communications in MSMQ?

What are Volatile queues?

What are Dead letter queues?

What is a poison message?

What is WPF?

What is XAML?

What are dependency properties?

Are XAML file compiled or built on runtime?

Can you explain how we can separate code and XAML?

How can we access XAML objects in behind code?

What kind of documents are supported in WPF?

What is Windows Workflow Foundation?

What is a Workflow?

What are different types of Workflow in Windows Workflow foundation?

When should we use a sequential workflow and when should we use state machines?

How do we create workflows using designer?

How do we specify conditions in Work flow?

How do you handle exceptions in workflow?

What is the use of XOML files.

How can we pass parameters to workflow?

What problem does Ajax solve?

What is Ajax?

What is the fundamental behind Ajax?

What is JSON?

How do we use XMLHttpRequest object in JavaScript?

How do we do asynchronous processing using Ajax?

What are the various states in XMLHttpRequest and how do we check the same?

How can we get response text?

How can we send request to the server using the XMLHttpRequest component?

How do we pass parameters to the server?

How can we create a class in JavaScript using Atlas?

How do we do inheritance-using Atlas?

How do we define interfaces using Atlas?

How do we reference HTML controls using Atlas?

Can you explain Scriptmanager control in Ajax?

Can you explain Enablepartialrendering and UpdatePanel control in Ajax?

Can you explain the concept of triggers in 'UpdatePanel' control?

Can you explain the 'UpdateProgress' component?

How can you do validations in Ajax?

How do we do exception handling in Ajax?

How do we consume web service in Atlas?

How can we consume data directly in web services?

How do we access crystal reports in .NET?

What are the various components in crystal reports?

What basic steps are needed to display a simple report in crystal?

Can crystal reports be published as a web service?

How do we invoke the crystal report web service?

How do we add formulas using crystal reports?

How do we pass parameters to crystal reports?

How do we export from crystal reports?

How do we print to printer using crystal?

How do we generate cross tab reports?

How can we do grouping in crystal?

Can you explain three-pass reporting which crystal report uses?

Can you explain reporting services architecture?

We have two IIS application 'Reports' and 'Reportserver' what do they do ?

Can you explain Report definition language (RDL) file in reporting services?

What is the basic process of making a report in reporting services?

How can we consume reports in ASP.NET?

Can you explain the difference between private and shared data sources?

How does reports caching in reporting services work ?

What are the major differences between Crystal and SQL reporting services?

What improvements are provided in ASP.NET 2.0?

How does ASP.NET 2.0 eliminate tedious coding?

How do we encrypt web.config files in ASP.NET 2.0 ?

With the above technique can you encrypt everything in the web.config file?

In .NET .X how was the encryption implemented for config files?

Can you explain membership and role providers in ASP.Net 2.0?

What kind of security web controls are introduced in ASP.NET 2.0?

Can you explain master pages concept in ASP.NET?

What is the concept of Web parts?

What are the different components of the web part framework?

What are partial classes in ASP.NET ?

Can you explain generics in .NET ?

Can you explain the concept of generic collection?

How do you send a email using ASP.NET ?

How did you deployment and setup in ASP.NET ?

Define LINQ ?

We already have common data access model what is special about LINQ?

How can you make entity classes from the table itself ?

How can we transform LINQ to objects ?

How to transform LINQ to ADO.NET ?

How to transform LINQ to SQL ?

How to transform LINQ to XML ?

How to transform LINQ to entities ?

Can you explain Delegate Instantiation?

Can you explain Anonymous methods ?

What is Yield in LINQ ?

Can you explain Lambda Expressions ?

What are Instance methods and Extension methods ?

What are Anonymous types ?

Revision of Simple Query syntax for LINQ ?

What is silver light?

9

Java Interview Questions

OOPS and CORE JAVA

What is JVM (Java Virtual Machine)?

What is JIT (Just-in-Time) Compilation?

What is Object Oriented Programming?

What's a Class?

What's an Object?

What's the relation between Classes and Objects?

What are different properties provided by Object-oriented systems?

How do you implement inheritance in Java?

How can we implement polymorphism in Java?

What's an interface and how will you go about implementing an interface?

What is an Abstract class?

What are Abstract methods?

What's the difference between "Abstract" classes and "Interfaces"?

What's difference between Static and Non-Static fields of a class?

What are inner classes and what's the practical implementation of inner classes?

What are packages?

What is a constructor in class?

Can constructors be parameterized?

Can you explain transient and volatile modifiers?

What is the use if "instanceof " keyword?

What are Native methods in Java?

Explain in depth Garbage collector?

How does the garbage collector determine that the object has to be marked for deletion?

Can you explain "finalize()" method?

How can we force the garbage collector to run?

What's the main difference between "Switch" and "If " comparison?

What's the use of JAVAP tool?

What are applets?

In which package is the applet class located?

What are native interfaces in Java?

What are Class loader's?

What is Bootstrap, Extension and System Class loader?

Can you explain the flow between bootstrap, extension and system class loader?

Can you explain how can you practically do dynamic loading?

How can you copy one array in to a different array?

Can you explain the core collection interfaces?

Can you explain in brief the collection classes which implement the collection interfaces?

What's the difference between standard JAVA array and ArrayList class?

What's the use of "ensureCapacity" in ArrayList class?

How can we obtain an array from an ArrayList class?

What is "LinkedList" class for?

Can you explain HashSet class in collections?

What is LinkedHashSet class?

What is a TreeSet class?

What's the use of Comparator Interface?

How can we access elements of a collection?

What is Map and SortedMap Interface?

Have you used any collection algorithm?

Why do we use collections when we had traditional ways for collection?

Can you name the legacy classes and interface for collections?

What is Enumeration Interface?

What's the main difference between ArrayList / HashMap and Vector / Hashtable?

Are String object Immutable, Can you explain the concept?

What is a StringBuffer class and how does it differs from String class?

What is the difference between StringBuilder and StringBuffer class?

What is Pass by Value and Pass by reference? How does JAVA handle the same?

What are access modifiers?

What is Assertion?

Can you explain the fundamentals of deep and shallow Cloning?

How do we implement Shallow cloning?

How do we implement deep cloning?

What's the impact of private constructor?

What are the situations you will need a constructor to be private?

Can you explain final modifier?

What are static Initializers?

If we have multiple static initializer blocks how is the sequence handled?

Define casting? What are the different types of Casting?

Can you explain Widening conversion and Narrowing conversion?

Can we assign parent object to child objects?

Define exceptions?

Can you explain in short how JAVA exception handling works?

Can you explain different exception types?

Can you explain checked and unchecked exceptions?

Can we create our own exception class?

What are chained exceptions?

What is serialization?

How do we implement serialization actually?

What's the use of Externalizable Interface?

Threading

What's difference between thread and process?

What is thread safety and synchronization?

What is semaphore?

What are monitors?

What's the importance of synchronized blocks?

How do we create threads?

What's the difference in using runnable and extends in threads?

Can you explain Thread.sleep?

How to stop a thread?

What is wait() and notify() ?

Can you explain how Scheduling and Priority works in threads?

Can you explain Yielding in threading?

What are daemon threads?

JDBC

How does JAVA interact with databases?

Can we interact with non-relational sources using JDBC?

Can you explain in depth the different sections in JDBC?

Can you explain in short how you go about using JDBC API in code?

How do you handle SQL exceptions?

If there is more than one exception in SQLException" class how to go about displaying it?

Explain Type1, Type2, Type3 and Type4 drivers in JDBC?

What are the advantages and disadvantages of using JDBC-ODBC bridge driver?

What are the advantages and disadvantages of using Native-API/ Partially Java Driver?

What are the advantages and disadvantages of using Net-Protocol/ All-Java driver?

What are the advantages and disadvantages of using Native-protocol/ All-Java driver?

Define meta-data?

What is DatabaseMetaData?

Can you explain "ConnectionFactory" class?

I want to display tables of a database how do I do it?

Define "ResultSetMetaData"?

What is the difference between "ResultSet" and "RowSet"?

Can "ResultSet" objects be serialized?

Can you explain "ResultSet", "RowSet", "CachedRowset", "JdbcRowset" and "WebRowSet" relation ship?

What are the different types of resultset?

Explain the concept of "PreparedStatement "statement interface?

What's the difference between "Statement" and "PreparedStatement"?

How can we call stored procedure using JDBC?

Can you explain "CallableStatement" interface in detail?

How do you get a resultset object from stored procedure?

How can we do batch updates using "CallableStatement" Interface?

Define transactions?

What is ACID in transaction?

What are the four essential properties of a transaction?

Explain concurrency and locking?

What are different types of locks?

What are the different types of levels of resource on which locks can be placed?

Define lock escalation?

What is Table level and Row level locking?

What are the problems that can occur if you do not implement locking properly?

What are different transaction levels?

Twist: what are different types of locks?

What is difference between optimistic and pessimistic locking?

What are deadlocks?

How can we set transaction level through JDBC API?

Can you explain transaction control in JDBC?

What are Savepoints in a transaction?

Servlets and JSP

What are Servlets?

What are advantages of servlets over CGI?

Can you explain Servlet life cycle?

What are the two important API's in for Servlets?

Can you explain in detail "javax.servlet" package?

What's the use of ServletContext?

How do we define an application level scope for servlet?

What's the difference between GenericServlet and HttpServlet?

Can you explain in detail javax.servlet.http package?

What's the architecture of a Servlet package?

Why is HTTP protocol called as a stateless protocol?

What are the different ways we can maintain state between requests?

What is URL rewriting?

What are cookies?

What are sessions in Servlets?

What's the difference between getSession(true) and getSession(false) ?

What's the difference between "doPost" and "doGet" methods?

Which are the different ways you can communicate between servlets?

What is functionality of "RequestDispatcher" object?

How do we share data using "getServletContext ()"?

Explain the concept of SSI?

What are filters in JAVA?

Can you explain in short how do you go about implementing filters using Apache Tomcat?

Twist: Explain step by step of how to implement filters?

What's the difference between Authentication and authorization?

Explain in brief the directory structure of a web application?

Can you explain JSP page life cycle?

What is EL?

How does EL search for an attribute?

What are the implicit EL objects in JSP?

How can we disable EL?

What is JSTL?

Can you explain in short what the different types of JSTL tags are?

How can we use beans in JSP?

What is <jsp:forward> tag for ?

What are JSP directives?

What are Page directives?

What are include directives?

Can you explain taglib directives?

How does JSP engines instantiate tag handler classes instances?

What's the difference between JavaBeans and taglib directives?

What are the different scopes an object can have in a JSP page?

What are different implicit objects of JSP?

What are different Authentication Options available in servlets?

Can you explain how do we practically implement security on a resource?

How do we practically implement form based authentication?

How do we authenticate using JDBC?

Can you explain JDBCRealm?

Can you explain how do you configure JNDIRealm?

How did you implement caching in JSP?

EJB

What is EJB?

What are the different kind of EJB's?

You are designing architecture for a project how do you decide whether you should use session, entity or message driven bean?

Can you explain "EJBHome" and "EJBObject" in EJB?

Can client directly create object of session or entity beans?

Can you explain the concept of local interfaces?

What are the limitations of using Local object?

Which application server have you used for EJB ?

Can you explain step by step practically developing and deploying EJB component?

What is Passivation and Activation in EJB?

Can beans who are involved in transaction have "Passivation" process?

How does the server decide which beans to passivate and activate?

In what format is the conversational data written to the disk?

Can you explain in brief Life cycle for Stateless and Stateful beans?

Struts

What's MVC pattern?

Define struts?

Can you explain the directory structure for a struts folder in brief ?

Can you give an overview of how a struts application flows?

Twist: What are action and action form classes in Struts?

XML and WebServices

What is XML?

What is the version information in XML?

What is ROOT element in XML?

If XML does not have closing tag will it work?

Is XML case sensitive?

What is the difference between XML and HTML?

Is XML meant to replace HTML?

Can you explain why your project needed XML?

What is DTD (Document Type definition)?

What is well formed XML?

What is a valid XML?

What is CDATA section in XML?

What is CSS?

What is XSL?

What is element and attributes in XML?

What are the standard ways of parsing XML document?

In What scenarios will you use a DOM parser and SAX parser?

What is XSLT?

Define XPATH?

What is the concept of XPOINTER?

What is a Web Service ?

What is DISCO ?

What is SOAP ?

What is WSDL ?

Can you explain UDDI ?

Can you explain JAXP ?

What is a XML registry?

What is JAXR?

What is JAXM?

Can you explain how JAXM messaging model works?

Can you explain JAX-RPC?

Internationalization

Can you explain i18n and l10n?

Can you explain internationalization and localization?

What is Locale?

How do we display numbers, currency and Dates according to proper Locale format?

What are resource bundles?

How do we load a resource bundle file?

How can we do inheritance in resource bundles?

JNI

What is Native Interface in JAVA?

Can you say in brief steps required to implement Native interfaces in Java?

Can JNI be used for VB6, C# or VB.NET directly?

What are JNI functions and pointers?

How does the garbage collector know JNI objects are no more used?

Twist: What are the different types of references JNI supports?

Twist: How to do you delete global objects?

How does the native language C or C++ understand data types in JAVA?

Can you explain exception handling in JNI?

What are limitations for "JNIEnv" pointer in multi-threading scenarios?

What are the advantages and disadvantages of using "JNI"?

Architecture

What are design patterns ?

What is the difference between Factory and Abstract Factory Patterns?

What is MVC pattern?

Twist: How can you implement MVC pattern in Servlets and JSP?

How can we implement singleton pattern in JAVA?

How do you implement prototype pattern in JAVA?

Twist: How to implement cloning in JAVA? What is shallow copy and deep copy ?

Can you give a practical implementation of FAÇADE patterns?

How can we implement observer pattern in JAVA?

What is three tier architecture?

What is Service Oriented architecture?

What is aspect oriented programming?

Project Management

What is project management?

Is spending in IT projects constant through out the project?

Who is a stakeholder ?

Can you explain project life cycle ?

Twist: How many phases are there in software project ?

Are risk constant through out the project ?

Can you explain different software development life cycles ?

What is triple constraint triangle in project management ?

What is a project baselines ?

What is effort variance?

How is normally a project management plan document organized ?

How do you estimate a project?

What is CAR (Causal Analysis and Resolution)?

What is DAR (Decision Analysis and Resolution) ?

What is a fish bone diagram ?

Twist: What is Ishikawa diagram ?

What is pareto principle ?

Twist: What is 80/20 principle ?

How do you handle change request?

What is internal change request?

What is difference between SITP and UTP in testing ?

What is the software you have used for project management?

What are the metrics followed in project management?

Twist: What metrics will you look at in order to see the project is moving successfully?

You have people in your team who do not meet there deadlines or do not perform what are the actions you will take ?

Twist: Two of your resources have conflicts between them how would you sort it out ?

What is black box testing and White box testing?

What's the difference between Unit testing, Assembly testing and Regression testing?

What is V model in testing?

How do you start a project?

How did you do resource allocations?

How will you do code reviews ?

What is CMMI?

What are the five levels in CMMI?

What is continuous and staged representation?

Can you explain the process areas?

What is SIX sigma?

What is DMAIC and DMADV ?

What are the various roles in Six Sigma implementation?

What are function points?

Twist: Define Elementary process in FPA?

What are the different types of elementary process in FPA?

What are the different elements in Functions points?

Can you explain in GSC and VAF in function points?

What are unadjusted function points and how is it calculated?

Can you explain steps in function points?

What is the FP per day in your current company?

Twist: What is your company's productivity factor ?

Do you know Use Case points?

What is COCOMO I, COCOMOII and COCOMOIII?

What is SMC approach of estimation?

How do you estimate maintenance project and change requests?

UML

What is UML?

How many types of diagrams are there in UML ?

Twist: Explain in short all types of diagrams in UML ?

What are advantages of using UML?

Twist: What is Modeling and why UML ?

What is the sequence of UML diagrams in project?

Twist: How did you implement UML in your project?

Just a small Twist: Do I need all UML diagrams in a project?

Give a small brief explanation of all Elements in activity diagrams?

Explain Different elements of a collaboration diagram ?

Explain Component diagrams ?

Explain all parts of a deployment diagram?

Describe the various components in sequence diagrams?

What are the element in State Chart diagrams ?

Describe different elements in Static Chart diagrams ?

Explain the different elements of a Use Case ?

Twist: What is the difference between Activity and sequence diagrams?(I leave this to the readers)

10

Questions Left

Belo sections will be covered in the second edition of this book:

- Togaf
- Different types of standard enterprise architects.
- Security aspects to be considered while doing architecture
- Processes like CMMI , and Six sigma
- Specific architecture implementation according to vendor like Microsoft, IBM and SUN.

If you think any question or section which is not attended in this book please email us at shiv_koirala@yahoo.com , we will try to cover the same in the second edition.